The Bankrupt, the Conman, the Mafia and the Irish Connection

The Bankrupt, the Conman, the Mafia and the Irish Connection

Chris Moore

Gill & Macmillan

Gill & Macmillan Ltd
Hume Avenue, Park West, Dublin 12
with associated companies throughout the world
www.gillmacmillan.ie
© Chris Moore 2003
0 7171 3594 2

Index compiled by Cover To Cover
Design and print origination by Carole Lynch
Printed and bound by Nørhaven Paperback A/S, Denmark

This book is typeset in Goudy 10.5 on 14.5pt.

*The paper used in this book comes from the wood pulp
of managed forests. For every tree felled, at least one tree
is planted, thereby renewing natural resources.*

A CIP catalogue record for this book is available
from the British Library.

1 3 5 4 2

This book is dedicated to my old man, Billy Moore.
As he approaches his eightieth year, his enthusiasm for life
in general, and writing in particular, remains undiminished.
One day his book of short stories will be published.

Contents

The Preface

Colin Lees is survived by some of the companies he left for dead. They prosper under different ownership, of course, while he languishes in a prison cell . . . a fraudster and money laundering drug smuggler . . . a common criminal.

Lees was the entrepreneurial darling of the 1980s with the then Tory direct rulers of Northern Ireland. But when his mismanaged Mid-Ulster based business empire cracked under the strains of rapid expansion without commensurate profit margins, bankruptcy finally exposed the darker side of Colin Lees.

His Scottish business kingdom had been the first to topple, warning him of the impending doom of a total spectacular collapse.

For behind the veneer of the successful multi-millionaire lurked the other Colin Lees: this was the secret Colin Lees — the crooked, corrupt and deceitful drug running criminal he preferred to keep hidden away from the public glare.

Lees was once top of the heap in his hometown, Magherafelt. He lorded it over his fellow citizens: the crumbs from his table provided jobs for almost 500 at his group of companies.

He is, and was, an enigma. He enjoyed winning. A motor racing champion living life to the full, the trappings of success were evident: lavish parties, powerful friends, first-class travel . . . after all, he could afford the fast lane.

Indeed, it was for his racing skills rather than his business acumen that he was honoured in his hometown. Magherafelt Council laid on a civic reception for him in February 1985 to mark his many achievements in motor sports. At the time, council chairman Paddy Sweeney was quoted as saying that Colin Lees had been to the forefront of Irish motor racing since 1976 and had made such a big impact that the council was proud to honour him.

Today, however, you would be hard pushed to find members of Magherafelt Council willing to admit they elected to honour Lees. Many will be surprised to learn that local MP William McCrea of the DUP says he knew of him but didn't know him.

Perhaps when Lees is released from prison in October 2003, he will bear in mind that those who once devoured crumbs from his table or who valued his entrepreneurial skills today shun him — terrified of being in any way identified with a common criminal.

And perhaps he will have time to reflect on those he left shattered emotionally from the pain he inflicted by his willingness to hoodwink them into believing his bullshit. These are the very individuals who would have done anything to help him because they trusted him and believed in him and were ultimately betrayed by him. Lees was as cunning as a fox, extremely plausible when dealing with high financiers, government ministers and businessmen at one level, and with his employees and workers at another level. He used many false names and passports to keep secret his world of criminal conspiracy. Lees used his finely honed skills of deception to convince people he was what he said he was. In short, he was the consummate 'con' man.

Lees' fall from grace was spectacular. Things began to go wrong in the spring of 1992. The business king's crown began to slip with the arrival of Scottish police officers. They were investigating fraud in his Scottish group of companies. He bluffed it out, telling newspapers that he would recover from this setback. But the reality was that his businesses were already at death's door and he was increasingly at risk of being exposed as a corrupt and crooked citizen.

By November 1992, Lees' companies in Northern Ireland were declared bankrupt. What emerged in the aftermath of the collapse of his empire, with debts of £35 million, was an incredible story about a man who had it all — powerful and influential friends in government, links to British secret services and yet also associates in the underworld of Mafia crime families.

From the top of the business heap in Northern Ireland, Colin Lees plunged to the depths of the criminal world by connecting with men who plied their trade in the Mafia occupied sewers of New York. What you are about to read is the tale of a man who specialised in living well at other people's expense.

This was a greedy man who took £23 million in fraudulent business transactions with banks and finance houses in Northern Ireland alone. There was more fraud in Scotland, although he managed to sidestep responsibility for most of it and left two people who once trusted him to face the consequences in a Scottish court — Stuart Baillie got a jail sentence and his father, Malcolm Baillie, died in January 2002, a broke and broken man.

Even while declared bankrupt and under investigation in Scotland and Northern Ireland for fraud, Lees slipped in and out of the country to the United States to fleece a Dallas businessman of nearly $1 million. He had to keep his hand in, as they say. Lees was dogged in his determination to take from others what he could have legitimately earned himself had he applied his undoubted talents in the right direction. But he didn't want to wait for the rich rewards of his labours; he moved into the fast lane to become a multi-millionaire. What he didn't steal, he made on the lucrative drugs market — mixing with known drug runners and dealers. One convicted drug dealer told stunned police that Colin Lees, the multi-millionaire entrepreneur, bankrolled his drug deals.

This was the same Colin Lees who at one time in the late 1980s was prepared to risk his life by setting up business on a remote Scottish island to help the British government beat the IRA. There, he furtively manufactured special concrete panels for use in RUC stations, well away from the trigger-happy fingers of Provisional IRA gunmen at a time when they would happily murder anyone for as much as supplying a light bulb to a security base.

Lees' silver spoon had been to take over from his late father, William Alexander Lees, a modestly successful sawmill and concrete works in Magherafelt. But in spite of this comfortable cushion, Lees wanted more. Lees drove his business ambitions as hard as the Formula Ford racing car he took to championship success.

Today Colin Lees is locked up behind bars. But the police service in Northern Ireland is still trying to track down millions of pounds unaccounted for. One attempt at securing a confiscation order failed in court but new legislation might yet enable the police to finally close the file on Colin Lees by successfully going after his money.

Lees, meanwhile, is confident he will be released to enjoy the proceeds of his crimes. But that remains to be seen.

What is certain is that William John Colin Lees will go down in history as one of the most prolific Irish criminals of our time. A glittering business career was undoubtedly compromised by his desire to race to the top, and that in turn propelled him into stretching his business empire to breaking point whilst he gorged himself on the illegal fruits of his furtive labours.

The Preface

To this day it is difficult for many of his former employees to accept that Colin Lees was a crook. But perhaps they will be clear in their minds once they read the story of his criminal exploits . . . of his 'Race to Destruction'!

Chris Moore
September 2003

Acknowledgments

There are very many people to thank for their help in the preparation of this book. Clichéd as it might be, it is necessary to state clearly that without the assistance of this determined bunch, the book would not have been possible. There are those who have chosen anonymity — many from Lees' hometown in Co. Derry, Magherafelt. Others not wishing to be identified include a couple of very fine police officers.

And mention of police officers brings to mind the special thanks owed to the 'Money Laundering Anorak'. That's Det. Const. John Horan, formerly of the RUC and now with the Police Service of Northern Ireland (PSNI). John has a wicked sense of humour and is a tremendous communicator and storyteller. His enthusiasm for his work was an inspiration and his knowledge was invaluable in helping me understand just how difficult it is for the police, in spite of all their resources, to keep up with determined money launderers. Also in this category are Det. Ch. Supt Jimmy Molloy (now retired) and Det. Const. Margaret Connor. This trio of officers showed great forbearance and humour in trying to answer the seemingly endless list of questions I needed to ask about what was an extremely complicated investigation. What's more, in the process of covering the story of Colin Lees, I now have three very good friends that I didn't have before.

In the writing of this book I am grateful to a number of what I will call 'guinea pigs' — those who very kindly assisted by reading the early versions of the manuscript and who offered up support, encouragement and helpful suggestions. Among this rare breed are: my father Billy, my son Steven, my wife Fiona and Dr Justin O'Brien, author and former colleague and editor of the UTV *Insight* programme.

Of course, my present colleagues at *Insight* have been extremely supportive — from the present editor Trevor Birney to producers Mary Curry and Stephen Riley, who expertly produced the Lees film for UTV, 'Racing to Destruction'; and to Michael Fanning, our determined researcher who is rapidly heading in the direction of becoming a producer.

I am also grateful to Renee and Stuart Baillie for their co-operation and, of course, to the late Malcolm Baillie. Mickey Donnelly was of great assistance in unravelling the courtroom complexities in the Lees case. And finally, my thanks go to top *Sunday World* photographer Conor McCaughley for his usual professional service with a smile.

The Timeline

1952
1 October: Colin Lees is born in Magherafelt.

1969
Lees joins his father's company.

1987
IRA murder campaign against building contractors stepped up so Lees sets up secret production of special concrete panels on North Uist, Scottish island . . . but ends up owning fish farms and Scotpole, a timber company. Has lorries with 'Lees Group Scotland' painted on the side.

1991
26 January: Lees appears at news conference in Derry to announce new pulp mill to make product for Scandinavia. Alongside him at White Horse Hotel are John Hume, MP for the area, and the then Industry Minister Richard Needham.

5 September: Needham cuts tape at opening of Lees' Meadow Lane Shopping Centre in Magherafelt.

1992
March: Scottish police begin investigation of Lees' Scottish companies for fraud.

November: Lees is declared bankrupt in Northern Ireland with debts of £35 million. Price Waterhouse examines books and discovers fraud to the tune of £23 million. The RUC Fraud Squad is called in to begin investigation.

1993
Dallas businessman Richard Worthy says he has his first encounter with Lees in the spring of this year . . . they met at a concrete plant in Florida — Emerald Pre-Cast Concrete — owned by the Brannan family, friends of Lees' late father.

1994
Lees is charged with £23 million fraud and is given bail but on condition he surrenders his British passport.

Lees and his new American business associate, Derek Jones, fleece Richard Worthy of almost $1 million.

In late 1994 Lees returns to Northern Ireland with Derek Jones (who sets up home in Ballymena).

1996
March: Derek Jones opens Ulster Bank account in Ballymena with over £50,000 cash which he carries into the bank in a briefcase. The bank is therefore obliged under law to inform the police of such suspicious activity. So from this point on the RUC are watching the comings and goings of Jones and his sixty-eight bank

accounts all over the world. The RUC investigation is given a name: Operation Kilbreck.

June: John Ferguson gets eight years in jail on drugs charges. He tells police: 'Lees was my banker.'

6 August: Noel Morrison of Bradford Heights, Carrickfergus, buys equipment from Mullen Marine, Kinnego Marina, Oxford Island, Lurgan, to the value of £5,000, although receipt says: 'Received from Billy Mullen . . .' On the same day A. Megeen Enterprises Ltd, Skey Hill, Dundela, Dundalk, spends £11,064 on a speedster and trailer.

18 September: Lees agrees purchase of boat from couple in Gibraltar (Serge and Angelique Bonet) — they agree purchase to be completed by 10 October. Payments sent from Ballymena account by Jones. Deposit sent on **23 September** for £5,500. On **4 October** the balance of £50,000 is sent to Gibraltar through the Ulster Bank in Dublin. RUC Constable Horan sees money transfer to Gibraltar and is beginning to check up on what deal had been done.

25 October: RIB boat bought from Red Bay Boats, Cushendall, by Noel Morrison under the name of A. Meegean & Co., Sky Hill, Dundalk for £11,815.42. On same day Mullen Marine sells six sleeping bags and four hand-held radio transmitters for £1,000.

30 October: Five Co. Antrim men arrested at Malin Head. They say they were washed ashore on their RIB boat. They are questioned and released but their Land Rover is confiscated as is the boat. They are released next day without charge.

1 November: The *Plongeur Wisky* limps into Kilrush Harbour in Co. Clare with engine problems. Customs board for routine search and discover cannabis with street value of £17 million (1.7 tons of the stuff). Following this find, the Gardaí send routine fax to RUC when they discover that the drug-laden ship had been bought through money transfers to a Derek Jones and they wondered if anyone in the RUC was checking up on Jones. Horan asks the Gardaí for a meeting at which he explains he does not want any arrests just yet . . . the Gardaí agree to hold off pending further inquiries up North.

1997

10 June: Police raid house at 19a Riley Avenue, Blackpool, in relation to a drink scam. They find passport pictures of Lees with the birth certificate for a complete stranger, Andrew Hankin. When they check with passport authorities, it is confirmed that a passport in this name had recently been issued . . . and the pictures are those of Colin Lees. Lees denies he ever had the passport. On this day police forces all over the UK and Ireland take part in raids. Derek Jones is one of those arrested.

10 October: Colin Lees is arrested coming into Belfast on a flight from Manchester.

November: US authorities visit Northern Ireland to view documents found by police in Derek Jones' home and which help the Americans secure a conviction against bent New York stock-broker Jonathan Lyons.

1998

19 March: Northern Ireland police (John Horan and Jimmy

Molloy) interview Jonathan Lyons in New York as they continue to build a case against Colin Lees, Derek Jones and others.

1999

12 April: Colin Lees makes first court appearance, admitting forty-seven charges of theft and fraud totalling £20 million from his own group of companies.

7 September: Lees appears in court again, this time to plead guilty to involvement in the £2 million drinks scam in which he evaded paying duty.

9 September: Derek Jones goes on trial for his involvement in the drinks scam. It ends on **29 September** with his acquittal on eight charges and the jury hung on eleven others.

30 September: Colin Lees pleads guilty in court to the £17 million drug smuggling operation.

10 October: Jones goes on trial for the drug smuggling and is acquitted on **27 October.** A reporting ban is imposed by the judge on coverage of this trial because Jones faces other charges of money laundering for the Mafia and a retrial on the drinks charges.

6 December: Jones is convicted and banned from being a company director for seven years. But he is set free and his current jail terms of four and five years are suspended for three years. Reporting of his case is still banned because of the money laundering charges yet to be dealt with in the Lees case.

In the wake of Jones' release, Lees dismisses his former lawyers and successfully applies to the High Court to set aside his guilty pleas and to again plead not guilty on all charges. Reporting ban reinforced because of prospect of four jury trials.

2000

September: Lees' trial on the drug charges begins . . . but is aborted for legal reasons. Retrial follows within weeks and on **19 October** Lees is convicted. Reporting ban still holds.

23 November: Lees pleads guilty to forty-seven charges of theft and fraud; nineteen on the drinks scam and two of money laundering. Reporting ban still holds because of trials of others still to take place.

30 November: Lees is finally sentenced. He gets twelve years for the drug offences and lesser sentences to run concurrently on the other charges. As he indicates he might appeal the drugs conviction, the reporting restrictions remain in place. However, the BBC ask the judge to reconsider and the judge allows the media to report the fact that Lees has been convicted of the drugs offences. But all other reporting restrictions remain, preventing the media from reporting the full extent of Lees' criminal past.

2002

October: Lees finally indicates that he will not be going ahead with an appeal and the reporting restrictions are finally lifted.

2003

10 October: Having been in prison since 1997, Lees will qualify for release on this date as the system in Northern Ireland allows for 50/50 remission.

The Prologue

S itting at his desk, the wheeler-dealer pondered excitedly on the scale of the business scam he was about to execute, dwelling on the massive profit he would derive should he bring it off.

He doodled on a notepad, going over and over the figures, again and again, never arriving at the same costing twice. This was a complicated and audacious business plan.

Here, in one corner of a sheet of paper, he wrote: Boat £55,000; bank £300; solicitor £300; surveyor/yard £350; crew plus retainers £3,000; Noel expenses equipment plus £2,500; travel crew expenses £1,500; company front £5,000 . . . total £68,500 rounded up to £70k. Beside this figure he wrote 18 October 1996.

Then, on another part of the same page he scribbled another set of figures: Crew £50,000; John plus 1, £25,000; unloaders/security 4 times 5, £20,000 . . .

This was going to be a very profitable deal — risky but exceedingly profitable — if everything went according to plan. He had to make sure everything was taken care of, every eventuality catered for, every cost accounted for to ensure maximum profit. It made good business sense. That's why he was a multi-millionaire. Bankrupt, but a millionaire. He'd taken risks before, played for high stakes and lost. He wasn't going to lose this one.

He took time to reflect on his humble origins, the family businesses set up by his father. But that was before he took control and used his skills to expand and bring about the rewards of success — the racing cars, the helicopter. That was all before the crash, the bankruptcy, the fraud squad investigations, the humiliation.

He stared at the figures and began once again. On a clean corner of the page he started writing.

This time he figured it . . . boat £55,500; crew times . . . £3,000; £3,000 again and £3,000 again; £2,000; £2,000 again; home £11,000; rib etc. £9,000 — giving a total of £88,500 plus another £1,000. Underneath were the names Noel/Colin and the date, 28 October 1996.

And so it came to pass that on 29 October 1996, the 'Noel' mentioned above was arrested along with four other 'unloaders' along the Donegal coast. He was there to make sure the businessman's cargo was safely offloaded from the mother ship, but his RIB boat, an inflatable with a rigid hull, ran aground. Then the mother ship, the *Plongeur Wisky*, limped into harbour in Co. Clare before it could reach its destination with 'Noel' and his team in Donegal. The cargo discovered during a routine search of the mother ship staggered customs officers in Clare. On board they found 1.7 tons of cannabis.

The 'Colin' referred to on the bankrupt businessman's notations was himself — Colin Lees, one time champion racing driver and king of Northern Ireland's entrepreneurs. He had lost again — this time denied by the fates and a couple of diligent customs officers. He wasn't now going to pocket the massive profit he was anticipating from the sale of the cannabis he was smuggling into Ireland. Street value was estimated at £17 million. Very soon the world would know that he wasn't just another failed, bankrupt businessman. And soon he would have time, twelve years to be precise, to doodle and scribble notes to himself, working out what went wrong with all his careful planning. Twelve years to rue his foolishness at having committed his daring business plan to paper in his own handwriting. His prosecutors later referred in court to these notes as the 'game plan' for the enormous drugs shipment.

Yet it had all begun so differently when as a teenager he had joined his father's company en route to the top — in sole control and in pole position.

1 Life in the Fast Lane

'Colin's father brought him in to the company to help him run the business . . . it was a bit like inviting the cuckoo into the nest.'

The words of one of Colin Lees' former employees.

❦

I t was 6 a.m. The toaster popped. Colin Lees grabbed a knife and began buttering furiously. Watching and waiting were his faithful management staff.

They had gathered around him in the company offices in Magherafelt for what was not an untypical start to a working day for management at the Lees Group of companies.

Breakfast meetings were a particular favourite of the man regarded as a business messiah among those favoured with management positions in his companies. As one of them, Michael

1

Wightman, recollects, Lees brought vigour to these meetings. He just 'bristled with ideas'.

❧◦❧

William John Colin Lees was born in Magherafelt on 1 October 1952. His father, William Alexander Lees, was a respected figure in his local community. A joiner by trade, he had set up his own business in partnership with a friend, George Stewart, just after World War Two, around 1946 or so. Lees-Stewart, as the company was known, built houses and opened a concrete works that made bricks for the building trade. William Lees became a long-serving member of Magherafelt Rural District Council, representing the Unionist Party. He had five children. Colin was the only son.

According to local journalist Tommy Walls, William Lees was proud of his family home — a bungalow on the Moneymore Road. Situated on the highest point of the town of Magherafelt, it bore the grandiose moniker of Mount Zion. Tommy Walls says the old man used to boast proudly that on a clear day you could see five counties around Lough Neagh from his home.

Lees grew up in a caring and comfortable middle-class family environment. The old man's business venture steadily grew in stature and the partnership with George Stewart survived for over twenty years before a disagreement resulted in William Lees buying outright control of the business. Before the end of the 1960s, William Lees set up the sawmill that he managed successfully and profitably as well.

Colin Lees attended Rainey Endowed Grammar School. A contemporary of the time recalls starting her secondary education at Rainey in 1964 in the same class as Lees. She remembers him as an extremely bright, intelligent and pleasant pupil.

Lees, she remembers, had an ability to make others 'feel stupid' with his general knowledge and his grasp of current affairs. He was right up to date with everything on television and he was just, to use her words, 'very smart'. But she stressed that he was not a 'swot' or teachers' pet. The young Colin Lees wasn't just naturally bright; he was 'sociable, easy to get on with and in no way shy or backward . . . just normal'.

Academia held no attraction for Lees. As a teenager he was already driving a forklift truck around the yard of his father's concrete works. 1969 became a watershed year for the teenager. After completing his O Level examinations, he spent the summer working in the yard and, although he had every intention of going back to study for his A Levels, Lees found it difficult to drag himself away from his paid employment, especially as his father's health was suffering. He stayed on to help, and it wasn't long before he was making his mark. But as one former employee remarked wryly, 'Colin's father brought him in to the company to help him run the business . . . it was a bit like inviting the cuckoo into the nest.'

Another former member of staff at the company watched as Colin set about taking over. As he told me: 'Lees was ambitious. The father was happy to go on making money at the same rate and living comfortably, but Colin wanted more and he wanted it quicker than the father could deliver. So Colin effectively took over running the business. He drove the father wild with the astronomical costs he incurred.' Undoubtedly, one of Lees' most expensive costs was to lease and maintain a helicopter.

Tommy Walls remembers Lees' helicopter and one clear example of how he used it in a charitable venture. 'One year,' he told me, 'Colin used the helicopter to play Santa Claus for kids at the special care school in the town. He had the helicopter land in the school grounds and he stepped out dressed as Santa Claus to deliver sacks of presents. It was an amazing sight.'

Of course, the townspeople of Magherafelt had long grown accustomed to amazing sights when it came to the young Colin Lees. From the mid-1970s, when he was in his twenties, he enjoyed the comforts of the wealth his father had accumulated. Now that he was earning good money in the family business, he could afford to drive around town in the kind of flash cars his peers could only dream of. He was a bit of a 'Jack-the-Lad' who felt that his growing influence in the Lees company gave him an air of invincibility.

The helicoptor was seen as an extension of his other expensive hobby — racing cars. Lees had been enjoying the high-speed risks of the racing track from the 1970s. When he bought a brand new car to race in Formula Ford, Lees proudly put it on display in the disused salesroom of a property bought over by his father's company on the Moneymore Road in Magherafelt. 'He had it painted black,' Tommy Walls recalls, 'and it sat in what was formerly a car sales showroom so that it was on view to the general public through the big window facing the street.'

Colin Lees made his racing debut in the mid-1970s driving behind the wheel of a much more modest form of transport, an Alfa Romeo GT. But within twelve months he had switched to single-seat racing cars where he immediately made an impact. He led the Kent Messenger Championship in the South of England until the final round. He had demonstrated exciting driving skills and qualities in his debut year and, although pipped at the post, it was recognised that before long he would become a champion. Lees was building a reputation for his aggressiveness on the racetrack, an attribute that soon made him a champion. For his opponents, he set the standards. He *was* the man to beat. Generally regarded as the quiet man of Irish racing off the track, Lees enjoyed a reputation as being a hard, uncompromising racer who, according to some of his opponents, 'grows horns once behind the wheel'.

In 1979 he won over twenty races in the Irish Championship and appeared destined for his first major title victory. One of his fiercest rivals in those early days was Arnie Black. He regarded Colin Lees as a very tough competitor. He remembers having his first ever racetrack accident with Lees during a Formula Ford event: 'As he was getting out of the car, he got bigger and bigger, and I thought, "I better learn how to run pretty fast." But in all fairness he was always a front-running driver. I think he could have gone on internationally to be a very good driver.'

However, in November 1979, with the Irish Nationwide Formula Ford Championship seemingly in his hands, victory was snatched away before Lees could get his hands on the trophy. The beneficiary of an extraordinary piece of bad luck for Lees was his closest rival Arnie Black. The Irish Racing Drivers Association (IRDA) took away the points gained by Lees in three races because of an infringement of the rules, even though the IRDA found Lees to be an innocent party in the affair. After winning the Leinster Trophy meeting at Mondello that September, the engine of his Katzenberger Crossle was sealed for checking by an RAC scrutineer along with those of the other top three finishers. Some time later a mechanic broke the wire seals in Lees' absence. By doing so, the mechanic had broken the rules by removing the scrutineer's seals before the scrutineer had checked the engine. When the scrutineer did check it, he found that it had not been tampered with but even so, Lees lost the points and the title. The consequence was that Lees dropped into second place behind Arnie Black. Even worse, Lees lost the Ulster Championship in the last race of the season, pipped again by Arnie Black. But he soon bounced back.

The 1980 season was his. He easily claimed the Ulster title as well as the Irish Formula Ford Festival. It is perhaps worth pointing out that in the Formula Ford 1600 racing class, Lees was at one time or another competing against future Formula One drivers Martin Donnelly and Eddie Irvine. Another of Lees' opponents was Kenneth Acheson, a regular winner, who once had this to say about Lees' ability as a racing driver: 'The thing about Colin is, if you can beat him, then you know you can go into England with your confidence boosted. Your won't meet anyone tougher there.'

The 1980 racing season was significant for another reason. Arch-rival Arnie Black was so impressed with Lees' driving form that he recommended the mid-Ulster businessman to Goodwin Racing boss Ivor Goodwin. As the UK distributor for Delta Cars, Goodwin was looking for an Irishman to take the wheel of a Delta in a Formula Ford 2000 race at Phoenix Park in Dublin. Black, the 1979 Irish Champion, had no hesitation in putting Lees' name forward. Not only had Lees never raced in this class before, he did not catch sight of the Delta car he was to drive until the night before the race. But none of this prevented him from hounding Jason Pollock in his works Crossle all the way, setting a lap record and only conceding victory on the last lap, apparently because of a missed gear change.

Lees had done enough to convince Ivor Goodwin to take him back to England for a few more races. At Brands Hatch, Lees qualified on the front row of the grid and was leading the race by nearly six seconds when he was shunted off the track by a back marker he was trying to lap at the time. Ivor Goodwin was quoted in the *Belfast Telegraph* as saying: 'I reckoned I had found a potential star and when the opportunity arose to run this new Argo in the Atlantic Championship I lost no time in offering the drive to Colin, even though I think he has only raced an Atlantic car once before.' This was just the news that Lees had always wanted.

He had accelerated his racing career into a sponsored works car. He told the *Belfast Telegraph* he saw this as an unexpected chance to break into big-time racing. Described as a '27-year-old company director', Lees was quoted in the March 1981 article as adding: 'Up until now I have been responsible for my own racing — buying the car, looking after it, finding the money to run it — but now all I have to do is race. It's up to me and it's a marvellous opportunity.' The challenge for Lees was to compete in the 13-round British Championship, beginning at Brands Hatch. Unfortunately, 1981 did not turn out well for Lees — at least on the racetrack. Car Care, his sponsors, went bust halfway through the disappointing season. The car never displayed the kind of competitiveness so evident in its driver. But Lees had had a taste of the big time and he was determined he would not be denied. If he could not beat them on the track then, like any right thinking, wealthy Premiership manager, he would buy success!

When Lees returned to the Irish Atlantic Championship circuit for the 1982 season, he brought with him the car that had consistently hammered him during his curtailed British Championship bid the previous year. The Ralt RT4 had been driven to British Championship success by Ray Mallock — winning a staggering eleven of its fourteen races. So Lees was certainly familiar with the car he had spent most of the previous season tailing! What Lees paid for it is unknown, but the fact that he chose to purchase the championship-winning car is a clear indication of his overweening ambition.

In order to fund the purchase of the Ralt in the first instance, Lees had already secured sponsorship from the family firm, William A. Lees (Concrete) Ltd., and Katzenberger Products Ltd, a UK subsidiary of a German company specialising in concrete flooring. Lees manufactured the product under licence and in time he would mix business with pleasure by buying over the UK subsidiary of the German company. Katzenberger Products Ltd became wholly owned by Dynaspan (UK) Ltd — one of the companies in Lees' empire.

In January 1982, he revealed to *Belfast Telegraph* reporter Sammy Hamill: 'I will be doing the nine races in the championship and obviously I feel this is the right car. Certainly there was nothing to touch it when Mallock was driving it last season.' But he had more ambitious plans for the car: 'When I bought the car I also bought a Hart kit for Formula Two racing and I would like to tackle some of the European championship rounds. I am aiming to put together a deal which would allow me to drive in the two English rounds and hopefully two more on the Continent. But everything depends on getting sufficient sponsorship. I'm working on it . . .'

He informed the reporter that his new Ralt car was far from outclassed when Mallock ran it in some Formula Two races, even though the engine was not regarded as being up to scratch. Lees clearly indicated his ambitions when he added: 'I'll be talking to some engine builders and we will see what can be done. Obviously a Honda engine is the thing to have but financially that is out of the question. If I can get something worthwhile from Hart or Swindon or wherever, I certainly want to give F2 a try.'

All the effort appeared to be paying off. By August 1982 Lees was making history at Phoenix Park in Dublin — scoring a unique double victory in Formula Ford 2000 and Formula Atlantic. But his success in the Ralt RT4 came only after an incident at a hair-pin bend that left runner-up Gary Gibson feeling angry and upset. Lees had led the race from start to finish but Gibson was on the verge of overtaking him on lap eight. Gibson told reporters: 'Lees ran wide at Ratha [the hairpin bend] and I think he got his wheels on the grass. I had the inside line and had better traction and I went for the gap but he turned straight back into the side of my car. There was no excuse for it.' Gibson's car was sent into a spin and Lees raced away to victory. Lees insisted he did not see Gibson's car coming up on the inside.

Even though Lees was by now well known in racing circles, his opponents had little knowledge of his business activities, as Arnie Black recalled: 'When motor racing guys come together, you know them at the circuit, and you may not see them for six months or until the season starts . . . I knew he [Lees] ran a large company in Magherafelt, and that's about all I knew.'

Had Arnie Black or any members of the racing fraternity taken the trouble to find out about Colin Lees, they would have discovered that his business ambition off the track was as ruthless as his driving on it . . . and, in fact, he was busy using his racing connections to further his business activities. Aside from his acquisition of the UK subsidiary of German company Katzenberger, in 1983 Lees joined the board of Mondiale, a Co. Down company that designed and manufactured racing cars for some of the classes in which Lees raced. He also went on to race their designs competitively.

In 1990, Lees was quoted in a company magazine about his hobby and his role as a director of the Mondiale Car Company based in Bangor: 'That's another great Northern Ireland story. We started a small company in 1984 and now it's employing 20 people and exporting cars all over the world.' He was clearly proud of Mondiale and his involvement with the firm. But there would come a time when Mondiale were not so keen to be associated with Lees.

Mondiale's managing director Leslie Drysdale recalled Lees putting up a financial stake in the company when he joined the board. He could not remember how much. He told me Lees remained a director when his own companies got into financial trouble in the early 1990s. He could not remember exactly when, but recalled that Lees was approached to resign by concerned directors, concerned at the potential damage that a scandal could cause to Mondiale's reputation. 'We went to him at the time. It had become well known that he was having problems with his own companies and as far as I recall we made our approaches before he had officially gone bankrupt. Once bankrupt he would have been banned from holding directorships in any company but I think we took our action before it got to that stage.'

Throughout the 1980s, Lees built up an impressive list of company directorships both inside and outside his own family group. Records in Companies House in Belfast reveal his company interests as follows: W.A.L. Holdings Ltd; William A. Lees Concrete Ltd; William A. Lees Sawmills Ltd; W.A.L. Woodland Products Ltd; W.A.L. Forest Services Ltd; W.A.L. Wood Fibre Ltd; Dynaspan (UK) Ltd; Mondiale Car Company Ltd; Mondiale Aviation Ltd; Katzenberger Products Ltd; Celtic Forestry (NI) Ltd; Samuel Gilchrist (Lenaderg) Ltd; and Lees Pulp Ltd. With the exception of the two Mondiale directorships, all the other companies were subsidiaries of W.A.L. Holdings Ltd. His late father was listed as having directorships in all the 'W.A.L.' companies and Dynaspan (UK) Ltd, while his sister Dorothy Hartley held directorships in all of the companies with the exception of the two Mondiale companies and Katzenberger Products Ltd. For many years she was described as company secretary. She and Lees were also listed as sole directors of Dynaquip Engineering Ltd, a company established in 1987, principally to operate the mobile plant used by the Lees Group of companies. Dynaquip Ltd never employed anyone and almost without exception all its dealings were with the Lees Group.

Other companies were formed in the United Kingdom and the Republic of Ireland — and were controlled by Lees personally. The true significance of these companies would not become apparent until much later, when police fraud squad officers would discover the true role they played in Lees' criminal activities. One of these companies was Structocrete Ireland Ltd. Another was Plant Corporation of Ireland (PCI), formed in 1986. For a short period Lees and his late father William, who died in January 1992, were directors. Colin Lees, as he had with the family companies, soon nudged his father aside and took control for himself whilst at the same time creating the impression among his staff in Northern Ireland that it was his father, and not he, who owned PCI. Michael Schuster was also a director until his death in 1990, although he never knew Lees had named him as a director. PCI used the offices of an accountancy firm in Dublin, Manley and O'Reilly, and had bank accounts with Allied Irish Banks at Uxbridge in Middlesex and at Ballsbridge in Dublin. Another company with the same address as PCI was Creteplant Ltd, similarly controlled by Lees personally. Enormous amounts of money passed through these accounts under the complete control of Colin Lees. But as we shall learn later, not all the money raised on behalf of W.A.L. Holdings went to the company's accounts.

While she was still alive, Lees' mother was also listed as a director of the core companies. But after her death, there were signs of tension within the family that, as one police officer told me, resulted in Lees 'sacking' his father William. A former employee recalled: 'When the mother died, and I can't remember when that happened, the old man became a lonely figure. He found a female companion and I am not sure if that spooked the family into dealing with the ownership issue. But there was a period when the family appeared to be in a panic.' Apparently up to this point, the old man had had a free hand and he was always on site and was always working. As another former staff member told me, 'He did not do a bad job.' Effectively, he became Colin Lees' manager on site and took control of the building work and it was all done properly but 'at great expense'.

When the big break-up came a mediator was sought — someone trusted by both parties. It proved to be a successful move. Within a month or so of the mediator talking to both Colin Lees and his father William, they were back on speaking terms. The father was soon back on site as the new office block on the Ballyronan Road was under construction. The old man was spending money but Colin Lees did not mind just how much. 'As long as the old man is happy,' he remarked.

While staff enjoyed the vitality of the chief executive and major shareholder in the Lees Group, some acknowledged that the unorthodox manner in which Lees ran company affairs worked against the kind of progression that could and should have been achieved. Michael Wightman was twenty-four years of age when he joined the Lees company in Magherafelt in 1985 as a management accountant. He acknowledges that he was ill-equipped for the job: 'way in over my head with just one year's exams,' was how he put it. But he said that was not an uncommon feature of the employment practice at the time.

'If Colin Lees had had a proper management structure I am certain he would not have experienced half the difficulties he eventually had to face,' he says, adding: 'But he was the golden boy of the Industrial Development Board. Everything he touched seemed to turn to gold and to be fair, up to 1991 when things started to go wrong, it was a great company to work for. Colin had great personality and a wonderful ability to speak to anyone on any level. He could speak intelligently to government ministers, to the leaders of high finance and could go to a bar and talk to a lorry driver about the steering mechanisms on the lorry.'

Lees worked hard. He did not expect of his workforce a level of effort and commitment that he himself was not prepared to give. Another Lees employee says that even though Lees began work at 6 a.m., preparing breakfast for his management team, he would finish late at night — nine or ten most commonly. Few were surprised he had created a company that, on paper at least, showed expediential growth.

In 1984 Colin Lees took steps to upgrade his management team. Lees by then had a disparate group of seven or eight small companies operating in what one employee described as 'financial disarray with no accountancy system at all'. It was difficult for those tasked with the financial reconstruction of the companies to find a starting point. There was a lack of a proper accountancy system. It just did not exist.

As a freelance management consultant, Joe Cole was one of the key figures in re-shaping Lees' companies, going on to become a financial director for a number of years. Joe Cole declined to talk about his experiences with W.A.L. Holdings, but others who worked for Lees describe Cole's contribution as vital in bringing order out of chaos. Cole travelled extensively with Colin Lees. Like others, I was told, he was impressed by Lees' work rate even if a little concerned that some of the shortcuts taken by Lees would take him close to the line.

New auditors were brought in to help make important changes in the way W.A. Lees did business. One source told me that the new auditors had a query with the old auditor about PAYE. He apparently said he needed some time to get an answer to the question. When he called back a few days later he said, 'That was a figure Dorothy [Lees' sister Dorothy Dickson Hartley] gave me.'

It just seemed to be the way an old country practice had worked.

As a family-run concern, W.A. Lees had a less than formal way of conducting its affairs. Christmas bonuses were paid in cash . . . and there were some substantial amounts handed over to loyal members of the company, particularly on the management side.

Lees' companies paid their staff weekly, on Fridays, and in cash. It was the way it was done before computers, cash cards and electronic money transactions. Every Friday, staff would go to the company bank and draw sufficient cash to make up the wage bill. A number of the staff would lock themselves in an office and count out the cash into pay packets. Nothing out of the ordinary in that . . . except! One Friday, unexpectedly, an employee was somewhat taken aback as he walked through the office: 'I saw two trays of pay packets set out on the desk. I happened to look at the first name on one tray and when I did the same on the second tray, I noticed the same name again. Was someone getting two pay packets? I asked one of the girls who then explained that the second packet was the overtime. She said they paid any overtime in cash. They didn't put it through the books. I asked where the cash came from and was told it was collected at weekends from farmers who came in to pay bills and buy materials and they paid cash to avoid VAT.' That was another of the practices that changed under the new system of accountancy.

The new auditors soon had a solution to some of Colin Lees' problems. They had identified inefficiencies in the way the companies were run and suggested it would be better for tax purposes if Lees established a group of companies. It was decided to go with this plan. It was around this time that the family determined that Colin Lees should take over ownership of the companies. He took 51 per cent controlling share, leaving the remainder of the shares divided between other family members. Although he had relinquished control of his companies, William Lees continued to be involved in the day-to-day running of the business, working effectively as manager.

The groundwork was prepared for the establishment of W.A.L. Holdings. Records at Companies House in Belfast show that the holding company was registered on 29 January 1986. The W.A.L. was for William Alexander Lees, Colin's father, who had established the concrete works and sawmill some years before.

It was an exciting time for the Lees Group of companies. Lees' work rate continued to impress those who worked with him. But some of the new financial thinkers in the company found it difficult to work with him in one respect.

Michael Wightman, as commercial director, was in a good position to observe Lees' management style: 'The management team never had the full picture of what was going on. Only Lees had the full picture. He did not have the right people in the right jobs. But every one of the 400 he employed at his peak thought the world of him.'

However, while that may have been the experience of those managers employed by Lees, it was not the case for other employees, according to other sources. *Mid-Ulster Mail* reporter Stanley Campbell told me: 'The workers were not allowed to look him in the eye. Most of them regarded him as an obnoxious man.' Another former worker said both Colin Lees and his father William had little idea about good industrial relations. He told me that if they tried to run the company today as they did then, they would be put out of business on health and safety grounds alone. 'The story around Magherafelt was that the Lees would not employ cripples — they made them,' he said, adding: 'The machinery was dangerous and by today's standards was inadequately protected by guards.'

Some people living in Magherafelt watched Lees closely and agreed that he was generous when drinking in bars around the town. 'Of course he would buy drink,' said one resident, 'but he liked to publicly display this generous side to his nature. It's amazing what buying a couple of pints for someone in a bar can do. It buys patronage and some strange kind of loyalty, even though in the workplace Lees and his companies were absolutely ruthless in the way they treated workers. On pay-day the workers would be kept waiting in a queue outside the offices to collect their wages — and they could stand around for ages in the pouring rain. That's the kind of care they were shown.'

Some of the key management personnel in Lees' companies found the lack of consultation, as identified by Michael Wightman, the most frustrating aspect of their work. But the new auditors brought about change. As one former staff member told me: 'Lees was challenged about his system of management. For example, the issue of board meetings or the lack of them was something that needed to be changed. Lees and his family, his father, mother, sister, would run the group of companies with meetings around the fireside on Sundays. They did not bother with the formality of board meetings, although that is one of the things that changed when the new holding company was established.'

One of Lees' managers told me he was surprised that he did not pick up on Colin Lees' shady dealings. With hindsight he, like so many others, realises that Lees apparently could compartmentalise his life. He had the ability to deal with people function by function. 'We never all got together as a committee,' my source recalled. 'Lees was sitting in the hub of the wheel and he alone was keeping people around the wheel informed . . . which of course kept them busy without them realising the degree to which they were involved.'

'What worries me,' he added, 'is that I should have picked up on what was going on. You know, sometimes it is something intellectual that triggers a concern but other times it is a gut reaction. I got neither. In the last year Lees was not involving the team around him and he was becoming increasingly isolated. Two or three left and others still working there were looking for opportunities to get out. That casual, dependable feeling that people had in Lees had gone . . . it was accelerated. But these things brought to my attention were nothing on the scale of the stuff that emerged. I still have difficulty accepting the scale of things.'

With wealth comes power, responsibility and temptation. As he continued his business expansion in the 1980s, Lees was beginning to display signs that he was struggling to cope with the power that came with his wealth and success. Increasingly there was tension in his private life. According to a variety of sources, Lees had a number of mistresses in the Mid-Ulster area. There were definite signs of strain on his marriage, as witnessed by employees. One told me: 'I met the wife and kids. It was a good family set up. As best I could judge it, everything was hunky dory. This would have been about two years or just a bit more before the companies collapsed. During that period, I arrived for work on a couple of mornings and was told by others I had missed the action. Apparently a couple of mornings Mrs Lees had turned up with Colin's clothes packed into suitcases which she then deposited. She was throwing them about the place.'

On another occasion, according to a Magherafelt resident, Lees' wife found out about an affair and exacted revenge by getting all his good suits and placing them on the muddy laneway leading to their home. She then drove the family car up and down the lane.

Eventually, Lees moved out of the family home and settled with Zara — a former bank worker who became his personal assistant. One woman who knew her told me: 'Zara worked for him. She had been employed at the Northern Bank because that's my bank and I used to see her working there as a teller. Her name was Hyndman. I remember when the job was advertised — for a personal assistant to the managing director. I think my manager at the time applied for it. It was a career girl's dream job. I might have thought about it myself. It was advertised in the *Mid-Ulster Mail*.'

In spite of the pressures, the family difficulties and the continuing growth of his group of companies, Colin Lees successfully managed to juggle all these problems. By the mid-1980s he was actively involved in securing business loans from banks, most notably the Ulster Bank and Bank of Ireland in Magherafelt. The banks were convinced that Lees' business plans were credible, so Lees enjoyed their confidence and their money. So too finance houses and leasing companies advanced millions of pounds to Lees in the belief that his capital investments in plant and equipment had tied up large amounts of hard cash.

Lees apparently even managed to convince some famous celebrities to invest in the future. In the mid-1980s his forestry management company was contracted to look after acres and acres of forests in Ireland, North and South. At the time Lees said in a television interview: 'I think that the timber when it matures in some thirty, forty, forty-five years time will be a worldwide commodity that will be in demand, very much in demand. And I think Ireland at that stage will probably be self-supporting in timber.' BBC staff recall Lees mentioning a number of VIPs who had or were thinking about investing in this futuristic plan — among them rock singer Roger Daltry. Whether or not they actually put money into the project is far from clear.

In a glossy brochure promoting the company and giving something of its history, Colin Lees spelt out his vision for Irish forestry:

18

'Trees grow faster in Ireland than anywhere else in the British Isles and at three times the speed they grow in Scandinavia. However, there is only 5% afforestation [sic]. This growth rate, coupled with the lack of afforestation [sic] presents a tremendous opportunity for the whole timber industry.'

However, more significantly, Lees had the confidence of the government. Throughout the 1980s, Lees was working feverishly towards one of his most ambitious projects, a £6m shopping centre for his hometown. The plan was to build the shopping complex on the site occupied by the Lees company on the Moneymore Road. He intended to build new company offices on the Ballyronan Road.

Government cash was by now starting to pour into the Lees company coffers to assist in the continued growth as envisaged by Lees. Between 1985 and 1992, he received offers of government financial aid totalling £2,279,300, according to official figures provided by the Industrial Development Board (IDB). First to benefit was Dynaspan (UK) Ltd in 1985, with further monies paid to W.A.L. Holdings Ltd in 1992 and Lees Sawmills Ltd between 1985 and 1992. The IDB said they actually paid him £1,667,954.65p before he went bust. When the shutters came down on the king of the entrepreneurs, the government was entitled to recover £823,481.84p — but managed only to claw back £173,514.39p — leaving Lees with a tidy profit of £1,494,440.30p!

Lees was on target to persuade his friends in government to give the go-ahead for the shopping centre. But first, there was the small matter of IRA gun and bomb attacks against companies and the workmen they employed doing jobs for the Crown. This was a major difficulty for the government, and assistance was needed to resolve the problem. Lees was willing to provide his services to help. And so it came to pass that in 1987, during an escalating IRA murder campaign against anyone working on the construction or rebuilding of security bases damaged in bomb attacks, Lees was prepared to carry out work for the security services by secretly setting up an operation in Scotland. Unknown to the government and its ministers was the fact that behind the veneer of success, Lees was already struggling to make ends meet and had by then already taken his first steps into criminality . . .

2 *The Scottish Misadventure*

'I really didn't understand what he was talking about until he produced this revolver from the back of his trouser belt and my wife came in with coffee for everybody, saw the gun and took fright . . . and they were immediately put away. I spoke to Colin Lees and his view was they were just a couple of lads playing cowboys and Indians. He said if there were any problems, he would see they would be attended to and so I took it from that he had connections which were real connections.'
The late Malcolm Baillie describing an early business meeting at which Lees outlined a secret plan to deceive the IRA.

❖

Renee Baillie nearly dropped the tray of tea and biscuits when she saw the loaded revolver sitting on the dining room table in front of her husband Malcolm and his business associates.

21

Renee struggled to disguise her fright as she caught her startled husband's eye. He shrugged his shoulders. She deposited the tray and returned to the kitchen of their terraced Inverness home. After all, she thought, Malcolm had been told the business deal under discussion was top-secret and involved MI6 in a venture designed to assist the British government to hoodwink the IRA. It was April 1987 and Malcolm Baillie was simply answering a call to stand up to be counted at his country's time of need.

That call for help had come the previous autumn — in November to be precise; just a month or so after the IRA had murdered another workman involved in carrying out work for the security forces.

On 24 October 1986, the IRA took Kenneth Johnston's life. He was a 25-year-old shop manager, married with one child. He died at the wheel of a car owned by his employer who, most likely, was the intended target of the gunmen. He was taking a salesman to lunch at his boss's behest. The sales rep was slightly wounded. The IRA said the firm was carrying out work for the security forces and claimed the company had ignored repeated warnings to desist. The shop owner said the IRA knew that Kenny Johnston managed his shop and that he had no connection to the work being done for the security forces by other sections of the company. Kenneth Johnston was the first of a number of employees connected with the Magherafelt-based firm Henry Brothers to be murdered by the Provos.

Colin Lees' companies were at the time also involved in work for the security forces from their premises in Magherafelt. Attacks on other firms in the town made Lees and his staff ever more vigilant. IRA attacks on workers employed by companies contracted to provide services to what the terrorists described as 'agents of the Crown' were rapidly becoming a matter of growing concern. Like many other businessmen, Colin Lees was extremely worried about his own safety and that of his workforce. Advice on basic personal security measures was provided in leaflets issued by police which had been prepared some years earlier with VIPs in mind. Now they had become essential reading for building workers and tradesmen going about their everyday routine of earning a crust to keep their families fed and clothed. Within weeks of Kenneth Johnston's murder, Lees took steps to remove the threat of IRA attacks — with the help of ministerial friends in the ruling Conservative government, which by then regarded Lees as a valued and trusted entrepreneurial partner in business. Now that partnership was about to answer the country's call in a time of need.

And sixty-year-old Malcolm Baillie in Inverness had become the key to outwitting the IRA. In ill-health, he had just accepted a redundancy package from the Highlands and Islands Development Board (HIDB) for whom he had been employed as an accountant. His job had been to investigate companies seeking to set up in business with HIDB funding.

Like anyone approached for help by their State, Malcolm Baillie believed he could, even in retirement, make a meaningful contribution to Queen and Country. That is how he viewed this approach. He felt flattered to be asked. He understood the risks. The adventure began in November 1986 — less than a month after Kenneth Johnston's murder — with a telephone call from Chris Nicholson, an Englishman who owned the Scottish island of Easdale and a small shipping company appropriately named Easdale Shipping. Malcolm Baillie had already met Nicholson, shortly after the Englishman bought the island and was seeking help from the HIDB to buy the *Eilean Eisdeal*, a puffer — the Glasgow name for small cargo boats that plied their trade on the River Clyde. But now Nicholson wanted to talk about an exciting new venture, one in which Malcolm Baillie would have an important role to play.

Nicholson said he had been negotiating a shipping contract with someone in Northern Ireland but had come across a bigger 'hush-hush development' taking place and if it came to pass he, Nicholson, would be back in touch. Baillie was intrigued.

But even as Lees planned his furtive construction work on a Scottish island, there came a tragic reminder of why such extreme measures were necessary to protect building workers. On 21 April 1987, the IRA struck again in Lees' hometown. This time the victim of five IRA gunmen was Harry Henry, a 52-year-old married man with six children. The Provos said he was targeted because his brother's building firm was still doing work for the security forces. An IRA statement said: 'Such people are a more prime target than the foot soldier or the RUC constable because of the crucial function they perform.' The gunmen had broken into his home and dragged him away from his wife and family to shoot him dead in the garden outside.

By this stage, Chris Nicholson had already kept his promise to telephone Malcolm Baillie. The 'hush-hush' deal was about to be done and he wanted to set up a meeting between Malcolm and a highly successful Northern Ireland businessman, Colin Lees. Nicholson explained that Lees' companies had been involved in providing building materials to the security forces to repair bases damaged in terrorist bomb attacks. But now that the IRA considered building companies and their workers 'legitimate targets', the attacks were becoming more frequent and the body count was mounting. Given the very real threat that now existed, Lees was well advanced with plans to continue working for the security forces but at a new location well out of view of the terrorists.

Malcolm Baillie may not have appreciated the urgency of the business meeting hosted at his home in Inverness in April 1987. But Lees' bid to out-manoeuvre the IRA was moving apace and could only do so with the help of government agencies, including the secret services.

Before arriving at the Baillie's home that April afternoon, Colin Lees took his party of business advisers and associates to a meeting with the HIDB to find out if the new business venture could qualify for grant aid to establish a special concrete production plant on a remote Scottish island. Interestingly, according to Malcolm Baillie, the HIDB agreed to make funding available but because of the political sensitivities involved and in order to maintain secrecy among the islanders, chose to pass the paperwork to the Scottish Development Agency in Glasgow. Eventually, financial assistance to the value of £248,000 was offered but Malcolm Baillie claimed the new company didn't take it up — principally because in his view, as managing director of the new company, insufficient work was done to justify accepting the cash.

Agreement to establish the new company — Marine Structures Ltd — was reached following the HIDB meeting when Lees' high-powered business team gathered in the comfort of the Baillie's terraced home high above Inverness. The talk was of plans for Lees' new commercial venture at Lochmaddy on the western isle of North Uist, population 3,000. The Baillies recall those present as Alan Dunlop, representing William Reid Shipping Agents in Belfast; Chris Nicholson of Easdale Shipping; Professor Jim Magowan, the then Dean of External Affairs at the University of Ulster, and, of course, Colin Lees.

From the beginning, some members of the group were keen to boast about their 'connections'. Certainly at the initial meetings in the Baillies' home, the production of a gun added a whiff of danger to the whole affair. According to Malcolm Baillie, Chris Nicholson was keen to emphasise his links to the British secret service, MI6. Malcolm Baillie told me: 'The only connection that

I know of was that Chris Nicholson seemed to be involved with the security services. But Chris being Chris, it could have been correct or it might have been Walter Mitty. He certainly produced a gun along with Alan Dunlop, the shipping agent, which was a ratherfrightening experience. We were in the dining room and Alan Dunlop kept saying, "Are you carrying?" And I really didn't understand what he was talking about until he [Nicholson] produced this revolver from the back of his trouser belt and my wife came in with coffee for everybody, saw the gun[s] and took fright . . . and they were immediately put away. I spoke to Colin Lees and his view was they were just a couple of lads playing cowboys and Indians. He said if there were any problems, he would see they would be attended to and so I took it from that he had connections which were real connections.'

Agreement was reached to establish a holding company, Wharton Trading Ltd, which was incorporated on the Isle of Man. The company came into existence on 12 June 1987. In order to cover his involvement, Lees had asked a firm of company agents Jordan & Sons to assist. In fact, Jordan & Sons became the nominated shareholders, while the directors were initially listed as Susan Mary Allen, of High Street, Port St Mary, Isle of Man, and Nicola Janet Kermode, of Glen Maye, Isle of Man. Jordan & Sons (Isle of Man) Ltd were listed as company secretary. But by 8 August, Allen and Kermode had resigned. Pierre Labesse, whose address was given as Rue de Revilly, Paris, and Jean Bloch, from Meyrin, Switzerland, immediately replaced them as directors. Marine Structures Ltd was a wholly owned subsidiary of Wharton Trading. The company had authorised share capital of one million shares at £1 each; of which 500,000 were allotted, issued and fully paid up.

Malcolm Baillie described his role as follows: 'He [Lees] offered me the job as a book-keeper at £12,500 a year but because of the security angle he had to hide his name. That was the reason for the company being set up in the Isle of Man. There were two shares in the company in fictitious names in order to hide Colin Lees' involvement. I fronted it as the managing director. Colin Lees' name was kept out of it.' Malcolm Baillie later travelled over to Magherafelt to be briefed on the duties he was expected to carry out.

I contacted those identified by the Baillies as being present at the initial meeting in Inverness. Alan Dunlop told me he had 'absolutely no comment' to make. He said he wanted to leave his past connections with Colin Lees in the past and just wanted to 'move on.' Professor Magowan said he could recall the HIDB meeting but had no recollection of the meeting in the Baillies' house. He certainly had no memory of a gun being produced at any meeting. 'I would certainly have remembered that,' he said.

Chris Nicholson was at his home in Warwickshire when I called. Wearing green overalls, he emerged from the stables at the top of his laneway and invited me to have a cuppa with him in his kitchen. He denied any links with MI6, stating: 'I would not say if I was, at least, I would have thought not.' He also very clearly denied having a gun. 'I did not produce a gun,' he stated emphatically.

Chris Nicholson, in spite of his claims otherwise, was no stranger to guns. On two other occasions Renee Baillie witnessed him with handguns — both times at Nicholson's Warwickshire home when the Baillies were staying there. Malcolm Baillie also told me of these two occasions during that trip. Firstly, they say Nicholson produced a handgun and shot dead a rat found in one of his outbuildings. Renee and Nicholson's partner had uncovered a rat's nest while tidying up one of the barns. Then during the early hours of the morning, a courting couple parked at the bottom of the laneway leading to Nicholson's home — setting off alarms. Lights went on around the house and, according to the Baillies, Nicholson appeared with a handgun. Police arrived within minutes. 'He was certainly well protected,' said Malcolm Baillie.

One other person told me of an occasion when Nicholson produced a weapon. A member of the Lees management in Magherafelt remembers collecting Nicholson off a flight from England at Lees' behest. 'That man was bonkers,' he said. 'Colin asked me to go to the airport one day and pick Nicholson up. I was to take him to his hotel and then we would meet him next morning. I took him to the hotel and got him checked in. He asked me to join him for dinner that evening. I agreed; I didn't think it right he should be dining alone. At one point we were in the gents and as we peed, he asked me what I carried. I didn't know what he was on about. "What are you carrying?" he would ask. Then he produced a big handgun from beneath his jacket. I told him to put it away.'

Nicholson said it was Alan Dunlop, the shipping agent, who introduced him to Colin Lees. 'He [Dunlop] had been asked to find work for us,' said Nicholson. 'We were desperate for work and Lees induced us to buy a 600-ton vessel and he would fit it with a crane to load and unload logs and timber. I was double-crossed by Lees. All the freights we did for him have never been paid. I ended up paying for the crane myself.' Nicholson said he was not party to the discussion that took place at Malcolm Baillie's house because he left the room and spent time in the kitchen with Renee. 'I introduced Lees to Malcolm and I left the room,' he said.

Whatever the truth of the competing claims, what was certain was that Lees had security clearance because of his secret work on the police rebuilding programme and appeared to be exceptionally well connected. How well connected would not become apparent for some time.

Colin Lees did not act alone in making the move to North Uist to produce concrete panels for police stations in Northern Ireland. He needed government approval to attempt such a dangerous security operation intended to hoodwink the IRA. He had the backing of British secret services and elected politicians. By 1987, Colin Lees was regarded highly by British government ministers sent to administer Westminster's direct rule. He had been involved in negotiations with them about the construction of a shopping centre in his hometown — to be built on the site of his own offices. In those days of extreme IRA violence, the government needed all the friends it could get and in Colin Lees they found someone prepared to put his money where his mouth was and to actually invest in a programme of expansion that helped create jobs. Lees was shaping up to be a major employer in the north-west area of Northern Ireland. Colin Lees was lured to the Scottish highlands and islands by a government that admired his business acumen. In their time of need, he was prepared to help them. Scratching each other's backs was a means of maintaining the outward appearance that terrorism was not going to be allowed to win; either by stopping rebuilding work on security bases or by putting companies that did such work out of business. Such talk helped convince and inspire the Baillies that they would be doing their bit to assist in the defeat of terrorism.

But what also emerged at the crucial 1987 meeting in the Baillies' home was the fact that the concrete to be manufactured had special qualities developed in Northern Ireland in a bid to help the government and the security forces keep one step ahead of their enemies, the IRA. Colin Lees did not disguise the dangers that potentially lay ahead. 'In fairness,' Malcolm Baillie recalled, 'Colin Lees did say there was a slight element of danger; he said certainly if you were in Northern Ireland, but to a much lesser extent here in Scotland, and I should think about it before decid-ing. Which I did. And I decided to go ahead with it. However, I was clearly advised at the time.' And it wasn't just Lees' evident candour that impressed Malcolm Baillie: 'He was very businesslike. He travelled with his own private plane and conducted business very efficiently and capably. He was a very good businessman and it's just unfortunate that he went down the wrong road. I wouldn't discredit him in any way from his ability to carry out business.'

Malcolm Baillie had a very clear understanding that what was to be secretly manufactured were special concrete panels designed and tested to powder on impact rather than fragment into large dangerous chunks that had the potential to kill when thrown high into the air by the force of an explosion before crashing down on those beneath. 'The actual concrete panels consisted of a material known as fabric reinforcement,' Malcolm Baillie recalled. 'The polypropylene mesh was filled with concrete inside the steel plate. If it was struck by an explosive, instead of concrete flying about the place it just pouted and therefore did not do any harm to people inside the building. That was the purpose of using it; plus by constructing these panels you could use them to erect fabric buildings in twenty-four hours.' He said this had been demon-strated to him during his visit to Northern Ireland.

Professor Magowan knew more about the history of the new concrete product Lees was proposing to produce in North Uist. Lees had approached him some months earlier after learning from an official in the Local Enterprise Development Unit (LEDU) that a new concrete product had been patented. Professor Magowan said: 'Lees called me and asked for a meeting. The patent belonged to two guys from the civil engineering department and Lees said he would like to try to develop the patent. We thought the best way forward was if he had any applications for it he could develop it, but in order to do that he would have to take out a licence for permission to use it and exploit the patent. And that's exactly what he did.'

But the patent — which cost Lees around £5,000 a year in licence fees — was actually shared jointly between the University of Ulster and the Lambeg Industrial Research Association based near Lisburn. A number of former Lees employees remembered it was a man called Harry Green who pioneered the work on the concrete. Green's expertise lay in the development of a product called Kevlar, a crucial component used in the production of bullet-proof vests. Green was first to identify the potential for developing some kind of Kevlar weave into concrete. Once Lees had the licence to exploit this new development, he applied for research and development money. Around a dozen panels were made for testing up at Magilligan Strand in Co. Derry. One former employee recalled: 'The Army hit them with stuff of a similar strength to that being used by the IRA. It was all witnessed by the senior military personnel. But the Industrial Development Board refused to pay out because we had no panels left to show them!'

The panels had great potential with far-reaching, life-saving applications in conflict zones all over the world. Much later, after he had produced the concrete on North Uist, Lees was delighted to learn of interest from consultants representing the Ministry of Defence (MOD) in London. Lees sent a delegation to London to meet the procurement officer. I understand that during the meeting one of Lees' executives helpfully suggested that the panels would provide good protection if used in the construction of aircraft hangars. But one of the MOD boffins was quick to respond: 'Fuck that. We want to build huts for pilots. We can get another plane in six months, but it takes six years to train a pilot.'

Time was of the essence. The meeting to finalise details for setting up the factory on North Uist had taken place in April 1987, and one of the first jobs for the new managing director of Marine Structures Ltd was to advertise for staff in the local newspaper, the *West Highland Free Press*. At the same time Malcolm Baillie informed the newspaper that his company had just acquired the old seaweed-drying factory at Sponish just a few miles away from the island's main town and ferry port, Lochmaddy.

In an interview with the Skye-based paper, Malcolm spoke about business worth £40m being generated over the next few years, with the potential to create 100 new jobs. Obviously, these were the stated targets of the new company as expressed by the real 'behind-the-scenes' management. They made the bullets; Malcolm Baillie's job was to fire them into the public domain. Whilst talking to the reporter, Malcolm even unwittingly gave the newspaper the carefully concocted cover story to disguise to everyone, including the future workforce, the true reason for the establishment of the concrete business. He informed readers of the *West Highland Free Press* that the first customer for the concrete panels was based in the Middle East. They were required for marine breakwater and harbour facilities. Interestingly, the editor apparently later received a call from the Israeli secret service Mossad inquiring about the materials being supplied from North Uist to Oman!

Soon potential workers surrounded the Lochmaddy Hotel where Marine Structures' interview panel was in session. People, starved of work, had come from far and wide, attracted by the creation of what they had been promised was a secure business with fantastic growth potential. North Uist resident Donald MacIsaac remembers the day well: 'There were long queues of people there, one hundred or more. I couldn't say exactly how many but there were a lot. When I turned up there were a lot of people ahead of me and by the time I left there were still a lot of people waiting to be interviewed.' According to Donald MacIsaac, Chris Nicholson sat on the interview panel alongside two Lees employees from Northern Ireland and Malcolm Baillie. Nicholson admitted he sat in on the interviews but told me: 'I was present at the interviews on North Uist because I brought the work to the island. I was delighted. I was involved in introducing Colin Lees and Malcolm Baillie. People trusted me because I had been bringing coal to the island at a better rate. I was transporting coal to the island and selling it at £75 per ton when others were charging £120 a ton.' Former employees like Donald MacIsaac believed Nicholson's role on the interview panel was connected to a fact that emerged much later, which revealed that everyone employed at the Sponish works had been secretly vetted by the security services. Nicholson denies he had any involvement in the vetting procedure.

A trained engineer, Donald MacIsaac was hired by the interview panel. But still the work was too 'hush-hush' to share with him or the eventual small number of recruits chosen at the hotel interviews. 'They were making concrete that used a fabric reinforcement,' Donald MacIsaac said. 'It all fitted together in a steel frame. They were all bolted to a steel frame. All sections, roof and ceiling and walls, everything was pre-cast. There were layers of polypropylene mesh sprayed with mortar, a silica-sand cement mix and layer upon layer of that on the external surfaces. It was for strengthening against impact. We were shown the document from the Sultanate of Oman showing figures for impact resistance and just technical details for the panels. But it was to withstand or resist shell attacks or for use in bunkers. We got very little detail from the company about what was going on.'

Production began in the summer of 1987 with an initial twelve or thirteen people hired to work at the old seaweed factory, although that number may have quickly increased to around twenty according to one former worker there. Two batches of panels were constructed and 'despatched to the Middle East!' But it didn't take the workforce too long to establish that this top-secret production work — given the codename the 'Luton Airport Project' — was not all that it seemed to be. Nor indeed were the people sent over from Lees' parent company in Ireland all that they said they were. As the workers at Sponish discovered, some of the Irishmen were using false names.

'We knew that once we had the buildings complete that they had been erected fairly quickly because we had feedback from Neil Morris — one of the Irish workers sent over to North Uist,' recalled Donald MacIsaac, 'so we knew that they hadn't gone to the Middle East anyway. So we assumed that they had gone to Ireland because they had been . . . over a weekend they had been erected, I believe. And, so that we kind of knew something else was going on but we didn't know what it was.' What was even more disconcerting for the small workforce was the discovery that some of the workers sent across from Lees' Northern Ireland company were not using their real names. For example, Donald MacIsaac was stunned to find out that initially Neil Morris was not identified or introduced as Neil Morris. 'It was odd that that was going on,' he told me. 'Malcolm Baillie described him as Morris Neill, so I think it was a Neil, yes, but I am not sure. They had, I think, fallen out somewhat, Malcolm Baillie and Neil Morris, so I guess maybe it was a while after that before everything was starting to fall into place, you know. I didn't realise and although I worked here, it was a short time and I had probably left, you know, when we started to find out about these things. They should have told us. As I've said, they were hiding behind false names and other things and if it was perhaps dangerous, they should have told the workforce here. Perhaps everyone here was putting themselves in an element of danger.' Colin Lees often used false names in his business dealings, citing security as a reason when eventually challenged by the police to explain this particular trait.

In any event, according to Malcolm Baillie the production of concrete panels continued for a short time, maybe eight to ten months. Shipment of the finished product to Northern Ireland was the responsibility of Chris Nicholson's company, Easdale Shipping. The first and only delivery of panels by Easdale Shipping was destined for the RUC station at Castlederg in Co. Tyrone. Chris Nicholson told me he remembered it well, although given his involvement in helping to bring Lees to North Uist in the first place, his recollection of the events surrounding the first delivery is, to say the least, somewhat baffling.

This is what he told me: 'One of our ships took the first load to Belfast. It was to go to a secure wharf at Harland and Wolff. We did not get that information until we were in Belfast Lough. When we radioed to Harland and Wolff to tell them we had 600 tons of concrete blocks, we were told to "fuck off". So we took the load to a wharf in the city centre and were met with loads of cops. It was then we learned exactly what we were carrying and we refused to do it anymore. I thought we had been absolutely duped. If terrorists found out about North Uist and our involvement in the shipments of material for police stations in Northern Ireland, then we would have become targets.' Nicholson claimed that he refused to make any more deliveries and that six subsequent loads were shipped to Northern Ireland by another shipping company based in Glasgow.

But a Lees employee in Magherafelt had a different recollection of the first delivery by Easdale Shipping, based on a conversation he said he had at the time with Malcolm Baillie: 'Then there was the first load of panels from Scotland. Nicholson, who owned an island and a shipping line, had the contract to deliver the stuff made on North Uist to Belfast for onward shipment to Castlederg. He was on the boat with the panels, carrying an Uzi sub-machinegun. But after he entered the mouth of Belfast Lough he told the captain to turn the ship around and head back. A secure dock had been set aside at Harland & Wolff. The army was waiting to ensure safe delivery. He had to be contacted and told to turn the boat back, which he eventually did.'

Production of the concrete panels ceased late in 1988, according to the annual company accounts for that year, finally produced some years later, when the IRA apparently discovered the secret operation and made a threat against Colin Lees. Malcolm Baillie remembered that at the time negotiations in relation to a big contract were taking place. One contract for £700,000 had been paid, he said, and a second was under negotiation for £3,500,000. But even though production had stopped, the IRA retained an interest in Lees and more threats were made. Michael Wightman remembered the threats that led to the end of the Scottish concrete production: 'It came to a halt when the IRA found out what was going on and threatened Lees many times. One time he received a Mass card. He called a staff meeting and because of the attacks on other businesses in the area by the IRA, it was agreed that production on North Uist would cease.'

Malcolm Baillie had a clear recollection of a serious threat in December 1989. 'At that time,' he said, 'as I understood it, Colin Lees came under threat from the IRA and he placed an advert in a newspaper to say that he was no longer involved in that activity and that's how the activity was terminated, or the reason for it.'

It was on 11 January 1990 that Lees' solicitors published the following advertisement in the *Mid-Ulster Mail*: 'Statement issued by Millar Shearer and Black Solicitors on behalf of the Lees Group of Companies. William A. Lees Concrete Limited wish it to be known that they are NOT, nor will they supply ANY materials to ANY contractor or persons known to them to be carrying on or involved in security work from ANY of their premises including: Ballyronan Road, Magherafelt; Kildress, Cookstown; Glasgort Road, Aghadowey; Maralin Quarry, Banbridge. This statement applies to all member Companies of the Lees Group.'

The codename 'Luton Airport Project' had proved to be inadequate in protecting Colin Lees' secret operation. The IRA had somehow broken the code. With his clandestine activities exposed, Lees moved quickly to stop the work. The workers, however, were left in the dark. Donald MacIsaac assumed orders had been cancelled. 'But there was no reason given to us,' he said. We assumed that they weren't very successful and that they weren't going to continue building that. It was a long time afterwards that we found out that Colin Lees had been threatened by the IRA.'

Colin Lees may have been forced to close production of his concrete works on North Uist, but he wasn't someone to pass up the chance to make money. In fact, his deteriorating business empire ensured that he had to. For by 1989, behind the veneer of being a respectable businessman and exceptional sportsman, Colin Lees had begun to commit fraud on a grand scale back home in Northern Ireland and, as it happens, in Scotland as well. With the concrete production having run aground, an undeterred Lees spotted an opportunity to exploit the sea — buying up fish farms on the island and taking some of his Scottish workforce with him. One of them was Archie McCorkindale, who has fond memories of his only encounter with Lees: 'He came up here for a Christmas function and he seemed to be a very nice person. He got involved in the night and went round and met all the people that were working for him, introduced himself, and he seemed a very genuine person; thoroughly enjoyed his evening with us. He was a fine man, aye yes. We got on fine. I was only talking to him for maybe half an hour or so but he was interested in the island and the people and the fish farm that he had started, yeah.'

According to Malcolm Baillie, who by now had his son Stuart working with him as well, there was a need to find a means of 'earning our keep in order to pay the debts that were incurred in Marine Structures'. The 'debts' had arisen out of the leasing arrangements made by Lees and the Baillies, who were given what an employee of the Lees Group in Ireland later described as 'carte blanche' to expand Lees' Scottish interests. Repayments had to be made on the money advanced by banks and lending houses. So, of course Lees was happy with the fish farms. It was another opportunity for him to exploit banks and finance houses. As Malcolm Baillie told me: 'We went into fish farming and we leased, purchased and leased fish cages and that developed the whole of the fish farming business, which ultimately was about the fourth largest in Europe with fish farms in Harris, Lochmaddy and down the west coast of Ireland.' Soon a fleet of lorries were traversing Scottish roads with 'Lees Group Scotland' emblazoned on their sides. Like Marine Structures, Lees Group Scotland was established under the holding company, Wharton Trading Ltd.

The Trustees Savings Bank in Inverness held the Lees Group Scotland accounts and soon they noticed the rapidly expanding company portfolio. In 1989, the bank prepared a tree diagram of the various companies under the control of Lees' Scottish Group, noting the percentage share the Lees Group had in each. It read as follows: Lochportain Fish Farms Ltd (100%); Tarbert Fisheries Ltd (90%); Uist Shellfish Ltd (100%); Shin Game Dealers

(Scotland) Ltd (60%); Scotfish (Int) Ltd (75%); Webb Marine (Int) Ltd (64%); and Scotpole (International) Ltd (100%).

The programme of expansion continued with the purchase in June 1989 of a company called Blum Scot, based in the Scottish Highlands. Lees renamed the firm Scotpole (International) Ltd. As evidence of how plausible Lees was, the Highlands and Islands Development Board actually approached him about buying the company. The Board had, of course, met Lees when he was in the process of establishing the concrete factory on North Uist. Aware of his timber interests back in Northern Ireland, HIDB thought Lees might be interested in taking over the Blum Scot operation. Production there had ceased and the plant and machinery lay idle. The HIDB had invested heavily in Blum Scot, a company set up by a wealthy Swiss businessman to make telegraph poles for export to Eastern Europe. The Swiss businessman had spent around £5m developing the production plant. According to Stuart Baillie, Lees sent his own plane over to Inverness to collect Malcolm Baillie and two of the HIDB's investment managers and bring them to his Magherafelt offices for discussions.

'We paid £180,000 for Scotpole,' recalled Malcolm Baillie. 'The arrangement was that Colin Lees would take the whole thing over completely, rebuild it and create a sawmill. It was a telegraph pole company and he had plans to start a sawmill as well. It never actually developed at all and as it turned out he had no intention of developing it . . . but we didn't know that at the time.' According to Malcolm Baillie, Lees persuaded him and his son Stuart to put their names on the Scotpole bank account with the TSB Bank in Inverness. 'He conned us,' Malcolm told me, 'by saying "You put your names on the Scotpole account and I'll take them off with two directors when we direct — it makes the picture look rosy." We had no interest whatsoever in a sawmill;

knew nothing about it and just were accommodating him. He asked if we would do this to help him and we said yes. And then what you find is he doesn't do it. That's how he defrauds people. He will not do what he says or even anything remotely like it.'

But according to a former Lees employee, Colin Lees' intentions were to asset strip Scotpole to raise capital and to utilise tax losses available to that company. Lees also intended to use Scotpole's trade in timber products as a lever to obtain supplies of Scottish timber for Irish consumption. But Lees had a secret reason to be grateful for having acquired Scotpole — it would soon feature in his fraudulent deals and would become an important 'asset' for laundering his money.

Everyone noticed that Lees was busy building up an impressive list of companies in his ever-expanding empire. But what they did not notice was that many of these small firms were either paper companies that did not trade or were bogus companies set up by Lees for his own nefarious purposes.

It all began in 1986. The keys to these deceptions were the 'paper' companies Lees had established, most notably PCI Ltd, to raise large sums of money. Remember, PCI Ltd and another company, Creteplant Ltd, were controlled by Lees personally and they used as an address of convenience the Dublin offices of accountants Manley and O'Reilly. Another company set up around this time was Structocrete Ireland Ltd. But most important of all, Lees controlled the bank accounts of these companies. PCI Ltd had Allied Irish Bank accounts at Uxbridge in Middlesex and at Ballsbridge in Dublin.

On 30 September 1986, Royal Scot Leasing Ltd paid £479,246.36 to PCI Ltd on foot of an invoice from PCI Ltd showing that the company had supplied, delivered and erected on site for William A. Lees (Sawmills) Ltd, a new Aumund portal crane at a cost of

£438,000. Of course, PCI Ltd had supplied nothing at all . . . apart from the false invoice that was generated on Lees' instructions. Lees ran his Dublin-based PCI company from his Magherafelt offices, giving directions and instructions to Manley and O'Reilly's by telephone or fax. Aumund, the German manufacturers of the crane described in the PCI invoice, had supplied such a crane directly to W.A.L. (Sawmills) Ltd just a week earlier at a price of £166,000 which included delivery and erection. Lees later told police he didn't know who he had dealt with in PCI or why the crane had been bought through PCI! Of course, having been advanced nearly half a million pounds, Lees had committed his company to repaying, with interest, by instalments. What happened to the £480,000 in the PCI bank account that he alone controlled is not clear. However, there were other instances where it has been possible to establish how he spent the cash generated by false invoicing.

Lees was clearly impressed by the ease with which he had managed to secure half a million pounds, and nine months later he was back to help himself to more of the same. This time he managed to get Norwich Union Equipment Finance Ltd to put £448,000 into the coffers of PCI. This was again after an invoice from PCI had been produced to show that PCI had supplied and installed an Aumund crane for Dynaspan (UK) Ltd. Interestingly, the tender number quoted in the PCI invoice was identified by Aumund as a drawing number, while the serial number mentioned related to a double load bridge crane supplied to a customer in Mulheim, Germany. Lees signed the leasing agreement and other documents, and on 7 July 1987, he signed a cheque removing £350,000 from the PCI account just seven days after the Norwich Union money was paid into it. Where it went, no one knows.

On 6 October 1987, the Investment Bank of Ireland Ltd issued a bank draft in the sum of £119,000 in favour of Creteplant Ltd.

This was done after Creteplant produced an invoice to show that a piece of plant had been supplied to Dynaspan (UK) Ltd at a cost of £119,000. The Creteplant invoice was generated by Lees and presented to the leasing company as a genuine piece of equipment purchased at the stated price. It was nonsense of course. The piece of equipment in question actually existed but had been supplied by the manufacturers directly to the Lees Group of Companies some time before. Again Lees signed a lease agreement to repay by instalments, plus interest, of course. £119,000 was a modest figure judging by the standards he had already set through leasing arrangements . . . and compared to what he was to go on to secure. Five months later, in March 1988, Lees set his sights a little higher.

This time he drew up an invoice in the name of PCI Ltd showing that plant, including a 670-foot self-stressing bed, had been supplied to the Lees company, having been purchased from Dynamold, a US company. Of course Dynamold never sold any equipment to PCI — but, remarkably, had supplied similar plant to Lees in 1981! This time a company known as SOCGEN advanced £575,000 to PCI Ltd. With this money in his privately controlled PCI bank account, Lees signed a number of cheques. On 4 March, he paid £110,000 to Lees (Sawmills). Three weeks later he paid his American Express account £947.93, and three days after settling that account, he paid £8,000 to his own personal account. A cheque made payable to Colin Lees and signed on behalf of PCI Ltd by Colin Lees! But it didn't raise any suspicions within his bank. Out of the same PCI account he paid £55,000 to Forest Services Ltd and £54,000 to a firm called Gremo. Amazingly, when Lees was later questioned by police about this transaction he was to tell detectives he thought PCI was a company that supplied plant. He 'thought' they were a southern Irish company but to the best of his recollection he had no involvement with that company in 1988!

Having found this method of getting rich quick, Lees was not about to rest on his laurels. Soon he would go for six-figure sums as his overstretched businesses faced difficult choices. He wanted more and he just kept getting his companies into deeper and deeper debt — they had the repayments to make on any leasing deal he signed up to. At first it was barely noticeable because his companies were turning a healthy profit.

And he needed profits to sustain his expensive hobbies, although it was noticeable through the 1980s that Lees' motor racing career took a back seat as he concentrated on building his business empire. At the end of the decade he told the *Belfast Telegraph* that his new Mondiale car, the M90S, was 'the best we have produced and is certainly capable of matching anything that Reynard and Van Diemen have to offer'. Lees conceded to the reporter that he had been 'fed up' with racing a couple of years earlier and took the very deliberate step of cutting down. He said: 'I decided to cut out the testing, only doing the Kirkistown meetings and one or two races in England or south of the border. Now I'm really enjoying it again.'

But by then Colin Lees' companies were already suffering from the first symptoms of financial stress and he had begun his criminal career as a fraudster. His lifestyle — the helicopter, the racing cars, the first class travel, the entertaining of clients to corporate hospitality days at British sporting occasions such as rugby internationals and motor racing events, the strip shows and visits to nightclubs such as Stringfellows in London — all this was eventually going to put a financial strain on the companies. But in the meantime, Lees lived well on the proceeds of his criminal exploits. On one visit to London with Lees, Stuart Baillie was lavishly wined and dined. Lees was entertaining on that visit. Stuart Baillie witnessed business contacts of Lees being treated sumptuously at a hospitality suite at Brands' Hatch racing circuit. The evening finished at Stringfellows nightclub where Lees bought champagne. Lees had a couple of girls on his arm. He disappeared with them and arrived late the next day at Brands' Hatch looking the worse for wear. Later police discovered cards from prostitutes in Lees' possession — tucked inside his wallet; the lurid kind of calling cards left in public telephone boxes by hookers and their pimps. Apparently he had quite a collection!

But still, there are those who worked for Lees who to this day will not accept that his involvement in defrauding finance houses and banks was for personal gain. They believe he used the money to try to develop his business interests. Well, that might have happened to some extent, but there is evidence that he personally gained.

For example, in June 1988, he went back to SOCGEN and persuaded them to pay PCI £519,000 for equipment to help in concrete production. What's most interesting about this particular fraud is the way Lees spent the money paid into his PCI account. Cheques signed by Lees were paid out to the following:

Dorothy Hartley (his sister)	£2,500	June 20
W.A.L. Forest Services	£91,000	June 21
American Express	£593.40	June 20
Colin Lees (personally)	£225,000	June 21
Dorothy Hartley	£4,000	June 23
Brian Burnett	£45,000	June 27
W.A.L. Forest Services	£97,000	June 28
Dorothy Hartley	£16,500	June 30
Associated Trust Co.	£300	June 21
Robert Campbell	£2,000	July 5

Clearly, some of the money went into his companies, some went to settle debts with individuals who had no idea how Lees had acquired the cash. No one knew what was really going on — only Lees had the answer and he was not sharing it with people in his offices in Magherafelt. But certainly, the largest payment was to his personal bank account — indisputable evidence of how he benefited directly. Three cheques were paid to his sister Dorothy, and his brother-in-law Brian Burnett received one cheque. With PCI providing such 'sterling' service for Lees, he now began to turn his attention to Scotland. Although the concrete business had collapsed, new opportunities were presenting themselves, not only for fraud there but also as a means of laundering some of his ill-gotten gains in Northern Ireland.

Lees now had a complex set of business and banking arrangements that would be difficult to track down. With control of Wharton Trading Ltd, and with the nominee directors, Malcolm Baillie and later his son Stuart, running its subsidiary Marine Structures Ltd, Lees had the ability to shift large amounts of money from one business venture to another. The purchases of the fish farms and the other small businesses in Scotland created opportunities to move and hide the proceeds of his crime. The Lees Group Scotland (LGS) was not part of W.A.L. Holdings Ltd. LGS was set up under Wharton Trading Ltd and would later, between late 1989 and 1990, become the subject of intense and difficult negotiation involving the Lees Group of Companies in Northern Ireland and the Baillies, who effectively ran and controlled LGS, although they had no financial stake in the company. The plan was for W.A.L. Holdings to buy 75 per cent of the LGS shares from Wharton Trading Ltd, with the Baillies to purchase the remaining 25 per cent of shares. In spite of the fact that Malcolm Baillie had taken no financial risk in the establishment of LGS, Colin Lees told his negotiators that 'morally' he was entitled to 50 per cent. But as we shall learn later, by the time this negotiation was taking place, relations between the Baillies and the Lees had hit rock bottom.

Although Colin Lees had secured the help of his Northern Ireland financial advisers such as Joe Cole and Ralph Chalmers to negotiate the LGS deal, he had successfully concealed his true involvement with his Scottish interests, just as he was concealing the fraudulent deals with lending institutions back home. The key to making all this work to his advantage was not to let anyone around him know exactly what was going on. Colin Lees was living his life in compartments, with the people in each of those compartments unaware of what was going on in the other compartments. He had to operate this way if he was going to succeed in building up his business empire quickly and without having to do too much work to make it happen. He had, after all, expensive tastes.

According to Stuart Baillie, as soon as Lees got Marine Structures Ltd up and running at Sponish on North Uist, he began setting up leasing agreements initially through PCI, of course. The first leasing deal brought in £750,000, but Malcolm Baillie told me Lees immediately took £500,000 out himself. 'Lees insisted I write a cheque for half a million pounds,' Malcolm Baillie told me. Stuart confirmed that Lees had taken the money and left Marine Structures to meet the repayments of around £50,000 a quarter. 'Lees' way of financing a business was through leasing,' said Stuart. 'He put little or nothing of his own money into the companies. Through an agent he guaranteed the leases.' The £750,000 was arranged through a leasing company, Atlantic Computers plc. The company specialised in leasing IBM computers but had decided to branch out into other areas. 'Atlantic's Scottish manager Peter Nicholl contacted us and gave instructions on how we were to prepare an inventory of equipment on Marine Structures headed paper,' Stuart Baillie recalled. The Baillies never saw any of the equipment that was subject of the lease agreements, but they believed Lees' assurances that the equipment existed in Northern Ireland. Certainly what had been brought over to North Uist for the production of the concrete panels was not new but plant that had been used elsewhere for a number of years, a view borne out by Donald MacIsaac, who remembered the poor state of the equipment at Sponish.

But the use of PCI Ltd — a Dublin-based company — in his Scottish deals was something that might raise questions and concerns or at the very least attract unwanted attention that had the potential to expose Lees' involvement as the sole director and beneficiary of PCI. So Lees decided on another course of action that would protect his PCI operations and still provide another useful source of revenue. He already knew the benefit of having a 'shelf' company like PCI. So why not have one based on the British mainland?

Lees urged Stuart Baillie to set up a company called Nationwide Plant Corporation at the LGS offices in Inverness. Lees, however, decided on the directors — naming Stewart Lyle and James Lilley, apparently two men from Inverness who worked for him in Scotland but who were not informed of their status as company directors. Both men have criminal records and Lilley was later sent to prison in Scotland on drug charges; he was caught bringing drugs in from Amsterdam.

Nationwide opened a bank account in England with the Allied Trust Bank, formerly the Allied Arab Bank. 'As the Allied Arab Bank it had been set up through the Kuwaiti Investment Office,' Stuart told me. 'But it was sold to Barclays and that was when it changed its name to Allied Trust Bank.' Soon Nationwide Plant

Corporation was busy generating invoices and raising cash, with Stuart Baillie signing the agreements. But in order for Nationwide to function, Lees would get an agent, often Mark Harding, the managing director of Future Financial Services plc, to organise the guarantees. He also used Atlantic Computers plc, a company run by John Foulston. Lees knew Foulston and Harding as friends. No money could have been raised without Lees' signature as guarantor. Millions of pounds were raised and, according to Stuart Baillie, at least £5m made its way back to Lees' bank accounts in Ireland.

An early example of how he could put these bogus companies to good use can be traced back to the purchase of Scotpole. In early July 1989, he used Plant Corporation of Ireland (PCI) in Dublin to generate two false invoices, claiming that his companies had purchased two separate lots of concrete block making equipment from German manufacturers MASA. An invoice dated 4 July 1989 and numbered 4010 claimed that PCI had supplied 3325 moulding and handling bases at a cost of £200,000. Leaseplan UK was satisfied that this was a legitimate business transaction and on 11 July paid £200,000 into PCI's bank account. Another PCI invoice, also dated 4 July, but numbered 4011, was submitted to another leasing company, this time US Leasing Ltd, to show that PCI had supplied 3670 moulding and handling bases to Lees Concrete at a cost of £220,000. US Leasing Ltd paid £220,000 to PCI on 18 July. PCI issued a cheque for £220,000 to W.A. Lees Concrete on 24 July. A second PCI cheque for £200,000 was paid to Lees' companies on 3 August. Bringing in £420,000 was more than enough to cover the cost of the Scotpole purchase. But by this stage in 1989, Colin Lees was well accustomed to plundering the funds of finance houses and banks.

The purchase of Scotpole in 1989 pushed Lees into even

more frenetic activity on the leasing front. And it helped him perpetrate another scam. This time the target of his deception was the Eagle Star insurance company. In April 1989 there had been a fire at the Magherafelt sawmill on Ballyronan Road. Eagle Star's loss assessor made recommendations in relation to damage to the premises and a payment was made in settlement. There was no issue in relation to this part of the insurance claim. But when it came to seeking compensation for consequential loss, Lees had a plan to boost the sawmill company's income. To establish the consequential losses, it was necessary to examine the firm's turnover prior to the fire and then compare it to the turnover after the fire. If there was evidence of a shortfall in the projected turnover, the loss of profit could be estimated on the basis of lost turnover. At the time, an English company, Home Grown Timber Marketing Corporation Ltd (HGT) acted as sole UK agents for timber produced at Lees Sawmills in Magherafelt. In June, after Lees had bought Scotpole, HGT were persuaded to make part payments for that month's deliveries to Scotpole. They agreed to this subject to the provision of a VAT invoice relating to the particular deliveries. This arrangement continued for sixteen months. HGT were told the reason for this change in arrangements regarding payments was to help set up a trading record for Scotpole and for the purchase of round timber that was shipped from Scotland to Northern Ireland. But all the timber invoiced by Scotpole was produced and dispatched from Magherafelt. Scotpole did not have the capacity to produce the timber required. The net result of this arrangement was that during the sixteen months, HGT paid Scotpole £3.2m while Lees Sawmills received £2.2m. The loss adjustors were not told about the Scotpole situation. Instead they noticed a fall in the production at Magherafelt, so a consequential loss claim was enhanced to nearly £2m. There was no actual loss in production at all, but by involving Scotpole, Lees had managed to gain £1.2m to which he was not entitled.

Scotpole had its bank account with the TSB in Inverness. But in order to accommodate the theft from the Eagle Star insurance company, a Scotpole No. 2 account was opened on 13 October 1990. Among the initial office bearers was Colin Lees but at some stage during the life of the No. 2 account, Michael Wightman became an office bearer entitled to transact on the account. The No. 2 account was not needed for normal Scotpole business. But it was needed to launder the money from timber production that was being hidden from the consequential loss adjustor. Lees would write cheques from this account in favour of another of his companies, Dynaspan — and on one occasion Wightman signed a cheque for £230,000. In nineteen months, £3.5m was transferred from this account to the Lees Group through Dynaspan. Of course, the money coming into the Dynaspan account had to be accounted for. Witt Thornton, the auditors, asked for an explanation. The accounts department of about five or six people was under the supervision of Michael Wightman, and his involvement in covering up Lees' fraud was exposed first by the auditors and subsequently by the police. One of the staff was told to type up a number of invoices on Dynaspan headed paper, addressed to Scotpole International. He was given the amounts and told to work back the VAT. Subsequently these invoices were handed over to the auditors but only after repeated requests. For the time being, Lees had managed to avoid detection of this particular scam.

More importantly, with Wharton Trading, Marine Structures, Scotpole, Lees Group Scotland, PCI Ltd, Nationwide Plant Corporation, Structocrete and Creteplant all now established, Lees was able to generate false invoices and recoup vast sums of money in advances from banks and lending institutions. There was such a profusion of companies involved, with an equal proliferation of bank accounts, that it was easy for Lees to continue his fraudulent activities without detection. And Lees needed more money than his company profits could provide. Aside from his own personal needs to maintain his lifestyle, his companies' coffers were becoming more and more depleted with the repayments of his growing leasing deals. Yet no one ever questioned the growing debt and the ever-increasing monthly or quarterly repayments — not the auditors, nor the government that provided him with protection, nor the quangos who represent public interests in the absence of devolution. There was a massive dereliction of duty, and the squandering, as a result, of millions of pounds of taxpayers' monies; all to keep Lees in the style to which he had become accustomed.

The pressure was on to maintain his public persona as an exciting, go-ahead entrepreneur who was on the verge of greatness, with the construction of lavish new offices and the completion of his hometown's first shopping centre. His career was about to reach its peak at just about the same time as it was going into terminal decline!

3 Pure Pulp Fiction!

'This really is one of the most important announcements of the century — not just for the north-west, but for the whole of this island.'

John Hume MP and SDLP leader on 25 January 1991 describing Colin Lees' plan to set up a pulp mill in Derry producing wood chip to sell to Scandinavia.

❧⚜❧

Selling snow to Eskimos or coals to Newcastle are just two colourful descriptions commonly used to convey outrageously ambitious optimism or as a back-handed compliment directed towards the selling skills or personality of some 'Jack-the-Lad'; or perhaps an 'Arthur Daly' type of second-hand car salesman. But for a short time in the early 1990s the business adventures embarked upon by Colin Lees veered from the sublime to the ridiculous and back with effortless ease. He was planning to set up a pulp mill in Derry that would export its product to Scandinavia! It certainly was adventurous and attention-grabbing. And unlikely as it might seem, it was apparently a good plan with a viable future: a future that might have delivered the promised work and wealth had Colin Lees confined himself to ensuring prosperity through hard graft and endeavour.

By the time he was ready to announce his pulp mill plans, Lees had already secured the future of his shopping centre project, details of which were first announced on 26 June 1990. Terrorism and politics took a back seat as the *Belfast Telegraph*'s front-page lead story was devoted to news about two major shopping centre developments. The paper reported that Belfast Co-op, the retailing section in Northern Ireland of the Co-operative Wholesale Society, had announced its biggest-ever single investment in the city, £11m, to build two major stores on the site of the former Gallaher cigarette factory on the city's York Street. The 'Yorkgate' enterprise was to cost £30m in total; providing accommodation for speciality market units, a 36-lane ten-pin bowling alley, a leisure centre, a 10-screen cinema, and parking for 1,400 cars. Eventually, it was predicted, 1,500 people would have jobs there with between 300 and 400 for workers during construction.

News of a £6m shopping mall for Magherafelt might have seemed small beer by comparison, but that morning's announcement from the Lees Group had promised 300 jobs and, aside from a brief mention on the front page, a special feature appeared in the paper's business section.

The article, illustrated with an artist's impression of the new shopping facility, reported that Irish food and clothing retailer Dunnes Stores had already signed up as the anchor tenant in the 90,000 sq. ft. development. Tenders for the initial building contract worth £4m were to be opened the following day and, according to Lees Group managing director Colin Lees, all those who had tendered came from Northern Ireland with 'significant interest' from contractors in the town. The report explained the aesthetic value of the complex, as it would be constructed on the site of Lees' concrete works on the Cookstown Road. The company would be moving to new offices on a 30-acre site on the town's Ballyronan Road — taking with them Ireland's largest sawmill as well as the concrete manufacturing plant.

A very proud Colin Lees told the reporter about the company's first large property development project: 'We have been dabbling with small developments for the past two years but nothing on this scale. It's satisfying to get such a big prestigious development in our own area. It would have been very easy for us to sell the site. We see it as a big commitment to the area. It gives me great personal pleasure to be able to announce the development, which will give a much needed boost to the local economy and, even more importantly, new jobs for the people of Magherafelt.'

The newspaper reported that the Lees Group was expecting profits of £3m for the past year, on turnover of £20m'. Healthy indeed; if it was true. Only Colin Lees apparently knew the reality that the business was beginning to slowly crumble. Behind the façade of respectability and public adulation about his business prowess, the champion racing driver had his foot to the floor as he doggedly maintained the outward appearance of success.

Certainly, the first two years of the final decade of the twentieth century held no fears for the Magherafelt businessman. For even as he basked in the glory of announcing his beloved shopping centre and was busy planning his pulp mill extravaganza, behind the scenes Lees was juggling with the figures to keep everyone from discovering his secret distress . . . and, of course, his by now blossoming criminal career. Vast sums of cash had been spent on the shopping mall and the construction of plush new offices for the Lees Group on the Ballyronan Road in Magherafelt, all of which added to the financial stress within the companies. There were telltale signs, not least of which were the huge leasing commitments Lees had undertaken and which were now attracting the attention of some key figures at the company's main bankers, the Ulster Bank. Bank officials had begun to gently probe Lees' employees about what was going on in the Lees Group.

Consequently, the bank was quietly informed that a number of staff at Lees' offices were becoming increasingly concerned at what they described as Lees' 'commercial madness'. They had noticed with some small degree of alarm that Lees had become what one person described as 'fanatical' in his desire to have the newest products and the most up to date machinery. Yet it didn't seem to occur to anyone that much of this new equipment was distinctly noticeable by its absence.

Of course, Lees was by now cutting everyone around him out of the loop; key management figures found it increasingly difficult to stay in touch with Lees' business and financial arrangements. The promise made early on by Lees to his senior financial advisers after the formation of W.A.L. Holdings Ltd to produce monthly management accounts was not fulfilled. Monthly meetings took place but the level of inter-company activity made it difficult to provide accurate and up to date profit and loss figures. This lack of discipline suited Lees perfectly.

By isolating himself, Lees was able to manage his staff in compartments, never letting any one person know the full picture. It was the only way Lees could maintain secrecy about his leasing agreements. Some of his management colleagues thought it was time to bring him back into control, into the loop. The Ulster

Bank was told as much but, although it had the power to bring a halt to the 'commercial madness', nothing was done to rein him in. It was not until it was too late that the reality and the enormity of what Lees was up to emerged.

All this was taking place in spite of the fact that there had been questions asked by members of his own staff on a number of occasions about these leasing agreements — all of which were negotiated and handled by Colin Lees. Sometimes someone would raise queries after coming across paperwork that just did not seem to be in order.

I have been told of an occasion when one of the auditors had a query that possible double leasing had occurred. He sought advice from a senior manager: 'He asked me what I would do about it. I said I would be down at Colin's office door at 8 a.m. the next morning to get him to explain what was going on. So next day he went to see Colin and afterwards he called me to say there was an adequate explanation for it. Lees told him there was a piece of equipment costing £300,000 and no one would touch it . . . so he got two companies that would be prepared to take on £150,000 each. Now that is not a problem as long as both companies know about the arrangement.' Lees had successfully covered his tracks and convinced the auditor that all was well.

But there was no disguising the fact that the expenditure on the shopping mall and the new offices was beginning to put company finances under duress. Had Lees overstretched himself? There was also growing concern that the Scottish Group was an unnecessary weight around Colin Lees' business shoulders, given that the concrete operation there had ceased production. What alarmed Lees' financial advisers was the fact that, although on paper the Lees Group in Ireland owned only a percentage of the Scottish operation, Lees had signed guarantees for loans and leases there to the tune of several million, even as much as £8m, some company insiders estimated. There were those in his own company urging him to ditch the Scottish operation to get away from the guarantees that could, if things went badly in Scotland, leave the Irish companies exposed to the extent of almost certain insolvency.

But, of course, there was not any real understanding in the Magherafelt offices that Lees was the beneficiary of most of the financial deals over in Scotland. Wharton Trading Ltd had been registered on the Isle of Man and was controlled by Lees. Wharton Trading was a major beneficiary of the financial dealings of the Lees Group Scotland. That too would only emerge much later . . . and in the meantime, Lees' ambitious plans for his companies continued. While no one was prepared to question his 'commercial madness' he carried on living the lie he created on 25 January 1991. That was the date chosen for Lees to announce to the world that he had a marvellous scheme for Derry that had the potential to create hundreds of jobs.

A news conference was called in Derry. Selling home-grown Irish wood chips to Scandinavia was the kind of audacious plan that enhanced Colin Lees' reputation as an entrepreneur. Now Lees could see his business career move into top gear. At his side as he made this historic announcement in the 'Maiden City' was the local MP and leader of the Social, Democratic and Labour Party (SDLP), John Hume. Hume told reporters: 'This really is one of the most important announcements of the century — not just for the north-west, but for the whole of this island.' Lavish praise indeed, given genuinely by someone who cared more about his community than someone who cared only for himself. With the benefit of hindsight, of course, it was a comment later deeply regretted. Seated between Lees and John Hume was Industry

Minister Richard Needham. Like John Hume, he and his government department had been taken in by Lees' business acumen.

Lees stood before the assembled battery of television and newspaper cameras and said: 'We aim to build a CTMP pulp mill at a cost of £90m, which will be the first of its kind in Europe.' But sources close to Lees told me there was one person missing from the line-up at the top table.

It appears that by 1991, the one-time 'golden boy' of the Industrial Development Board (IDB) was not quite so much in favour. A seat had been reserved for a representative of the IDB, the body that would be responsible for considering financial aid to Lees for his pulp mill. But the seat remained unoccupied during the conference. It appears the IDB representative chose to seat himself in the audience rather than be seen anywhere near Lees. My understanding is that there was at this stage little trust in the IDB for Lees. Joe Cole, Lees' one-time financial director, was trusted, even though he was no longer a director of the Lees Group but briefly held a directorship in Lees Pulp Mill Ltd between 1990 and December 1991. It was explained to me that had Cole walked away from the project, the IDB would most likely have followed.

But of course the pulp mill plan was pure pulp fiction. Or at least that appears to have been the case. Joe Cole was still working closely with Lees on this project even though he had resigned as a director. Lees asked him to stay on specifically to help him with the pulp mill and Lees Group Scotland. According to an informed source, Joe Cole travelled to Sweden and the United States with Lees researching the pulp mill's potential. The scheme had the backing of Richard Needham. The source told me: 'Richard Needham had promised Lees £20m for the Derry pulp mill. Needham met with Nigel Thompson, John Moore, Colin Lees and Joe Cole. The plan was for each to present an aspect of the project using an overhead projector. Each did his bit, but before Colin could speak, Needham said: "Let's cut the crap, Colin — what do you need for this project?" "£20m," said Colin. Needham replied: "You satisfy the IDB and I'll get that money for you some-how — so you get on with the project.'"

Richard Needham was back by Colin Lees' side again on 5 September 1991, eight months after attending the pulp mill news conference. This time it was for a trip down Meadow Lane, the shopping mall built by Lees on the site of his old concrete works in Magherafelt. Standing shoulder to shoulder with Colin Lees before an enthusiastic crowd of shoppers, the government minister cut the ribbon to declare the centre open. Needham praised the Lees Group for its role in helping to regenerate the area. He said: 'It shows the private sector's confidence in local communities. Local businessmen in mid-Ulster are also playing their part in bring prosperity to this area and this latest develop-ment has attracted an impressive list of retailers.' On the same day television soap star Kevin Kennedy, who played Curly Watts in *Coronation Street*, opened another shopping centre in West Belfast . . . unaware that the real soap opera was being choreo-graphed and acted out fifty miles away in Magherafelt — a drama that was to embarrass a British government minister.

Richard Needham's first step towards ministerial power came in September 1985 when the Tory MP for North Wiltshire was appointed Parliamentary Under-Secretary at the Northern Ireland Office. Needham was the sixth Earl of Kilmorey, an Irish title he did not use. He remained in Northern Ireland until April 1992, thereby becoming the longest serving minister under direct rule. I was told that during his time here, he and Lees became friends and it was even suggested by some of Lees' former employees that the pair had dined together on occasion. But when I contacted

Richard Needham at his London home, he informed me initially that he did not remember anyone called Colin Lees. As we talked, he remembered Lees had something to do with a shopping centre. Then he said he had only met him once. I mentioned the pulp mill. He said he could not remember and pointed out that he had so many duties as a minister, he could not recall every detail of the meetings and functions arranged for him by civil servants. He certainly had no recollection of having dinner with Lees, although he did say that it could have happened. What is certain is that if the Northern Ireland Office had had any inkling of Lees' dark secret, he would never have had any contact with government ministers like Richard Needham, no matter how skilful an entrepreneur he might have been.

In any event, walking Richard Needham around his newly constructed shopping centre surely must have been Lees' finest hour in his hometown — a real 'local boy makes good' story. But behind the smiles was a mind in turmoil. Things had not been going that well in Scotland; the Baillies had rumbled his leasing scams, although they were both now deeply imbedded in the culture of corruption that Lees visited upon them and were having to press for funds to meet the repayments. Additionally, pressure was continuing to grow at home. Lees' bankers were becoming more nervous about the extent of the borrowings.

From April 1991 the Ulster Bank began asking tougher questions about what exactly was going on inside the Lees Group. The consequence was an indication from the bank that it was not prepared to go any further with the Lees Group. Lees was displeased, to say the least, and from that moment on had more or less made up his mind to change banks. But that's not something that can happen overnight. Nevertheless, things would never be the same again at the bank. The relationship had reached a watershed.

Whatever reservations the bank had at this stage, it nevertheless agreed that if Lees could provide projections and statements,
they would allow the lending facility to continue . . . or, as it happened, to increase. By the summer, however, the mood changed
sharply. In July the bank made it clear they wanted to put investigating accountants into the Lees Group unless the company's
auditors could provide a clean audit certificate. A few days later,
Paul Rowan turned up at the Ballyronan Road offices of the Lees
Group. Rowan was an accountant with Price Waterhouse. His
arrival followed a series of calls between Lees and the Ulster Bank
during which Lees said he wanted Rowan to be brought in at his
own expense — in other words, not as the bank's eyes and ears.
The bank, for once being forceful, told Lees that Rowan either
came in as their adviser or as a receiver. Lees was compelled to
back down and receive Rowan as the bank's agent, even though
he feared that news of his arrival had the potential to start ringing
alarm bells outside the company.

So beyond the veneer of success, only Lees himself knew how
he was struggling to keep his career on track. On the sidelines,
creditors were closing in at home while his Scottish adventure was
about to come to a dramatic end as well. It appears he may have
overstretched in his rush to become a multi-millionaire, or perhaps
it was the expensive lifestyle he led. Even today it is difficult for
former staff members loyal to Lees to accept that he was creaming
off funds for his own personal use. As one of his former loyal
employees told me, if Lees was involved in a massive fraud scam it
'could only have been to help fund his business plans'. As things
turned out, there was more than an element of truth in all of that.
Lees, from as early as 1986, had been engaged in massive fraud and
some of the funds he raised by that means were being funnelled
into some of his ailing companies.

Shortly after he had taken up his position at Lees' offices, Paul Rowan made a staggering discovery that rang alarm bells throughout the company and in the Ulster Bank as well. He arrived at the Magherafelt offices one day clutching a cheque from Plant Corporation Ireland, Colin Lees' own 'bogus' company based in Dublin with Colin Lees' signature on it! Whilst Lees had tried to create the impression among staff that his father and not he owned PCI, the charade ended when Rowan produced this cheque. At last someone had noticed that PCI cheques, made out to the Lees Group, were actually signed by the managing director of Lees Group! Apparently, with one notable exception, staff in Lees' office were aghast. This was one of so many clues as to what was really going on that had been missed in the past and at the very least raises questions about the manner in which auditors had conducted previous investigations — though they would not have had the same access to Colin Lees' personal bank account with Ulster Bank that Paul Rowan was given by the bank.

Former staff in Magherafelt recall that the first inkling that things might not be going as smoothly as they should be came from the Scottish venture. There was something 'iffy' about Scotland and if Lees was not up to something, his so-called partners were. That appeared to be a view shared by a number of key Lees personnel in Northern Ireland, although they had no idea of the extent of the leasing scams in Scotland, nor had they the means to find out.

For example, the directors of Scotpole, the Baillies, claim they knew nothing of the Scotpole No. 2 account — at least not at first. According to Malcolm, the No. 2 Scotpole account was discovered only after Colin Lees made a slip-up. 'He made a mistake,' Malcolm Baillie told me, 'when he slipped up with one cheque. It was made out to Scotpole instead of the Scotpole No. 2 account and when I discovered that, I put the cheque into the Scotpole No. 1 account. Colin was over from Ireland like a flash out of a gun asking what had happened and I said, "Well, that's the money that you owe us and I've just taken it." We argued and bargied but he didn't get it on that one.'

Stuart Baillie said thereafter cheques were regularly sent over from Northern Ireland with instructions that they were to be lodged into the No. 2 account. The Baillies were blissfully unaware of the manoeuvres going on to enhance the Eagle Star insurance claim . . . until much, much later. Of course, in the meanwhile, the Baillies needed money to make the repayments on borrowings from leases generated by PCI and Nationwide. Marine Structures was out of business but still had debts to pay. The other businesses — like the fish farms — also had to find funds to pay for leasing arrangements on the cages and other equipment.

'It became so difficult to finance the leasing that had been carried on previously,' Malcolm Baillie reflected. 'But because Lees had said should the company get into financial difficulties, he would finance any shortfall, we had no reason to believe that we wouldn't meet our commitments and, right up to about June 1991, we paid all our commitments; the repayments of leases, whether there was equipment or not. And the fact of the matter was it was known by the leasing companies that there wasn't equipment in some cases because some of the equipment was up at Scotpole and it's only fifty miles up the road and they never bothered to even go and look. They never bothered to check whether there was equipment. They weren't interested. They were interested in the guarantee and being repaid. So long as they were repaid they weren't interested.'

It does seem incredible that large financial organisations would lend money without first seeing for themselves the condition of the asset they were lending against. It was yet another example of how plausible Lees was . . . even when persuading hard-nosed businessmen to advance hard cash on old equipment or even on occasion against plant that quite simply did not exist. Looking back to the first lease raised by PCI for Marine Structures, Malcolm Baillie said the equipment, the batching plant, was second-hand and worth about £58,000 and yet Lees secured an advance of £750,000.

Like every good 'con' man, Colin Lees had an ability to sell himself. The financial institutions never questioned him, as Malcolm Baillie recalled: 'When Colin Lees appeared and presented the case, everything went quite smoothly. And remember we believed from the figures we had seen that we were dealing with a profitable company with £3m to £4m profit a year. The leasing companies never queried any application; the banks never queried. There were normal discussions. The bankers were taken over to Magherafelt and they were interviewed by or they interviewed Colin Lees, and they discussed the accounts and got his agreement to extend overdrafts and so on. There was never any question of a shortfall, quite the opposite, so there was no suspicion at that time because Colin kept Northern Ireland strictly in Northern Ireland. Nothing came out of Northern Ireland to us of what was going on there. We knew nothing about that. It was kept completely separate and I must say Colin was very good at that, very good.'

That Lees was able to go on arranging leases meant that his credit lines remained in good shape. In spite of concerns at the Ulster Bank about his 'commercial madness', his credit references remained good for some considerable time, although there was one occasion when the Ulster Bank supplied a reference that was not 'five star'. Lees was angered and during a confrontation with a bank representative had demanded to know why the reference had been downgraded. But even then, the bank did not take advantage of the fact that they held the covenants on Lees' loans, and the 'commercial madness' was allowed to continue — up to the point of destruction.

Leaving aside the gullible nature of the leasing companies and banks for a moment, the question also arises about just how easily led were the Baillies. Stuart Baillie said he and his father were quickly aware that the leases raised by them were not for the purchase of new equipment, or to release capital from the investment in plant; but rather that Lees was engaging extensively in balance sheet finance. According to Stuart, he and his father realised about six to nine months after becoming involved with Lees that some of these transactions were suspect.

As time went on, Lees had them more and more committed to helping him through leases raised by his British equivalent of PCI — the Nationwide Plant Corporation, which had a telephone in the Inverness offices of LGS that accepted incoming calls only and use of the LGS fax machine. The fax machine received Lees' instructions. 'He would send over to LGS a schedule of equipment to be typed up on Nationwide Plant Corporation headed paper,' Stuart Baillie told me, adding, 'and we were told to send this on to the leasing company.' As a rule of thumb, according to Stuart Baillie, money raised through Nationwide Plant Corporation remained in Scotland to pay the growing monthly repayments, but any cash raised through PCI was returned to PCI bank accounts and thereby into the sole control of Colin Lees.

Once the situation became clear to the Baillies, they did take steps to find out about their legal liability. Stuart Baillie said he once remarked to Colin Lees: 'The way you are going we are both going to end up in a prison cell . . . this is totally fraudulent. The only comfort we took was that we still believed we were dealing with a big company with £3m to £4m profits a year. We had been told that Barclays bank was preparing to put up £4m to £5m for the funding of the pulp mill project and of course we had Lees' constant assurances that the equipment did exist. When I made my comment to him about prison, he reminded me that he was guaranteeing all the arrangements; he was the one at risk and so I should not be so concerned. Again he assured me the equipment existed.'

But father and son were deeply concerned. It had begun to slowly dawn on them that Lees' pockets were not so much deep as almost empty. As Malcolm Baillie told me: 'If you looked at his accounts at that time, you would find nine out of ten accountants would invest in that company. It was big profits he was making and doing very well. No question of . . . no indication that he was short of money. And the reason I think was because he kept leasing as it's turned out. We now understand that the reason he always had money was because he kept leasing and the money kept coming in from the leasing companies. I can't for the life of me understand where it all went. It must have gone into the development in Magherafelt. Colin Lees didn't put a single penny into the Scottish operation. Not a penny. He took plenty out. But we were left to worry about making the repayments.'

Of course, the deeper Lees got in debt, the deeper the extent of his fraudulent dealings to pay his way with the previous deals. And the Baillies were by this time caught up totally in the whole illegal shambles. 'We were in so deep it was difficult to do anything,' Stuart Baillie told me. 'We actually made an appointment with a firm of solicitors in Scotland to seek advice. We explained what we thought had been going on and asked if it was time for us to go to the police. There was a barrister there, a QC, who has since become a judge.' The advice was not good. Basically, reporting

Colin Lees for his fraudulent activities would only serve to draw attention to their own involvement in his criminality. The Baillies felt they had to extricate themselves from the clutches of Colin Lees, and by now the relationship had soured considerably.

By this stage Marine Structures and LGS were paying a total of £200,000 a month in lease repayments. The money to repay them was not as easily found as before. The financial arrangements between LGS, Marine Structures and Wharton Trading had been designed to be deliberately opaque. For Lees, complexity was a key ally. The holding company, Wharton Trading, was consistently mentioned in Marine Structures accounts as a 'debtor' owing usually around the £1m mark each year. In accounts to September 1988, for example, Wharton Trading owes Marine Structures £800,000. Two years later Marine Structures accounts note that £1,202,688 is owed to them by Wharton Trading, along with £388,575 from LGS and £555,000 from Lees Group Northern Ireland. In return, Marine Structures owed Lees Group Northern Ireland £167,350 and Structocrete Ltd a staggering £486,431. And remember, Structocrete is one of the Dublin companies set up and controlled only by Colin Lees.

On paper at least, Marine Structures always showed a profit. This could only have been true by means of creative accounting. The company made nothing to profit from! From Colin Lees' point of view it was becoming easier to dazzle and confuse his workforce, his fellow directors, his accountants and even the auditors with the movement of monies from one company to another within the Lees Group at home and the Lees companies in Scotland. Aside from the fish farming business that was running at a small profit of around £100,000 a year, according to Stuart Baillie, the other businesses did not produce anything, let alone a profit. Scotpole was never intended to function and, as Malcolm Baillie told me, all it ever actually made during LGS's tenure were a few fence posts.

When LGS bought Scotpole, it inherited two night watchmen who naturally were concerned about their jobs. 'They were men in their fifties or maybe even their sixties,' said Malcolm Baillie, 'and they said, "We suppose we don't have a job once you take over." I told them there was nothing happening at the moment and asked them if they could earn a bob or two. One of them said, "Yeah we can. We've got a wee sawmill here and it's a lovely little thing." The blades were greased and polished and they told me they could make fence posts. I told them I'd buy the materials if they made the fence posts and sold them. If they made it pay enough for their wages, then they had a job, end of story. And that's what they did. They made the fence posts. They sold them to builders and to farmers. They put the money in an envelope every Friday and it came down from them to Inverness. It does your heart good to meet honest guys like that.'

Back in Northern Ireland in September 1991 when he opened the Meadow Lane shopping centre, Lees was battling for survival. Any hope that his pulp mill project would have a realistic chance of coming to fruition was being endangered by the growing pressure of trying to meet all the repayments both at home and in Scotland. His staff in Magherafelt were being told that the Baillies had gone off the rails, that they had been engaged in a campaign of fund-raising using leasing agreements (all of which Lees had guaranteed). There was no suspicion on Lees at all as far as his loyal staff were concerned. They simply saw that it was the Baillies who instigated and completed the leasing agreements — never, apparently, suspecting that Lees himself was directing their every move. And Lees was able to play this tune because of the growing confusion over company accounts and the difficulty everyone had of getting an accurate picture of the funding issues.

It was during this period that Lees was busy trying to bring LGS into the Lees Group Northern Ireland fold. Negotiations between Lees and the Baillies had been ongoing for many, many months. Documents obtained by the author show that the financial director, Joe Cole, had been deeply involved in trying to resolve the problems. But in spite of several agreements, nothing came of them. It appeared that every time there was a settlement, one or other side would want to change it.

When you look at details of a handwritten fax sent by Malcolm Baillie to Lees — dated 12 July 1990 — you learn something of the kind of discussions that were taking place. Malcolm Baillie wrote:

Following our recent telephone conversation and previous discussions I offer for sale my 25% holding in Lees Group Scotland which you want to add to your 50% holding.

1. Sale price £350,000 payable on or before 31st December 1990. (a) by release of £300,000 bond at TSB substituted by a W.A.L. Holdings Guarantee. (b) £50,000 payable by W.A.L. Holdings.
2. Agreement for SMB (Stuart Baillie) as attached.
3. MLB (Malcolm Baillie) to continue as consultant at £12,000 p.a.
4. Transfer of Marine Structures Ltd in [or 'to'] Southern Ireland as discussed and agreed.

On the second page of the fax are details relating to the second point mentioned above — namely terms and conditions of Baillie's continued involvement with Lees Group Scotland.

1. SM Baillie to be the managing director with responsibilities and salary consistent with his current position.

       Suggest £30,000 over 10 years.

2. Option to sell shares to W.A.L. Holdings on cessation of contract or between 6th and 10th year of contract of employment (Colin Lees underwriting purchase).

3. Valuation of shares pro-rata with total value of business. The valuation to be based on accounts and future maintainable earnings.

4. Lees Group (Scotland) Ltd to have its head office situated in Inverness. SM Baillie to have right to veto any change.

5. Each of SM Baillie's shares to have four votes attached on matters which may affect his position.

What is really interesting about this fax is any discussion and/or agreement to transfer Marine Structures Ltd to 'Southern Ireland'. This, it would seem, was going to be Colin Lees' first step towards burying all records with his fingerprints to his favourite location for his secret companies, Dublin. Marine Structures would become part of the PCI, Structocrete and Creteplant family of firms. This might have given him the chance to continue to hide from his employees at home the extent of his involvement with the leasing arrangements made in Scotland in the names of the Baillies, but on his behalf. Malcolm Baillie recalled: 'He never put a signature anywhere. You will not find his signature other than on the guarantees for the leases. He guaranteed every lease. He got the note of all the equipment. He knew exactly what was being done and he authorised it. Without his guarantee we wouldn't have got a penny.'

The fact that his staff in Magherafelt did not have a full picture of what was going on in Scotland appears to be confirmed in a memo sent to Lees by Joe Cole in response to the above fax.

Noting that legally Malcolm Baillie 'does not own any LGS shares, I understand that you consider that morally he owns 50%', Joe Cole goes on to write:

> You are aware of my thoughts and concerns expressed in previous memos, this fax to a degree heightens my concerns that to acquire control of LGS you will have to pay an inordinate price; particularly since as I understand affairs you have borne all the financial risk to date. I would have felt better inclined to MB [Malcolm Baillie] had he reflected the fact that his position has been that of director and employee and not that of owner.

What lies at the core of this dispute between Lees and the Baillies over what to do with Marine Structures and LGS, is the knowledge they alone share about Lees' crooked deals with leasing companies. Effectively, each had a hold over the other because of their shared knowledge that things had been done that would not reflect kindly on either party if exposed to public scrutiny. This was the secret agenda at all discussions. It was an unspoken but powerful negotiating tool. Why else would two company employees ever get to the stage of negotiating deals about ownership when they had not put forward any collateral to establish the companies in the first place? What gave them their strength in talks was the fact that Lees did not want his business empire to collapse at the very point of reaching its peak.

Similarly, it is worth asking the question: why would a ruthless businessman like Colin Lees be so keen to negotiate and purchase from two employees his own companies in which he had invested capital and had taken all the risks while they had not put in a penny? Again the answer is that he was trying to ensure their silence. Lees' staff in Magherafelt continued to press Lees to jetti-son the Baillies and deal with the problems of the leasing deals he had guaranteed. Little did they know of the secret knowledge that kept both sides pressing against each other, giving each a hold over the other.

Before any agreement was reached and signed concerning future arrangements of LGS, Colin Lees went to court in Edinburgh to get access to the LGS offices in Inverness. He claimed the Baillies had locked him out. At least that was the story in Magherafelt. Michael Wightman told me he believed the Baillies were 'ripping Lees off'. He said Lees was not a signatory to any of the accounts in Scotland. Of course, this was stated in spite of the fact that he, Wightman, and Lees were signatories on the Scotpole No. 2 account. Wightman said he and another member of staff, Alastair McCorkindale, who came from Scotland originally, were sent to Scotland by Lees to 'find out what the hell was going on over there'. Wightman said they were prevented from getting access to the company offices by the Baillies and eventually had to get a court order in Edinburgh to get into them. It was further compelling evidence of the extent to which the relationship between the two had eroded.

Joe Cole and Michael Wightman were dispatched to Scotland to get a court order. Cole left before the court case was heard, but Wightman stayed on and went into court, battling successfully to get an order giving access to the office. Michael Wightman was said to have found that things there were not hunky dory. For Michael Wightman to find things were not hunky dory is interesting in that he had met with the Baillies, was aware of the useful 'paper' company Nationwide Plant Corporation, and had even asked one of the Baillies on one occasion: 'How's Nationwide performing?' He went on to say that 'he would be putting more finance through there'.

As a signatory to the Scotpole No. 2 account, Wightman was certainly aware of the scheme to secret payment for sawmill supplies at Magherafelt in that account whilst the assessors sorted out the fire insurance claim. Hadn't he signed over a cheque for £230,000 out of that account to the Group in Northern Ireland?

But as we know, Lees had a habit of keeping his staff in the dark by refusing to allow any one person to know all of his business dealings. According to the Baillies, this opportunity to get into the Inverness office and remove vital paperwork had one net effect, as Stuart Baillie explained: 'Colin Lees wanted a schedule of all the leases in Scotland. It was a pretence. He was telling people in Northern Ireland that this was terrible. He put an injunction on my folks to stop them from selling their house and he told everyone he had to get entry to the office in Scotland. He always had access to it. They carted stuff away from the office in black bin liners.'

The injunction against Malcolm Baillie related to a retirement package that Malcolm Baillie told me had been agreed with Colin Lees. It was a golden handshake. Chris Nicholson supported that view when he said: 'Colin Lees sent a letter to Malcolm telling him to take £80,000 to £100,000 as bonus or pay! Malcolm took half of it. When the shit hit the fan he was told to pay it back because he could not find the letter. He had to re-mortgage the house to pay it back.' The Baillies had been thrifty enough to have had no mortgage on their house after Malcolm retired from the HIDB. But because of the dispute over the money taken by Malcolm, they had to re-mortgage their home to pay it back.

Malcolm Baillie said Lees took over control of the office and used the time to make sure of one thing: 'By September the bubble had burst and he came in on a court order and took over the company. In the six months that he was there, from September, he made sure that what he left in Station Square, Inverness, where our office was, incriminated us. And he took away all the stuff that incriminated him. He then stripped the company, selling all the assets . . . well he sold most of the fish that he could.'

But there was one more meeting between Malcolm Baillie and Lees — in December 1991. The Baillies travelled to Magherafelt for the confrontation. As Malcolm recalled: 'That was the last communication we had. That was a bit stormy, that meeting, because we were trying to point out the situation and he said he could run it and had the assets and he confirmed it in front of a lawyer I took over on my own behalf. And they obtained from him a written agreement that he had the assets and the finance to continue the business and there were no problems.'

December 1991 was not a good month for Colin Lees. By the time he met the Baillies he would, of course, have done anything to settle the Scottish affair because by then he was deep in negotiations to raise funding for the pulp mill. Barclays Bank was considering whether or not to commit to the proposal to the tune of £4m to £5m. Lees did not want anything to rock the boat. But it was another meeting in December that did not go in Lees' favour and which caused him even more heartache, just at the moment when he should have been basking in the glory of his new shopping centre, which had the capacity to bring in over £230,000 a year in rent.

It appears a management meeting ended in disarray because one accountant refused to accept Colin Lees' explanation about the difference between the cash books and the sales books. The accountant was adamant that no sales had been made. He wanted the books to be reconciled. Tempers flared, voices were raised. What the creative accounting system had done earlier in the year to cover the traces of Lees' activities, could now, at the end of

1991, no longer sustain the earlier position. Staff were becoming alarmed at the level of expenditure. Money was leaving faster than the companies could bring it in. And what was even more alarming was Lees' desire to go on leasing what the staff then believed to be 'every new piece of equipment that came on to the market'.

Such was the level of excessive expenditure that the Ulster Bank was becoming increasingly nervous about its involvement. Yet for some reason Lees was apparently able to get them to continue providing any leasing companies that approached with good references. And the first thing a leasing company would require would be a reference from the Group's bankers. In spite of the earlier downgraded reference that so upset Lees, there were meetings at the end of 1991 at which Lees sought and was granted assurances from the Ulster Bank that any other bank approached by Lees seeking to organise re-financing would be given first class references. Of course, this might have suited the Ulster Bank if it meant they could off-load the Lees Group from their by now very unbalanced books.

But by the end of 1991, Lees had other enemies who had him in their sights. He had also fallen out with Chris Nicholson. When I visited Nicholson at his Warwickshire home in the summer of 2002, he told me he never received a penny from Lees, in spite of the shipments he made for the Magherafelt man. He said he lost thousands on the freight business.

As Lees prepared to send in the receiver to his Scottish group of companies, someone from Warwickshire was making a complaint to the police about the fraudulent activities of a Northern Irish businessman in Scotland. Pulp fiction was about to become palpable fact in the law courts in Scotland and Northern Ireland!

4 The Bankrupt Millionaire

'Despite repeated requests, Mr Lees has not yet produced the necessary banking records of PCI and Structocrete to help substantiate his assertions. Until such statements are obtained and examined it is not possible to adequately explain how the funds were obtained and utilised. It is also not possible to assess the underlying trading performance and true financial position of each of the group companies.'

Paul Rowan, of Price Waterhouse, in a letter to creditors of the Lees Group of companies after he had become joint administrator when the Lees Group went bust owing £35m.

❦

Angus Chisholm stepped on to the tarmac of a rain-soaked Belfast International Airport. Watching and waiting for him inside the terminal building were two plainclothes members of the RUC. Det. Insp. Chisholm had travelled from Inverness in Scotland. After introductions to his RUC escorts — Frank Savage and Norman Hill of the Fraud Squad — he was soon being driven to the offices of Colin Lees' group of companies in Magherafelt via the Fraud Squad office in Belfast's Strandtown police station. Det. Insp. Chisholm was making his first ever visit to Northern Ireland to ask questions about financial irregularities uncovered in the accounts of LGS by the Aberdeen Receivers, Ernst & Young. They had been appointed on 6 March 1992. And he had questions arising from a complaint of criminal activity made by a businessman in England who once had business links to Colin Lees.

The car journey to Belfast took little more than half an hour through the green and wet countryside. There was some small talk with the two RUC officers. After a briefing in the Belfast police station, Det. Insp. Chisholm and his travelling companion, Det. Const. Alan McKenzie, then visited the Customs and Excise offices at Belfast Harbour. They, apparently, had already seized paperwork from Lees' offices in Magherafelt. Again, there was a short briefing before it was time to leave for his appointment with Colin Lees in Magherafelt.

It was a forty-minute drive to the Co. Derry town and the small talk continued with the Scottish officers' RUC escorts. They would occasionally point out some spot in a field or by the road-side associated with some fearful act of violent death during the troubled past. Their stories would be peppered with the word 'bastards'. In Northern Ireland the 'bastards' are always on the other side — no matter which side is hosting the 'terror tour'.

It was Thursday, 28 May 1992, as Det. Insp. Chisholm's car drove through the gates of the head office of the Lees Group. The Scottish detective could not help but be impressed by the large office block that overlooked the concrete works and sawmill, the core of the Lees business empire. Then he came face-to-face with the man who had called in the Scottish receivers, Colin Lees. They shook hands. Lees was, outwardly at least, in buoyant mood. Lees' sister Dorothy Hartley produced tea and biscuits.

It was a cordial meeting and Lees appeared to be friendly and helpful. He gave a smooth if not polished account of himself. He did not wilt when asked questions about his Scottish operation in general and about Nationwide Plant Corporation in particular. After all, he had been successful for a number of years in concealing from his own staff the exact nature of his Scottish business links and his secret fund-raising exploits at the expense of banks and leasing companies.

Exactly how Lees felt by the time Angus Chisholm left his offices to return to Scotland is unclear . . . but the significance of the visit was inescapable. Before leaving to check into a hotel along the North Down coast at Bangor in Co. Down, the Scottish police indicated they wanted to question Lees on tape and under caution at Antrim Road police station in Belfast on Saturday, 30 May. So he must have known that whatever he said to them at his offices clearly did not remove him from the list of suspects, nor had his ruse as the person who called in the receivers. The Inverness officers had many questions still to ask.

Colin Lees' secret criminal career was edging closer and closer to public exposure. His world was closing in around him. Creditors were applying pressure at home, his bank was becoming increasingly impatient, alarmed even, and members of his staff were openly challenging the manner in which Lees was handling his business affairs. Now the Scottish police were on his tail.

'It was 10 March 1992, we received a report that Lees Group Scotland had gone into receivership,' said Angus Chisholm, 'and we started our enquiries into Lees Group Scotland. In the early stages of our enquiries we travelled out to Northern Ireland to interview Mr Lees and to look at the Irish side of Colin Lees' companies.'

The Scottish police found the Lees companies in Ireland were working to full capacity and 'at that time, they were doing well'. Of course, the truth was that while the sawmill and concrete works were profitable, Lees' had placed the entire group of companies in jeopardy by what some of his staff and his bank had identified as his 'commercial madness'. Although he did not realise it at the time, Det. Insp. Chisholm was about to delve into the real reasons for Lees' 'commercial madness', his secret world of fraudulent leasing so expertly manipulated from his base in Magherafelt.

Just a matter of two months prior to Det. Insp. Chisholm's arrival in Magherafelt, Lees had fleeced De Lage Landen Leasing of almost £1.5m by means of a false invoice, in what turned out to be his last act of 'commercial madness'. This time PCI invoices claimed to have supplied new sawmill equipment. Now the Scottish detective was quizzing Lees about similar operations in Scotland.

'Colin Lees had been instrumental in setting up Lees Group Scotland,' Det. Insp. Chisholm told me, 'and now we were heavily involved in looking into their activities. Our interest was in their invoicing, and in the early stages some of it had come from Ireland, and he was involved in that aspect of it. It came to light because the receiver was called in. I suspect that probably Colin Lees' company in Ireland blew the whistle on it and called in the receivers. Ernst & Young, the receivers in Aberdeen, went in and looked at the books and quickly found that there was a huge number of false invoices there and they reported it to us then.'

The Scottish police were further encouraged to look into the LGS by the allegations of impropriety by the English businessman. The complaint originated in Warwickshire, where Chris

Nicholson lived, in embittered anger with Lees over non-payment of £300,000 for shipping services, although the complaint had come from another individual who had had dealings with Lees. Malcolm Baillie said Chris Nicholson had encouraged the other businessman in England to make the complaint. And it became obvious early in the Scottish police inquiries that Nicholson would have to be interviewed. The Scottish police travelled south to speak to Nicholson and I understand that Nicholson made it clear to the detectives he met that he was involved with MI6. I also understand that subsequent checks into Nicholson's claims by high-ranking Scottish police officers confirmed that he had indeed strong links to MI6.

The Northern Constabulary of the Scottish police does not have a Fraud Squad. It is the only force in Britain not to have one. So the investigation of LGS was a major challenge for Det. Ch. Insp. Chisholm. From the outset he was determined to make use of whatever resources he could find. He told me how he decided to go about this difficult task: 'From my initial meeting with the receiver it was apparent that this was a fraud on a massive scale, and I immediately implemented the HOLMES Database. HOLMES is a computerised database that police throughout Britain use to deal with major enquiries. It was set up in the aftermath of the Yorkshire Ripper enquiry and the initials stand for Home Office Large Major Enquiry System. HOLMES is usually used in murder enquiries but from the outset I recognised that a huge amount of paperwork would have to be sifted through and I felt that HOLMES would be the best way in which to manage it.'

On 11 March 1992, Det. Insp. Chisholm raided the Inverness offices of LGS at Highland Rail House, Station Square, and with the permission of the receivers he removed every scrap of paper relating to the company. 'This amounted to several van loads,' according to Det. Insp. Chisholm. Under the umbrella of the Lees Group there were a number of associated companies — South Harris Hatcheries Ltd; Lewis Salmon; Salar Smolt & Salmon; Tarbert Fisheries; Marine Structures Ltd; Webb Marine (Int) Ltd; Scotpole (Int) Ltd; Uist Shellfish Ltd; Lochportain Fish Farm; Shin Game and Whitefish (Int) Ltd. The administration of all these companies was also carried out from the offices at Station Square. The paperwork for all the companies was seized. Using the HOLMES database was a stroke of genius. Very quickly Det. Insp. Chisholm was able to identify the nature of the crime he was investigating.

'All of the paperwork was itemised and input to the HOLMES database,' he recalled. 'And as the details were fed in we were quickly able to identify duplicate invoices. We found many duplicate copies of invoices as a result of this exercise, but the one that sticks in my mind was an invoice for an Invergordon-based company called Aquatess (UK) Ltd. This company supplied Norwegian manufactured fish farm equipment.'

Det. Insp. Chisholm visited the offices of Aquatess and got their carbon copies of their original invoices. The original Aquatess invoice, numbered 01650, was dated 19 December 1990 and made out to Lees Group (Scotland) Ltd for the balance of a payment for four fish cages. The invoice totalled £48,160.85. As the police put details of all of the paperwork from the offices of Lees Group into the HOLMES database, they found the original of this invoice, which was indeed made out for £48,160.85. But the computer threw up some startling information, as Det. Insp. Chisholm recollected: 'We then discovered three further copies of this invoice, which had obviously been altered, and they were made out as follows:

- One was dated 6 January 1991 and it was made out to Nationwide Plant Corporation for £189,405.
- The next one was dated 16 February 1991 and it was also made out to Nationwide Plant Corporation for £235,980.
- The third was dated 17 November 1990 and it was also made out to Nationwide Plant Corporation for £737,472.'

Lees had been busy! Nearly £1.2m raised from these false invoices alone! Scottish police visited three different leasing companies in London and established that these altered invoices had been tendered to them as genuine and that they had made payments to Nationwide Plant Corporation.

To the Scottish detectives, it was now patently clear that Nationwide Plant Corporation Ltd was a bogus company and its sole purpose was to purport to leasing companies that they were a genuine equipment supplier and to present false invoices to them for equipment that did not exist. Det. Insp. Chisholm told me: 'The telephone relating to Nationwide Plant Corporation was in fact located within a lock fast room at the offices of Lees Group (Scotland) Ltd and certain people were allowed to answer this phone taking great care to say that callers were through to Nationwide Plant Corporation Ltd and not Lees Group.'

Det. Insp. Chisholm's team then visited each of the Lees Group sites and photographed and catalogued each piece of plant and equipment. Details of the equipment were also fed into the HOLMES database with interesting results. It immediately became apparent that many more items of equipment had been leased than actually existed.

When quizzed by the Inverness detectives in Belfast on 30 May, Lees had been evasive about his involvement with PCI and Nationwide Plant Corporation. 'We told him we would have to speak to him again,' said Det. Insp. Chisholm.

It took the Scottish police a year to complete their inquiries, by which time they had the Baillies firmly in their sights — more so than Lees, as Det. Insp. Chisholm explained: 'Colin Lees was heavily involved at the outset and he did set it up. But once it moved into fish farming, Colin Lees took a step back and, if you like, the Baillies took over that wing of the operation on their own really without too much assistance from Colin.'

There was evidence of Lees' activities with PCI in Scotland. Det. Insp. Chisholm told me: 'Certainly in the early stages it had been set up by Colin Lees but I think it would be fair to say that latterly the Baillies themselves set up their own sort of structures and continued in the same vein as Colin Lees had set up. Initially they were using Plant Corporation of Ireland, which was a fictitious company set up in Dublin, and false invoices were being raised through that. When the operation was set up in Scotland, Colin asked that they use that company at the outset. As things progressed they set up their own fraudulent company in Scotland, in Inverness here in fact, called Nationwide Plant Corporation, and the Scottish side then started raising their own fraudulent invoices through that. That may have upset Mr Lees, I don't know.'

The Baillies acknowledge their involvement in the false invoicing but claim the beneficiary was Lees. Lees, for his part, told his people in Magherafelt that the Baillies were taking advantage of his guarantees for their own financial gain.

So, if Lees was upset with the Baillies, he put on a brave face for the benefit of the Scottish police. But he could no longer go on hoodwinking his bankers or his staff in Magherafelt. Within weeks of the Scottish police visit, administrators were called into the Lees Group in Northern Ireland. Accumulated debts totalled £35m.

The administration order covered W.A.L. Holdings and three of its subsidiaries — the sawmill, the concrete works and Dynaspan (UK). The Lees empire was about to go into a tailspin from which it would never recover. Six days before the arrival of the Scottish detectives, on 22 May, a defiant and less than forthright Lees told the *Belfast Telegraph*: 'I am a fighter and I will keep on going.' The story was initiated because Lees had been questioned for five hours the day before by Scottish tax officers, although Lees stressed that his interview with Scottish Customs and Excise was unconnected to the recent financial difficulties that had hit the Lees Group.

The reporter referred to Lees as the managing director of 'the recession-hit Lees Group in Magherafelt'. The article reports Lees' assurance that the troubles at the Lees Group in Magherafelt and the inquiry by the Scottish officers were totally unrelated. Lees is quoted extensively in the remainder of the story: 'This has been very unfortunate timing. The Scottish inquiry and the administration of the Magherafelt companies are completely co-incidental. I realise the company could not have any worse of a public relations image that it has at the moment. So many things have come tumbling down around me in the past six months. These are difficult times but I am a fighter and I must keep going.'

Lees told the reporter he was encouraged by all the messages of support he had received from the public and was working with the administrators to try and keep the business trading as successfully as possible. But he failed to mention that his Scottish group of companies was in receivership and under police investigation. Det. Insp. Chisholm's team of eight detectives had found evidence of a £13m fraud in forty-two bogus leasing deals between May 1988 and October 1991. The same modus operandi as used by Lees in Northern Ireland featured in the Scottish police investigation, as Det. Insp. Chisholm explained: 'If you take the western isles, leasing fish cages was a huge thing where they were producing false invoices. When you are leasing, you, as Lees Group Scotland, would go to the company who supply them, mainly and say: "I am Lees Group Scotland. I am purchasing twenty fish cages at a cost of £150,000." You would say you are being supplied these fish cages by Nationwide Plant Corporation, which the leasers understood to be an independent company. Then Nationwide Plant Corporation would supply a fictitious invoice. Lees Group would send a receipt saying "yes we have received these fish cages and everything is in order" and the payment would be made to Nationwide Plant Corporation, who was in effect the Baillies, so the money went straight to them.'

But surely such a concerted plan of fraudulent activity could not go undetected for long, given that it involved companies that did not produce anything approaching the value of the leases. And what of the leasing companies? Didn't they check on the equipment? Det. Insp. Chisholm: 'To be fair, the leasing companies, many of them based in the heart of London, had a difficulty in checking their assets, particularly if it is fish cages we are talking about. They would fly up here on occasion, fly to Inverness, then fly out to Uist to look at these cages and invariably it would be wet and windy when they arrived there, and to be told that they were then taken on a half hour journey in a rowing boat out to the middle of a rough bay to look at fish cages would deter them somewhat, and even if they had got on the fish cages, there are no serial numbers on there so you wouldn't know whether they were your fish cages or not. Fish cages did exist but they were leased many times over.'

The Scottish police report was passed on to the Fraud Unit in Edinburgh in the spring of 1993. The file made it clear that Colin Lees was in the frame and should be considered for prosecution along with the Baillies.

Once it reached Edinburgh, the Fraud Unit began an inquiry of its own to build on the work done by the Inverness Constabulary. However the Fraud Unit decided to deal with Det. Insp. Chisholm's report, it clearly exercised them considerably because it was to be over six years before they brought a case to court . . . and Colin Lees was not one of the accused!

Det. Insp. Chisholm recalled: 'We certainly knew there was a lot of paperwork flying about but at the early stages we didn't know how much of it was fraudulent and yes it did ultimately turn out to be, I think it was the biggest fraud in Scotland. I assume that the people in the Fraud Unit in Edinburgh would have to go through all the paperwork in fine detail and get it ready for court, so the preparation in Edinburgh obviously took some time.'

With all this growing pressure, Colin Lees apparently became difficult to deal with in the Lees Group offices in Magherafelt. When I met Michael Wightman he claimed to have begun to realise things were not going right when he more and more found himself challenging and arguing with Lees at meetings where he knew things were not adding up. 'Lees was lying through his teeth about what was going on,' he said. 'Things didn't stack up. So one morning he called me and asked me to meet him for breakfast. Once there he said we were not "getting on" and that it was time to me to go. He gave me three months wages and I was told to go away.' That was in April 1992 — just weeks before the appointment of administrators. Wightman told me he went back to help the administrator Paul Rowan as best he could. But, of course, the truth is that Wightman himself knew all along that what he was doing with the books was outside the law.

Naturally, the Scottish police informed the RUC of the fraud they had uncovered in Lees' Scottish companies. The information came to the police in Northern Ireland at about the same time as they received a telephone call from the newly appointed administrators to the Lees Group in Magherafelt. Suddenly, Colin Lees found his businesses in Scotland and Northern Ireland in administration and under investigation for fraud by two police forces.

Almost a year after he had gone into the offices of the Lees Group at the behest of the by now anguished Ulster Bank, Paul Rowan of Price Waterhouse found himself appointed as joint administrator of the group of companies. He first arrived at Lees' offices in Magherafelt in July 1991, becoming joint administrator on 7 May 1992. It was a move that spelt the end for Lees' business empire, because it didn't take long for Rowan to discover that the Group's paper assets, with an estimated value of £46m, were actually worth closer to £18m. Debts totalled £35m. The Ulster Bank was owed just over £5.3m and the Bank of Ireland £1.7m.

In a letter to the creditors on 22 July 1992, the administrators stated that W.A.L. Holdings had expanded its operations significantly in recent years and had invested heavily in fixed assets. To illustrate this, the administrators noted that turnover in 1989 was nearly £15m with profits of almost £2m. Fixed asset expenditure was said to be £4.5m. But in 1990, turnover had risen to £19m; profits were up to nearly £4m and expenditure on fixed assets was up to £12m. The figures for 1991 showed turnover of almost £27m; profits just over £2m and fixed asset costs at £8.6m. The administrators explained to creditors:

The group has been under severe financial pressure since mid-1991 due principally to:

- poor general trading conditions affecting both concrete and timber products;

- extensive expenditure and commitments made by the directors in projects for which funding was not available; and
- the high level of repayments due on capital expenditure financed through leasing agreements.

The administrators also noted:

The directors attempted to re-finance the group and lengthy and ultimately unsuccessful discussions took place with Barclays Bank plc. The termination of those negotiations coupled with the appointment, in February 1992, of a Receiver in Lees Group Scotland Ltd and subsidiary companies, a related group of companies in respect of which W.A.L. [Holdings] had given guarantees in excess of £8m in connection with bank lending and leasing agreements, intensified the group's problems.

The administrators then attempted to explain to creditors what their role would be in dealing with the financial mess they had inherited. First they described the difference between administration and receivership:

Administration bears many similarities to receivership but has important differences. The appointment of an administrator is made by the Court. In addition to his other powers (such as management of the business and sale of the assets), should the company be capable of being reorganised, the administrator generally has the power to make proposals to creditors leading to a compromise of their claims. This provides the alternative of restoring a company to solvency by relieving the company of debt instead of selling the assets (as in receivership).

The statement to creditors continued:

> In April 1992, a review of W.A.L.'s financial position by KPMG Peat Marwick showed a £5m to 6m additional working capital requirement to the end of 1992 for continued trading outside a formal insolvency. There was no prospect of the group's bankers advancing any further funds and the directors then took steps to seek an administration order on W.A.L. and the main operating subsidiaries, namely William A. Lees (Concrete) Ltd, William A. Lees (Sawmills) Ltd and Dynaspan (UK) Ltd. The group's main banker, Ulster Bank Ltd, hold security which would have enabled it to appoint an administrative receiver. However, after discussions with both the leasing companies and the Industrial Development Board for Northern Ireland, Ulster Bank agreed not to exercise its right to appoint an administrative receiver but rather to support the appointment of an administrator. It was considered that the appointment of an administrator rather than a receiver would allow a more structured and orderly approach to dealing with the position of the secured creditors, which would in turn be in the best interests of all creditors.

The administrators declared that they would try to continue to trade the operating companies, but they felt that because of 'the absence of reliable management information' it was necessary to establish the trading performance of the group and its financial position. However, they noted that the objective of this approach

— to determine whether or not a voluntary arrangement would be feasible for all or part of the group of companies — was hampered greatly by the extremely poor state of the company's accounting records and the lack of clear information about a number of 'significant transactions'. Consequently, the administrators announced their intention to sell the assets, as, in their opinion, they could not propose a voluntary arrangement to the creditors.

It was hardly surprising that the administrators found it difficult to establish exactly what state of affairs the leasing arrangements were in at the Lees Group. They found that the book value of the outstanding finance in W.A.L. — before any additional amounts that might arise on termination of agreements — was £6m including amounts owed on assets used by the main operating companies. But the total for the Lees Group on a comparable basis was £17.7m, excluding £800,000 owed by Dynaquip Engineering Company Ltd, a related company owned and controlled by Colin Lees and his sister Dorothy Hartley.

As a result they wrote:

A number of difficulties have been encountered on a group basis in relation to the group's fixed assets and the associated leasing financing. Due principally to what we consider to be the improper accounting practices and records of the group and the failure of the directors to supply the necessary information to the administrators it is not generally possible to identify assets against finance agreements and to verify the associated cost price with the company's records.

Under the heading 'Suspense Account,' the administrators further informed creditors:

The liability shown of £9m represents sums received by any W.A.L. group company during the year ended 31st March 1992 from two companies associated with Mr. Lees, namely Plant Corporation of Ireland (PCI) and Structocrete (Ireland) Ltd (Structocrete). We have been informed by Mr. Lees that there is no liability owing to these companies and that the amounts received represent proceeds from the sale of plant and amounts received by PCI from leasing companies which was in turn owed to group companies. Mr. Lees stated that PCI, a company that we believe he effectively controls, would raise invoices to attract finance from leasing companies. After paying the original suppliers for goods PCI would then remit the balance to a W.A.L. group company to cover whatever expenditure that company had incurred directly. This has apparently been the practice for a number of years.

Despite repeated requests, Mr. Lees has not yet produced the necessary banking records of PCI and Structocrete to help substantiate his assertions. Until such statements are obtained and examined it is not possible to adequately explain how the funds were obtained and utilised. It is also not possible to assess the underlying trading performance and true financial position of each of the group companies.

Whatever the accountants were making of the books in Lees' offices, it had become abundantly clear to some of those working for the company that they had entered difficult days. There was an awareness that the Lees Group was under severe financial strain. One man told me he had been sub-contracted to work for Colin Lees' companies. His job was to travel with a small team harvesting trees in the growing number of forests Lees managed north and south of the border. In the early years payment was regular but around the time the Lees companies moved into their new offices to make way for the shopping centre, the financial position became unclear and getting payment was not at all easy. He told me: 'It became harder and harder to get money out of the Lees Group. We would be owed wages and accommodation. I remember going to the old offices for my wages and you usually got paid. But at the new offices it was a game of chance. I would sit in reception along with a group of others and only some would get paid, others wouldn't. Sometimes you had to go back the following week and hope you got paid. Sometimes you were lucky and other times not. Meanwhile, he [Lees] was flying around in a helicopter and the new offices were being built.' Of course by the summer of 1992, it wasn't just the workforce that was concerned about getting payments out of the Lees Group.

On the day the creditors were scheduled to meet, 6 August 1992, a substantial story appeared in the *Belfast Telegraph* highlighting what it described as the 'strained' relations between Colin Lees and the administrators. Lees was in defiant mood. He clearly wasn't going to go down without a fight, even though he must have known that his fraudulent activities were almost certainly going to be exposed. Rejecting the criticism that the administrators had found inadequate accounting practices and a failure by the directors of the Lees Group to supply them information, Lees hit back. He is quoted in the story as saying that the bookkeeping for the audit period up to 1991 was 'correct and up to date'. 'Unfortunately we took our eye off the ball,' he told the reporter, when explaining that bookkeeping had become muddled in the past year when the company moved offices and was busy with expansion plans.

The remainder of the story is worth repeating as it provides an insight into the mind of Colin Lees in the face of almost certain doom. It reads:

'Mr. Lees expressed concern about the fate of his company's concrete business. In June it was announced that the division would close down with the loss of over 100 jobs. Mr. Lees said the business was viable and should have been maintained or sold straight away to attain full market value. 'It's now been run down to the extent that it won't be worth very much. I'm disappointed that the trade creditors are not going to be paid out of it.' He confirmed a claim made yesterday by Mid-Ulster MP, the Rev. William McCrea, that a management team had made a bid for the concrete division. Mr. Lees himself has been working on plans to buy out the group's sawmills division. 'I'm trying to put together a new board structure to buy back the sawmills business.' And he hasn't given up on the company's involvement in a £90m pulp mill project planned for Londonderry. 'The pulp mill has to happen, whether we do it or someone else does it. That may sound too much like false optimism from me, but I really believe the project is still viable.' Mr. Lees said the future of the project and of the Lees Group would depend on the company's ability to regain public and commercial confidence.'

Public and commercial confidence? New board structure? Buying back the sawmills business? This from a man who knew his false invoicing activities were bound to be uncovered by the administrators and that it was his heavy borrowings from leasing companies and banks that had jeopardised the whole group of companies he had developed in the first place. He surely didn't believe he could bluster his way out of trouble this time or hide the fact that not all the money he raised by means of the false invoices was directed into the company coffers?

What the creditors made of the story before they gathered for their meeting that August afternoon is unclear. What is clear, however, is that the story did nothing to rebuild their confidence in the man who broke the banks and leasing companies and even his own companies. Nominated on to the creditors' committee were NMB Leasing (UK) Ltd; Lloyds Bowmaker Ltd; Pandoro Ltd; El-Ge Engineering Ltd and Hill Samuel Asset Finance Ltd. Given the history of their involvement with Lees in the past, it was unlikely that they would be prepared to take a chance on him again. And they didn't. The creditors opted to back the administrators' plan to sell off the operational companies.

On 24 August, Paul Rowan wrote to the creditors to report acceptance of the package put forward on 6 August. Paul Rowan used the letter to report what had happened at the meeting:

A statement on behalf of Mr. Colin Lees and Mrs. Dorothy [Dickson] Hartley was made to the meeting by their solicitor, Sir Oliver Napier, who stated that his clients categorically denied any lack of co-operation with the administrators and any impropriaty [sic] whatsoever in regard to leasing transactions. Sir Oliver further stated that, according to his clients' instructions, the Customs and Excise investigation was unconnected with the affairs of the company and a full disclosure had been made of all facts pertaining to the ongoing Inland Revenue investigation. Finally, with regard to Lees Group Scotland Ltd, Sir Oliver stated that his clients were shareholders but did not fulfil any administration function.

Clearly, Colin Lees did not inform his solicitor, the administrators or his creditors of his true association with the Scottish company. More importantly perhaps was his decision not to disclose the removal by him from the Inverness offices some twelve months or so earlier of a large quantity of documents that might have shown much closer links with the leasing fraud perpetrated in the name of his Scottish companies. And clearly, the categorical denial by Lees of any impropriety in relation to the leasing transactions was a final blast of bravado from a guilty man who perhaps had still not grasped the reality of the situation . . . that the end of the road was nigh!

While Colin Lees was now battling on several fronts at home and in Scotland to try to paper over the cracks in his by now crumbling empire, he was hit by another piece of bad news that did little to assist his cover-up of his secret life as a criminal. A BBC Scotland Gaelic current affairs programme, *Reothart*, transmitted a revealing story about the financial fraud that had been taking place out of the LGS offices in Inverness. Lees himself appeared in the programme to deny any wrongdoing. But the report told how false invoices were generated in the office in Inverness and how there was a telephone there that was only to be answered by one person who knew not to say 'Lees Group Scotland' when taking calls but rather 'Nationwide Plant Corporation'.

The BBC programme also reported that Lees' interests in Scotland had begun with the setting up of the secret concrete manufacturing base on North Uist in order to fool the IRA. The consequence of the BBC Scotland transmission was that the Belfast newspaper the *Irish News* contacted Lees for a comment. He did not hesitate to confirm his involvement in the secret concrete production company in which he had a 50 per cent share. Lees told the *Irish News*: 'We were involved in that. After some threats we stopped that work completely and insisted no other work like that would happen in Scotland. Those sorts of things only last a while and when word got out who was involved we just said, "Look, to pot with that, we've a big enough operation, we don't need to be doing this work," and after some personal threats we just gave up.' No one could have foreseen that it was to 'pot' that Lees would soon be turning his attention in order to maintain the fast lane lifestyle that was now under threat from police and financial investigations into his affairs.

In any event, it wasn't long before the administrators in Magherafelt discovered that the real reason for the financial squeeze on the Lees Group was the debt produced by Lees' so-called 'commercial madness'. They found that 'commercial madness' in reality meant fraud. Just as the receivers in Scotland had called on the police to investigate the activities of Lees' companies, so the administrators in Northern Ireland felt obliged to do the same.

Whatever limited knowledge the RUC Fraud Squad had on Lees' activities up to this point may have been restricted to what had been learned from the Scottish police. Now the RUC was to become involved in conducting its own investigation.

But news of the RUC investigation was not reported for some time. It eventually surfaced in the *Belfast Telegraph* on 17 November 1992. Under the headline 'Fraud Squad Probe', the story read:

> The RUC's Fraud Squad is investigating the affairs of four companies formerly run by the Magherafelt businessman Colin Lees, it emerged today. A file on the companies — W.A.L. Holdings, William A. Lees (Sawmills), William A. Lees (Concrete) and Dynaspan — was passed to the Fraud Squad by the Director of Public Prosecutions on November 12. The four firms were placed into administration on May 7

with debts of around £40m. Insolvency expert Paul Rowan from Price Waterhouse, who was appointed administrator to the companies, is now selling off the assets with the hope of raising enough cash to pay some of the creditors. Creditors include the Ulster Bank, which is owed £5.3m and the Bank of Ireland (£1.7m). A further £25m is owed to a group of 24 leasing companies. Other creditors account for around £7m. On paper the assets of the companies total about £46m, but the directors estimated that no more than £18m could be realised. The administrators have indicated that the final total will probably be considerably less, although they are confident of finding buyers for the sawmills and concrete businesses.

A week later the same newspaper had another story on Colin Lees' troubled businesses. Under the headline: 'Former Lees Boss Is Bankrupt, Says Court', a short story informed the public:

The Lees Group saga has taken another twist with the bankruptcy of Colin Lees, the former boss of the Magherafelt-based construction materials and timber company. An order against Mr. Lees as a director was made in the High Court yesterday after a creditors' petition was supported by leasing lenders including Ulster Bank and Lloyds Bowmaker Leasing. As a bankrupt, Mr. Lees cannot be a company director, nor can he open a bank account or obtain credit of more than £250. Four of the Lees Group companies — W.A.L. Holdings; Lees Concrete, Lees Sawmills and Dynaspan — were placed in administration last May. Debts are now estimated at around £35m to 40m. Administrator Paul Rowan from Price Waterhouse is trying to sell the assets of the companies in a bid to pay off the creditors, including Ulster Bank, which is owed £5.3m.

Revelations about Lees' debts and the subsequent failure of his companies had been causing widespread alarm in his hometown. Obviously the jobs created at the shopping centre were secure, but with Magherafelt's largest employer in trouble, the local economy faced financial hardship if the administrators failed to find buyers for the two most viable assets in the Lees Group of companies — the sawmill and concrete works.

In order to cut costs whilst seeking buyers, the administrators laid off some staff at the concrete works and sawmill. Given the earlier closure of a shirt factory in the town, Magherafelt was dreading the complete loss of all the jobs at the Lees Group. The local council had talks with the new Economy Minister Robert Atkins about the perilous state of affairs in Magherafelt. The council's vice-chairman Bertie Montgomery noted, 'but he has not come through with much yet'.

The *Mid-Ulster Mail*, which had so often in the past carried advertising features on the Lees Group and had so frequently been used as a recruitment device with full-page advertisements seeking new staff, now found itself examining the potential loss of between 350 and 500 jobs related to the Lees Group.

This then was the backdrop to the ongoing Scottish police investigation, which had by now been running for around eight months and which had uncovered a £13m fraud. Meanwhile, in Northern Ireland the RUC was in the process of unearthing fraud to the tune of £23m. The modus operandi in each jurisdiction was identical. Lees' companies had gone bust owing £35m. The situation could not have been any worse for someone once regarded so highly in business and government circles as the 'Messiah of

Mid-Ulster' and who was about to become the region's 'Darth Vader' — a man who had entertained lavishly at home and further afield. Det. Const. John Horan was attached to the then RUC's Economic Crime Bureau, now the Police Service of Northern Ireland (PSNI) when he began to search into the background of Colin Lees. He said Lees led the champagne lifestyle with lavish parties at his home and expensive entertainment on business assignments. He was, as John Horan put it: '. . . very high profile, very well known in the north-west, very well liked. Very much the coming man if you like, the up and coming entrepreneur who was going to rejuvenate the north-west.'

Det. Ch. Supt. Derek McLaughlin headed the Northern Ireland police Fraud Squad investigation. He said his officers quickly focused on the leasing of plant equipment. 'In particular,' he told me, 'one piece of equipment was used over and over again in this scam. It was a crane that ended up in Portugal. This crane was leased out over and over with fraudulent claims coming for damage by fire or in industrial accidents. Lees made millions out of this scam.' Another officer spoke of how another piece of equipment was double leased. It had different registration plates front and rear so that if anyone from either of the leasing companies came calling, the equipment would be parked in such a way as to allow them to see the markings that related to their leasing agreement.

The Scottish police inquiry was first to be completed — in the spring of 1993. Det. Insp. Chisholm sent his file from Inverness to the Fraud Unit in Edinburgh for further investigation. There was sufficient evidence to consider charges against Lees, as Det. Insp. Chisholm told me: 'He featured in our enquiries here and he was involved at the outset but we did report the matters to the Fraud Unit at the Crown Office but the decision was made there that only the two Baillies, Malcolm and his son Stuart, would be reported here and prosecuted here.'

Lees had got lucky! The fact that he was under serious investigation for similar activities in Northern Ireland was a factor taken into consideration. Given Lees' pending prosecution in Northern Ireland, the Scottish authorities took the view that there would be little point putting him on trial in Scotland — much to the chagrin of Malcolm and Stuart Baillie, who were left to eventually face the consequences of their, and Lees', criminal folly. Few could have predicted that it would take ten years before the courts in Scotland and Northern Ireland would finally deal with Colin Lees. And no one could tell from these early legal and financial skirmishes with the ever-defiant Colin Lees, just how determined he was to make crime pay.

Colin Lees' race to destruction still had some distance to go. Bankrupt and jobless, Lees didn't lose his drive or determination to fleece other people of their money. Even while under investigation by two fraud squads and while the administrators attempted to salvage something from his companies in Magherafelt, Colin Lees was busy perpetrating a crime outside the jurisdiction, well away from the prying eyes of police officers in Northern Ireland and Scotland. The land of the free beckoned!

5 The Bonanno Family

'Where didn't Derek Jones lead us? He led us initially to New York to a gentleman called Jonathon Lyons, and when we began to look at Mr Lyons, we contacted the law enforcement agencies in the United States and they informed us that Jonathon Lyons was in fact on indictment for being involved in the manipulation of the American stock market to the benefit of two Mafia crime families, the Genovese and Bonanno crime families . . . And they [Jones and Lyons] had a reasonably simple method of moving the money — it went from New York to Canada, Canada to Dublin, Dublin to Ballymena and Ballymena back to New York. And Derek Jones manipulated each stage it went through the system through a number of shell companies that he owned . . .'

Det. Const. John Horan, of the Economic Crime Bureau, Police Service of Northern Ireland, describing just one of the most amazing developments in the investigation of Colin Lees.

I t was the spring of 1993 when the telephone rang in Richard Worthy's plush office suite in downtown Dallas. 'It's a Lillies Hooi from Berkshire Financial Group,' said his secretary.

'I'll take it,' he said.

Berkshire Financial Group Inc. was a financial brokerage firm operating in Florida . . . probably a routine call, he thought.

Richard Worthy looked across his desk into the adjoining suite with its comfy leather sofas, huge coffee table in front of the fireplace with an enormous steer's head resplendent with enormous horns hanging high above, dominating the room — a pleasantly plush area for relaxation where many a business deal had been sealed over a glass of brandy. 'Richard Worthy,' he said into the phone. What happened over the next few minutes was to forever change Richard Worthy's outlook on life and leave him considerably poorer financially, although of course he did not see it that way at the time.

Initially, at least, it did indeed appear to be a routine call from a financial broker in Florida who wanted to introduce Worthy to a potential customer. Although he had once worked as a district attorney, Richard Worthy had long since given up court work to set up and run his own business, Metro Factors Inc. — a company that specialised in lending money to building contractors on foot of trade account receivables. In other words, his company would advance cash to constructors or manufacturers who in turn would agree to hand over stage payments to repay the loan. At the other end of the phone Ms Hooi explained that her company, based in the St Petersburg/Sarasota area of Florida, had a client, Emerald Pre-Cast Concrete, seeking financing on a product they were manufacturing. She made it sound interesting enough for Richard Worthy to arrange a visit to Florida to meet with Emerald Pre-Cast.

Richard Worthy had studied the law and had become a district attorney in his home state, Texas. He had specialised in prosecuting white-collar crime. The irony is that he got fleeced himself to the tune of almost $1m. The sucker punch, which he says he should have seen coming, but didn't, was delivered by a 41-year-old Irishman whom Richard Worthy found charming and 'every inch the gentleman'. Richard Worthy had become the victim of a white-collar criminal, an experienced 'con' man and fraudster had taken him in . . . albeit with a little help from his equally corrupt American business partner.

The irony of his situation is not lost on Richard Worthy: 'For eight years I was a prosecutor in charge of white collar prosecution and I was always coming in after the fact . . . whenever a bank had been defrauded or when investors had been defrauded. I was always able to view the situation of armchair quarterbacking . . . looking back if you will, and in each of those cases I would always say to myself, "I could have spotted that person walking in the door! Why didn't you people?" You find that it's very different when you're on the other side of the table and whenever you're out there on the front line making those immediate decisions and character decisions about people. And the result is that I have become a lot more sceptical of people. We do a lot more extensive background checking on people today than we would have before. I think we turn down applicants that we might not otherwise have turned down. That may in many cases mean turning down very good people. But we've had to raise our standards of background investigation and so I think it has made me a lot more sceptical.'

Richard Worthy came face to face with the reason for his ingrained scepticism at the Sarasota offices of Emerald Pre-Cast and a perfect example of how so many people are conned by white collar criminals . . . for it was here that he had his first meeting with the 'charming' Irishman, Colin Lees. It's a meeting remembered very clearly by Richard Worthy: 'My first impression of him was very favourable. He was very articulate, very much a gentleman and talked extensively about the success of his business in Ireland, which was similar in that it was engaged in the concrete flooring. Yeah, he made a very strong, good impression.'

With Scottish and Northern Irish police busy investigating him back home and with his business operations in Magherafelt decimated, Lees had designs on starting a new life in the land of the free. At least he had no intention of allowing his charm and ability to 'con' people go rusty . . . he had come to the United States to continue where he had been forced to leave off back in Northern Ireland. Richard Worthy just happened to be in the wrong place at the wrong time.

Having been questioned by police in Northern Ireland, Lees was released pending further inquiries. But he was not meant to leave the country. As he had dual nationality — that is, a British passport and an Irish one — Lees was able to sneak in and out of Ireland through Dublin using his Irish passport. This avoided the possibility of drawing attention to his movements by using his British passport.

As Det. Const. John Horan was later to remark when police eventually learned of Lees' visits to the United States: 'It's just amazing that being on police bail for one fraud you go across to the other side of the world and commit another fraud, while on bail! And in fact, at that time my understanding was that he had surrendered his passport to the authorities. But of course he had dual nationality, Irish and British, and he used the Irish passport.'

But what attracted Lees to Florida? The crucial link was Lees' late father William. It appears he had struck up a friendship with a family called Brannan in Sarasota, the owners of Emerald

Pre-Cast. The bond of friendship was forged because Lees senior and John Brannan were the proud owners of a particular piece of German-manufactured equipment used in the production of pre-cast concrete. At the time that the equipment was purchased, it was regarded as the 'state-of-the-art'. William Lees had visited the United States many times during the 1980s. Colin Lees visited America in 1980 at a time when he wanted to expand the company. The purpose of his trip was to see Dynamold — the specialist manufacturer of casting equipment. In Northern Ireland at that time, there was only one maker of concrete flooring spans. When Lees returned, he worked on setting up Dynaspan, which formally began trading in 1981.

When the Brannans approached retirement they wrote to William Lees to enquire if he was interested in buying their business, unaware that Mr Lees had died some time earlier. Of course, Colin Lees was by now running the family business and it was he who received the letter. Bankrupt and with the police breathing down his neck, the time was ripe for Colin Lees to travel to Florida with the prospect of taking over Emerald Pre-Cast. There he could conceal his disbarment from holding a directorship of any company due to his bankruptcy. The Brannans had no great love of Lees 'junior' but agreed to make a deal with him, handing over control of Emerald Pre-Cast. Like Richard Worthy, they would soon have reason to regret what they would later regard as a 'flawed judgement'.

Colin Lees' version of events differs slightly. When later questioned by police, he told them he was working for Temple Quarries Ltd in 1993 when John Brannan contacted him. Lees acknowledged that his father William, and John Brannan had long been friends through business. Apparently, according to Lees, John Brannan had heard that the Lees Group had gone bust.

Brannan, again according to Lees, then asked if he would be interested in a franchise in the United States, in Florida. Lees travelled over to the United States to have a look at Emerald Pre-Cast and, to use his words, 'did a deal to take the business over and try and run it over there'. Lees said his employer, the owner of Temple Quarries, then decided not to invest in the American venture, so Lees borrowed a small amount of money — £20,000 to £30,000 — he couldn't remember how much exactly, to invest in his new company in Florida.

Of course, as a bankrupt he could no longer be a director of a company and he could not arrange a loan for over £250, but here he was admitting that he broke both those rules. His admission came much later in a police interview room in Belfast during questioning about other offences. As he said to the police officer: 'I borrowed a small amount of money and the operative word being £20/30 thousand small to just get the start of the company, as it was, over the hump and get it trading, and that I would then get away from the Northern Ireland scene and go and work along that business out there.' To a man more accustomed to dealing in hundreds of thousands of pounds, even millions, of course the challenge of 'borrowing' twenty or thirty thousand pounds was 'small'.

Once safely ensconced in a rented apartment at 3516 North Village Court, The Village in the Pines, Sarasota, Lees set about his task of fleecing Emerald Pre-Cast for all it was worth with great relish. Lees brought his common-law wife Zara with him to Florida. He spent time ensuring that his credentials impressed Richard Worthy along with his business acumen and his dedication to the American 'God' . . . the US dollar.

What Richard Worthy saw on his visit to Emerald Pre-Cast in Florida was a healthy company in full production. He was suitably impressed, and by the summer of 1994 he was ready to do business with Lees. First Lees had to fill in a couple of forms for the Dallas businessman. The results make fascinating reading. Lees declared himself married and named his common-law wife Zara Caroline Lees as his spouse! In the section where he is asked to state the date and place of marriage, Lees wrote: '1987 Northern Ireland'. He is then asked to provide details of his personal history. He is asked to list chronologically his last three employers, beginning with the present. For his present employer he lists Temple Quarries (NI) Ltd and states his position as director/manager. For supervisor, he states 'self'. Then he states that between July 1984 and 1 January 1994, he worked for Colas (NI) Ltd as manager with the chief executive as his supervisor. Finally, he informs Richard Worthy's company that between 1974 and 1984 he 'worked in family business owned by father who is now deceased — business sold'. He declares his position in his father's company as trainee engineer/manager. As to his supervisor he writes: 'N/A.'

So in a couple of strokes of his pen, Lees had airbrushed from history his true role in the Lees Group of companies . . . namely that he led them to destruction with debts of £35m and a £23m fraud investigation that was still active. He continued in the same 'selective memory mode' on the next page when he answered a number of questions as follows:

1. Are you personally or is any business in which you are presently or have been an officer, owner, partner or share-holder or director, a defendant in any civil or criminal law suit or are any such actions presently being threatened?
    Yes ❏
    No ❏
    If yes, please state below the style of the suit, case number, court in which case is pending, cause of action,

amount of plaintiff's claim and if applicable the govern-
mental agency involved.

Lees ticked the 'No' box!

2. Have you personally or has any business in which you
   are presently or have been an officer, owner, partner,
   shareholder or director been a debtor in a bankruptcy
   proceeding or affected a composition of creditors during
   the last 14 years?
   Yes ❑
   No ❑
   If yes, please give details below.

Again, Lees ticked the 'No' box!

3. Have you ever been convicted of a felony criminal
   offence or a misdemeanour criminal offence involving
   theft, fraud, or moral turpitude?
   Yes ❑
   No ❑
   If yes, please explain below.

For once during this paper exercise Lees could truthfully tick the
'No' box! Well, he hadn't yet been convicted of charges relating
to theft or fraud. But he certainly did not appear willing to impart
any information about his current predicament back in Northern
Ireland and Scotland. In the space reserved for information in
relation to a 'Yes' answer to the above questions, Lees volunteered
the names of two United Kingdom references. He named B.
McCurran, of McCurran-Salkhon, Chartered Accountants;

Wimpole Street, London; and Ian Smith, of Technical & General Guarantee Co. Ltd., Fleet Street, London. He provided telephone numbers for both, one at an office and the other a mobile.

But the most fascinating information on Lees' American connections comes in the section where he is asked to give the names of personal references. There are spaces for three. He lists three individuals.

The first is Robert Montgomery, of Marina View in Nassau, the Bahamas. Asked to explain his relationship, Montgomery is listed as a trustee. His occupation is given as accountant and they apparently have known each other for six years.

The second individual listed is Derek Jones, of Consolidated General, Palm Beach, Florida. Jones is described as a financial consultant in both the 'relationship' and 'occupation' sections. He apparently has been acquainted with Lees for eight years. The third person listed as a reference is J. Toale of Sarasota. He, or she, is described as a lawyer of Lees' acquaintance for just six months. The most interesting of the three referees named by Lees is undoubtedly Derek Jones, of whom we will learn much more later in this chapter.

But back to the Metro Factors Inc. form. Lees continued to demonstrate marvellous dexterity when he came to the page that required a statement of his personal finances. In this section he completed the form on behalf of 'Colin and Zara Lees'. And he declared that they had three dependants. Under the section exploring assets, Lees was asked about cash on hand and in banks. He wrote $50,000, with the cash value of life insurance $100,000. In the section, 'real estate owned', Lees declared property worth $5.25m with personal property valued at $450,000. His total assets therefore amounted to $5.85m. He declared a salary of $90,000 a year with dividends and interest yielding $30,000, giving him an income of $120,000 per annum.

So far, so good. Figures like these would impress not just Richard Worthy, but also any lending institution. Of course, they must be viewed in relation to the 'liabilities'. In this section Lees declared he had accounts and bills payable to the value of $300,000 with real estate mortgages payable of $1.5m. Total liabilities, therefore, stood at $1.8m. Deduct liabilities from assets and Lees had declared himself to be worth £4.05m. As far as Richard Worthy's company, Metro Factors Inc, was concerned Lees could easily afford his declared income taxes of $15,000, insurance premiums of $10,000 and mortgage payments of $15,000 a year. Lees signed the form on 18 July 1994.

From the very first day he met Colin Lees, Richard Worthy knew exactly what the Irishman wanted, as he explained to me when I visited his Dallas offices: 'Metro Factors is in the business of factoring trade accounts receivable, which is an alternative form of financing. What he [Lees] wanted from us was to be able to sell us invoices for a product that he was manufacturing. The product was a pre-stressed concrete flooring and the factoring speeded up the cash flow so that what he wanted from us was to be able to sell the invoices to us within a couple of days of him having manufactured the product . . . and so he wanted our money.'

Satisfied that the information on the introductory forms Lees had completed was correct, Richard Worthy considered him a good risk. Emerald Pre-Cast had succeeded in securing finance based on invoices showing it had manufactured a marketable product. But wait a minute! Lees? Invoices? Cash advances? Back in Northern Ireland or Scotland it would have had an air of familiarity to anyone associated with Lees' companies, or the police investigating them or the administrators trying to salvage something from the ruins Lees left behind. But in Dallas, Texas, there was no 'previous' form on which to make a comparison. No alarm bells sounded as Emerald Pre-Cast was used to provide Colin Lees with yet another large dose of someone else's cash to fund his rich and varied lifestyle.

Lees turned his attention to his new company. It needed a makeover. Lees was about to turn the ignition key on the kind of personal drive that had made him such a success back home. He was about to accelerate the Colin Lees of old into the new world, the new order in the sun-kissed landscape of Florida. It was as though he had discovered a new compartment for his life . . . a place where he could forget about bankruptcy, police fraud investigations and the collapse of his once vibrant business empire.

The Colin Lees that Florida was about to meet was the man who was so eloquently and lavishly praised by his staff — albeit in a Lees Group publicity brochure dreamt up by some PR man in the early 1990s. In one section devoted to Colin Lees, the man of vision, praise is heaped upon the boss: 'For all its massive investment, however, the Lees Group is still about people and leadership. Its managing director's personal influence on the success of the Group comes across clearly in conversation with his staff, many of whom have known him since his boyhood. *"Colin leads from the front and we try to keep up with him!" "Colin puts the buzz in Lees!" "He's a great guy, he really cares about his workers!" "I'm only a driver here, but he lets me know my work is important!"* The managing director himself is modest about his Group's success. "Above all we have a good, loyal management team and workforce. There's no magic trick, it's the result of a lot of hard work and a little luck."' Glowing testimonials given freely . . . and before Lees almost brought about the total demise of his group of companies.

Ruminating in Florida about the new challenge of running Emerald Pre-Cast and picking up the pieces of his defunct invoice scams back home, Lees decided it would enhance his new business if he could incorporate something of his Irish business interests. Temple Quarries (NI) Ltd was his inspiration. Newly designed headed paper for his America adventure would reflect his origins. From now on, letters and, for that matter, invoices would appear under the following legend: 'EPC: Emerald Pre-cast Company — A Tradestyle of Temple Stone Inc — Structural Concrete Products.'

Everything was in place. It was time to execute 'the sting'. Mention of 'The Sting' instantly brings to mind that great Hollywood tribute to the 'grifters' of the Joplin era, starring Robert Redford, Paul Newman and Robert Shaw. In the film, Newman and Redford are the expert 'grifters', the confidence men who target Shaw as their 'mark', the victim, or intended victim, whom they plan to relieve of a large sum of his cash. In Florida in 1993, the 'mark' was Richard Worthy from Dallas, Texas, and the 'grifters' were Irishman Colin Lees and US citizen and one-time member of the American Screenwriters Guild, Derek Jones. Lees and Jones had the same aim as Newman and Redford . . . to remove as much of Richard Worthy's cash as they could before getting caught.

Perhaps the best description of the work of the 'grifter' appears in a book by David W. Maurer, *The Big Con: The classic story of the confidence man and the confidence trick*, published by Century in 1999. This is how the author described the art of the 'con' man:

> '*The Grift* has a gentle touch. It takes its toll from the verdant sucker by means of the skilled hand or the sharp wit. In this, it differs from all other forms of crime, and especially from the heavy-rackets. It never employs violence to separate the mark from his money. Of all the grifters, the confidence man is the aristocrat. Although the

confidence man is sometimes classed with professional thieves, pickpockets, and gamblers, he is really not a thief at all because he does no actual stealing. The trusting victim literally thrusts a fat bankroll into his hands. It is a point of pride with him that he does not have to steal. Confidence men are not 'crooks' in the ordinary sense of the word. They are suave, slick and capable. Their depredations are very much on the genteel side. Because of their high intelligence, their solid organisation, the widespread connivance of the law, and the fact that the victim must virtually admit criminal intentions himself if he wishes to prosecute, society has been neither willing nor able to avenge itself effectively.'

Of course, there are fundamental differences in the two types of scam referred to above. Newman and Redford used the greed of high-rolling gambler Shaw to make him believe he could have an easy win at cards . . . whereas Richard Worthy was simply engaging in what he thought was a legitimate business enterprise. But make no mistake about it: the intention of Lees and Jones was precisely the same as that of Newman and Redford. And the outcome was the same . . . the mark was relieved of a large amount of cash. Richard Worthy was set up as the mark by Lees the 'con' man, who told blatant lies on forms intended to help weed out the bad from the good. Unfortunately for Richard Worthy, his system of vetting proved to be inadequate. Paradoxically, what Richard Worthy regarded as his strength — the ability to judge character — was the very weakness that the manipulative skills of Colin Lees, the 'con man', were able to exploit.

A police officer described Lees' activities in this way: 'Factoring agencies are set up to mainly service the building trade.

How they operate is you have a building contract and this is a very simplistic explanation; you're on staged payments for that. Well, you need to free up capital to do the building work, so what you do is you go to a factoring company and you say I've got this contract, it was for three million dollars, but I'm not getting paid until the end for it, will you give my money up front, and then as I get paid in stages I will give you that money and you keep a percentage of it. It's a method of freeing up capital. So what Lees actually did was he created false invoices alleging that work had been done, they freed up money for him and of course the work hadn't been done.'

As you might expect, Richard Worthy was not best pleased: 'He [Lees] conveniently forgot to tell me about the fact that he was at that time a bankrupt. Forgot to tell me about his failed business experiences and when I say forgot, I'm being generous. Had he been truthful with me instead of creating the impression of being a very successful businessman, we never would have entered into this relationship to start with.'

Metro Factors began advancing money to Lees. Emerald Pre-Cast had secured a contract with DCC Constructors from Clearwater in Florida to design, manufacture and erect pre-cast concrete products at a building project at Regency Oaks Boulevard in Clearwater. Emerald Pre-Cast invoices soon started arriving at Metro's Dallas headquarters. Sample copies of false invoices I have obtained reveal that on 23 February 1995, Lees sent Metro Factors details of invoices numbered 174, 175 and 176 identifying the debtor as 'DCC Constructors, Regency Oaks'. The amounts concerned were $12,300, $35,380 and $18,500 . . . a total of $66,180. The paperwork was completed in Lees' own distinctive handwriting. It wasn't long before he had accumulated almost $1m of Metro Factors' cash.

Lees could not have managed to operate a scam on this level so quickly after arriving in the United States had it not been for some 'insider' knowledge. He found a kindred spirit in the chain-smoking 'financial consultant' Derek Jones. In researching this book I learned from FBI files that Jones had for some time been under scrutiny. A source told me: 'Every company Jones had been involved with in the United States, almost without exception, was being investigated for some sort of fraud or other.' Jones was a seasoned professional criminal specialising in concealing money offshore and stock fraud. The FBI's interest in Jones was first aroused when they connected him to fraud on Wall Street.

Jones lived at Osceola Drive, West Palm Beach, in a property owned by Carol Martino. She also had expertise in stock fraud and was also under investigation by the FBI. Jones had organised a number of offshore accounts for her so that she could avoid US tax laws. He used an account in the name of Consolidated General to move stocks and cash offshore. Along with Martino, Jones had special knowledge of Regulation 'S', which was an exemption from some of the rules in the United States for issuing stock for small companies. It was originally designed to provide a means for US companies to sell stock to purchasers outside the country in order to attract capital to the US markets. Originally adopted in the early 1990s, it lasted until the mid-1990s by which time it had become a major attraction for fraudulent stock dealing. The fraudsters would get fraudulent control of stock by issuing the stock to companies that were ostensibly offshore purchasers but in reality were nothing of the sort. Individuals like Martino and Jones manipulated the situation. It meant they could claim to have off-shore clients when in fact there was no offshore buyer. But large blocks of stock could be issued by this means without the stock being registered with the Security and Exchange Commission.

115

It seems Lees was fortunate in being able to call on the expertise of someone like Derek Jones. How and where Lees first met Jones is not clear. Lees declared in the forms he filled in for Metro Factors that he had known Jones for eight years. And, of course, Lees had visited the United States, and possibly Florida, in 1980 to view a particular method of making concrete flooring. But Lees later explained to police that he had been put in touch with Jones when preparing to travel to Florida to take over the running of Emerald Pre-Cast. He said the information came from a business associate in Northern Ireland.

Lees said Jones was introduced as someone in Palm Beach who could help him get his business off the ground in Florida — someone who knew local banking and business tax regulations. Jones was also used to continue running the company while Lees was back in Northern Ireland. But surprisingly, Richard Worthy was unaware of how important Derek Jones was to Colin Lees. And he certainly did not encounter Jones during the final days of Emerald Pre-Cast in the spring of 1995.

It was around this time that it was beginning to dawn on Metro Factors Inc. that there was a problem with Colin Lees. But try as they might they simply could not pin him down. Richard Worthy takes up the story: 'During the latter part of the ordeal Lees was supposedly out of the country. He had supposedly gone back to Ireland for just a short visit. But that visit kept getting prolonged and prolonged and prolonged. Lees did make a couple of phone calls I believe — long distance calls from Ireland during that time. But we needed him here in order to straighten out the problems we had. We were talking to the contractor and trying to find out, "Why aren't you paying these bills?" As it turned out Lees was selling us invoices for products that had not been manufactured and delivered. Bogus invoices. He had not finished work that he said he had finished and I needed him here to help get that straight but he wasn't here.'

What Richard Worthy did not know, of course, was that Lees was in trouble with the law back home, not to mention the continuing saga over the mess he had left his companies in. In December 1994, he had returned to Northern Ireland to meet with the police. They had uncovered his £2m fraud against the Eagle Star Insurance Company when he falsely claimed his wood production had been severely reduced as a result of a fire. On December 10 he could not possibly have answered any calls to return to the United States because he was otherwise occupied . . . he was making an appearance at Belfast Magistrates Court where Det. Sgt. Nigel Snell of the RUC Fraud Squad informed the magistrate that he had charged Lees at Strandtown police station with dishonestly obtaining £1.96m. Det. Sgt. Snell said that when charged Lees had replied: 'I am not guilty to that charge.'

Because the authorities had discovered that Lees was slipping in and out of the country against the conditions of his police bail and the restrictions laid down by the court when he became a bankrupt, the Director of Public Prosecutions applied to have Lees remanded in custody. The DPP lawyer told the court the charge was part of a much larger investigation, adding: 'The matters which police wish to interview him about represent a very large sum of money.' The lawyer said it was believed that Lees was involved in business in the United States and if he did not answer his bail it would hinder the police investigation.

Lees' lawyer, Brendan Kearney, asked Det. Sgt. Snell what figure the police believed was the proper consequential loss arising from the insurance claim. The detective replied: 'I can't say at this time.' Mr Kearney told the court that the charge would be contested and his firm instructions were that Lees did not intend to leave Northern Ireland. 'He lives with a lady with whom he has had a five-year relationship and they have two children, one born ten weeks ago,' Mr Kearney informed the court. He then added: 'This lady has a business in Florida and he was going back and forward as he was playing a role in it.' Lees' lawyer continued to tell the court that Lees had other ties locally. He explained that although not divorced from his wife, he regularly saw his four children. But magistrate Fergus McCartan said he was prepared to grant bail on certain conditions. He remanded Lees for a week on his own bail of £1,000, a cash surety of £10,000 and a second surety of £20,000. He also directed Lees to hand over his passports and report daily to police at Magherafelt. Even Concorde couldn't manage to move Lees back and forth across the Atlantic to meet his bail conditions. Lees had run out of passports.

There was much in the court hearing that would have answered so many questions for Richard Worthy. It was Zara Lees, not Colin, who was apparently running the company. At least that's what Lees wanted the court to think. Lees was accused of £2m fraud. He had no intentions of leaving Northern Ireland to return to the United States. But naturally, Lees did not take this opportunity to tell the truth. In his phone calls to the States, he singularly failed to mention anything about these very real difficulties confronting him. He told Richard Worthy that he had a daughter who was sick. He needed to stay at home in Ireland to take care of her. Richard Worthy recalled his reaction: 'That was certainly something as a parent that I understand. Things that I have heard since lead me to think that that was a cover and not really the reason. I think that perhaps he did have a situation with a daughter who was sick but I think he took a little bit of truth and stretched it a long way as to why he wasn't here.'

The truth finally arrived at Richard Worthy's office courtesy of

Lees' landlord in Sarasota, who sent the Dallas businessman a copy of an Irish newspaper. In his efforts to track Lees down, Richard Worthy had been in touch with the owner of the property Lees rented in Sarasota. And like Richard Worthy, the landlord also had an interest in finding Lees. He was owed rent. Richard Worthy was stunned by what he read in the newspaper: 'The Irish newspaper announced that Lees had been detained for an insurance fraud involving I believe arson and fraudulent insurance claims and that his passport had been revoked and that's when I really knew this problem would never get straightened out.'

Lees was proving to be the 'Scarlet Pimpernel' of white-collar crime. Just as he had evaded prosecution in Scotland, he had managed to do the same in the United States. Perhaps it was his regular appointments with the law back in Northern Ireland that ultimately saved his skin in the US because there's little doubt that had he not been left without passports and compelled to meet strict bail conditions like reporting daily to his local police station, Lees would have been arrested in Florida and prosecuted for stealing from Metro Factors Inc. and its owner Richard Worthy.

But Lees, of course, had a different interpretation as to why his American venture with Emerald Pre-Cast had come to an end. Talking about the problems of losing his freedom to travel back and forth to the United States, Lees said he and Jones tried to think how best to run Emerald Pre-Cast. This is what he said as he recalled his frustrations in trying to run the company by phone link with Derek Jones in Florida: 'We said try and sell it, thinking we could shoulder some of the losses and capital, but realistically after, I think, the period from me not going back and the subsequent three months, the business got into severe difficulties, we were in major contracts at the time which we were well on target with. Suddenly we ran days and days into arrears, we were on

119

24-hour penalty clause on our contract and every day you looked at it from the end of a telephone in Northern Ireland it was getting impossible, you know.'

So at forty-three years of age, Lees had been grounded like a naughty schoolboy by the authorities in Northern Ireland. But while he was almost $1m richer, the extent and scope of the investigations into his activities back home were constantly being widened as more detail of his deceptions came to light. Lees' American dream had come unstuck two years after he tried to create a new life for himself and, just as at home, the damage was inflicted by Lees himself. It was as if he had learned nothing from the experience of false invoicing in Northern Ireland and Scotland, except perhaps how to perfect his technique to defraud other unfortunates of their hard-earned cash. Certainly, Richard Worthy has been left counting the cost of his misfortune of ever having met Colin Lees . . . over and over and over again.

He explained to me that it wasn't just the loss of almost $1m in cash that impacted on his business: 'The immediate ramifications shook confidence in our bank, which lends us money to operate on. We operate on equity that we have built up in the business, plus a line of credit. We were able to withstand the storm, if you will, but the long-range effect is that after you net out the taxes that were involved, we will be balling in excess of a half million dollars a year for ad infinitum. So what started as a net loss after taxes of approximately $500,000 keeps compounding itself to the tune of about $40,000 a year, every year. So the loss will continue forever until when and if Colin Lees pays us the money that he stole from us . . . which I am not counting on.'

With Lees forced to remain at home, his business interests were for a time controlled by Derek Jones and his common-law wife Zara. But the game was up in the United States. Richard Worthy had begun taking steps to bring Lees to book, even though he knew in his heart that he would never again cast his eyes on the charming Irishman who had so successfully conned him.

Richard Worthy's thoughts turned to whether or not he would ever see Lees made accountable for his crimes in the United States. 'I believe he should be accountable here,' he told me. 'But on the other hand I am a realist. Having been a prosecutor I understand the limited resources of the prosecutorial agencies and the tendency for sentences to run concurrently. So unless it would result in a longer detention, then I think that law enforcement has to use its resources in the best way possible and probably it would not be an effective use of the law enforcement resources to pursue the matter.'

Denying he was bitter, Richard Worthy said he lived by a prayer that says, 'Lord, grant me the courage to change the things I can and the serenity to accept the things I can't and the wisdom to know the difference.' But while he won't let bitterness eat away at him, Richard Worthy confesses to feeling resentment towards Lees. When asked how he might spend a few minutes alone with Lees, he had this to say: 'Now we're talking about something different!' he laughs. 'Now we're talking about a little satisfaction. I would love to be alone in a room with him for a few minutes! So if he ever returns to the United States he better not come to see me!'

It's not just Richard Worthy who lost out to Lees. In an act of extreme insensitivity, he had not even paid the workers at Emerald Pre-Cast. The Brannans were horrified that their business and its good name should be treated in this shoddy fashion and even though they were no longer liable, they stepped in to pay the men so cruelly denied what was owed to them by the bankrupt millionaire from Northern Ireland.

So, given this legacy of corruption, Richard Worthy and the Emerald Pre-Cast employees are unlikely to ever get a few moments alone with Lees. His chances of ever being allowed back into the United States — even if he wanted to return — are zero. He left almost $1m richer, and was then forced by court order to remain at home in Northern Ireland. But Lees was soon driving his criminal ambitions harder than ever. He was by now looking nervously over his shoulder at the US authorities on his trail. He realised the game was up. But he brought back his American side-kick. Derek Jones was also by now glancing backwards, worried about the 'Feds' catching up with him. And he had good reason to be concerned; the FBI had already built up quite a file on Jones.

In any event, the bond of friendship between Lees and Jones had grown so strong that Jones was prepared to pack his bags and move to Northern Ireland. Jones drove a hard bargain — he got Lees to set him up comfortably in Ballymena, a Co. Antrim town in the heart of what was commonly referred to as Northern Ireland's 'Bible Belt'. It's highly unlikely that either of them were Bible readers, but when it came to criminal enterprise, they were undoubtedly singing from the same hymn sheet. The chain-smoking American became a familiar figure in the town, driving around in an old Rolls Royce. From Ballymena, Jones would continue to orchestrate his American business interests whilst at the same time being conveniently placed to work closely with Lees on a number of moneymaking schemes. Looking at the extent of the business relationship between the two men, Det. Const. John Horan observed: 'Exactly how they got together I have no idea. But Derek and he got together. I suppose like finds like!'

Lees' decision to bring Jones back to Northern Ireland was not one based entirely on friendship. There was a real purpose for the bankrupt and disgraced former managing director of one of Northern Ireland's largest companies. Det. Const. Horan explained: 'Colin Lees was a bankrupt, so in effect he really couldn't have any bank accounts. He couldn't leave an audit trail that we could easily follow so he needed somebody to act as his front man and that is how Derek Jones operated. Derek operated all the bank accounts; he managed all the money going into the bank accounts and out of the bank accounts. But he operated those bank accounts on the instructions of Colin Lees — he was very much the front man involved. And when Colin Lees bought a business, Derek fronted the business.'

More importantly, as we shall learn, the ability to provide off-shore banking had a much greater appeal for Lees, who by now had salted away a few millions in bank accounts around the world, most probably stashing a major portion in the Bahamas. Jones' connections had, potentially, the wherewithal to move, conceal, and scatter his ill-gotten gains. There was no way Lees was going to go back to work for a living. He had a talent for living well off other people's hard-earned cash and with Jones by his side he had the means of laundering his proceeds of crime. Det. Const. Horan said: 'Lees brought Jones back into the United Kingdom and back to Northern Ireland and in fact to Ballymena where Derek began a laundering operation on behalf of Mr Lees. And, in fact, it was a very good money laundering operation, and Mr Jones was quite good at it.'

With Jones in place, Lees had set up what became an unholy and ruthless triumvirate of thieves. Jones, it turned out, had been helping to launder Mafia money for the Genovese and Bonanno crime families. The vital link in this Mafia chain was crooked New York stockbroker Jonathan Lyons. Like Lees, he once had it all . . . fast cars to match his fast lane lifestyle. When caught doing business for the Mafia, he turned State's evidence. His charge sheet reads like a cast list for the Godfather movies. But it was some time after Jones' arrival in Northern Ireland that this information

123

filtered through to police officers investigating Colin Lees. Naturally, once it did, they too were keen to benefit from Lyons' apparent willingness to strike deals with law enforcement officers. But more of that later.

With Derek Jones on board, Colin Lees was about to gain promotion from the fourth division to the 'Premier League' of criminals. Soon Lees' financial empire in Northern Ireland, managed by his sidekick Jones, would also become a fulcrum of Mafia money laundering activity.

But the paradox of Derek Jones' arrival in Northern Ireland to 'front' for his bankrupt friend was that whilst Jones took Lees' criminal ambitions to a much wider sphere of operation that included the Mafia, it was a fundamental, almost schoolboy-ish error that put Lees into the frame for one of the biggest investigations ever undertaken by police in Northern Ireland . . . an operation that eventually involved more than twenty police constabularies and customs officers in Britain, Ireland, Europe, Canada and the United States.

Whatever crime Colin Lees was already under investigation for could only be considered 'petty' by comparison with the offences about to be uncovered as a result of Derek Jones' gaffe. His mistake? In March 1996, Jones boldly walked into the Ulster Bank in Ballymena with £55,000 cash to open an account. He told bank staff he wanted to buy a haulage company. The moment he set the briefcase bearing the cash on the counter, the Lees and Jones crime syndicate was doomed. The bank was compelled by law to declare any suspicious banking activity to the police. The intention was to make it difficult for criminals in general, and terrorists and their supporters in particular, to launder the proceeds of their crimes. The Ulster Bank duly contacted the police.

Enter Det. Const. John Horan, then of the RUC's Financial

Investigation Unit, now of the Economic Crime Bureau of the Police Service of Northern Ireland. It was at this point that he was assigned to a case that would dominate his thoughts for the next six years. Acknowledged by his peers as the top financial investigator, John Horan relished the challenge. Twenty-three years as a detective, nine of them investigating financial crime, could not have prepared John Horan for the rollercoaster journey he was about to make as he followed the trail left by Derek Jones.

Det. Const. Horan's special ability is to be able to follow money trails, and since the 1994 terrorist ceasefires in Northern Ireland his field of speciality had been identified as a vital weapon in the police effort to crack down on organised crime. A cursory check on Jones produced startling results, barely believable in rural Ballymena. The American had a startling number of very active bank accounts.

'Mr Jones had a multiplicity of bank accounts,' Det. Const. Horan told me during one of many briefings about the Lees story. 'I mean this guy had nineteen or twenty bank accounts in the UK. He had a lot of bank accounts in the United States. And when we started looking at him we came across a couple of payments, which we considered a wee bit odd, one was for £5,500 to people called Bonet who were living in Gibraltar who were French citizens, and we came across a second payment to them from his Dublin bank account for £50,000.' The second larger payment was also made to the Bonets in Gibraltar.

The police were intrigued. So intrigued that they set up 'Operation Kilbreck' under the leadership of Det. Ch. Supt. Jimmy Molloy. The purpose of establishing a major investigation and getting the Home Office in London to allocate its next available name, in much the same way hurricanes are given names in the United States, is to ensure that ownership and primacy in

125

any subsequent police operations remains with the applying force. All police forces and customs in Britain and Ireland, Europe and the United States were routinely informed of Operation Kilbreck and the Northern Ireland police interest.

And, of course, another consequence of having police officers who are intrigued, is that they use all the weapons at their disposal to satisfy their curiosity in a bid to end the intrigue. Surveillance on Derek Jones was to lead police to Colin Lees. Up to this point there had been nothing to connect Lees and Jones. It was only as a consequence of surveillance on Jones that suddenly the man facing investigation over a £23m leasing fraud was linked to a US citizen of, to say the least, dubious character.

But the surveillance was to produce even more startling results. The police, and particularly Det. Const. Horan, could barely believe some of what they uncovered so early in their investigation: 'Where didn't Derek Jones lead us? He led us initially to New York to a gentleman called Jonathon Lyons, and when we began to look at Mr Lyons, we contacted the law enforcement agencies in the United States and they informed us that Jonathon Lyons was in fact on indictment for being involved in the manipulation of the American stock market to the benefit of two Mafia crime families, the Genovese and Bonanno crime families. And they [Jones and Lyons] had a reasonably simple method of moving the money — it went from New York to Canada, Canada to Dublin, Dublin to Ballymena and Ballymena back to New York. And Derek Jones manipulated each stage it went through the system through a number of shell companies that he owned...'

New York. A crooked stockbroker. The Genovese and Bonanno crime families. This was too good to be true for a self-confessed money laundering anorak. What more could an investigator specialising in the financial aspects of organised crime need for motivation? Particularly since in his world, up to this point, organised crime related to the nefarious scams operated by cash-hungry paramilitaries from both the loyalist and republican communities. Now Det. Const. John Horan was to have the chance to test his expertise in the murky waters occupied by the originators of organised crime . . . the Mafia, the Cosa Nostra.

For a man who had worn a wire when undercover to expose loyalist racketeering and extortion, this was a golden opportunity to utilise his vast knowledge of organised crime's money laundering operations. Det. Const. John Horan is highly regarded within the police service where he is a force mentor. This means that he is regarded as an expert to be consulted for guidance and advice, especially for new recruits to financial investigation. He also reviews the work of new investigators. His expertise is also recognised by the newly established Assets Recovery Agency set up to financially cripple terrorists who profit from organised crime.

Born in Antrim town in 1955, John Horan is one of a rare breed, a Catholic proud to have served in the RUC and the Police Service of Northern Ireland. In March 1996, Derek Jones' gaffe was John Horan's gift.

What further compounded Derek Jones' mistake were two events over which he had no control and which, by pure chance, gave police even greater incentives to pursue their lines of inquiry. These chance police interventions in the Republic of Ireland really opened the throttle, and thrust Operation Kilbreck into overdrive . . .

John Horan was in his element!

6 *Dumped in Donegal!*

'Within weeks of finding out about the payments to bank accounts in Gibraltar, lo and behold the Plongeur Wisky comes ashore at Kilrush in Co. Clare, with nearly two tons of cannabis on board. So in effect, it appeared that Mr Jones had bought the Plongeur Wisky, which was loaded up with cannabis, I would assume in North Africa, and then was sent to the United Kingdom . . . albeit that it was captured in the Republic of Ireland. My own gut feeling is that the cannabis was for the UK market.'

Det. Const. John Horan — referring to the moment the police resolved the mystery payments made by Derek Jones to someone in Gibraltar.

❦

It was cold, damp and dark when their inflatable boat hit rocks off the Donegal coast at Malin Head.

They had miscalculated the waters . . . overestimated their sea-faring skills.

Now they had lost control and were being driven inexorably towards the jagged rocks.

As inexperienced sailors, fear gripped them momentarily.

Suddenly, the engine cut out as the propeller made contact with unseen rocks beneath.

They scrambled ashore . . . almost as anxious about remaining unseen as they were about their safety and surviving the sea's temper. This was, after all, an unannounced visit.

Terrified of discovery, they moved swiftly and silently in the darkness. Equipment was stashed on the stony beach. Binoculars, camouflage netting, two-way radios and even some foodstuffs were buried in rock pools. Their mobile phones they retained . . . essential tools in contacting help. Their immediate problem was in successfully describing their exact whereabouts to their friends further up the coast. They were not familiar with the Donegal coastline.

The date was 29 October 1996. They were lucky to survive . . . but their luck ran out the next day when a Garda came calling as a Good Samaritan. He simply wanted to help people in distress. But his policing instincts didn't desert him when he arrived at Bambas Crown in the townland of Backlands on the Malin Head peninsula.

Det. Sgt. Carroll had been on duty in Malin that day along with a colleague, Det. Garda Cafferkey. Around 4.00 p.m. another officer, Det. Garda Frain, approached to report that a boat had been washed up on rocks nearby and the men with it were seeking help to get it out of the water. He led his two colleagues to the stretch of rugged coastline that had so troubled the inexperienced sailors.

On arrival at Bambas Crown, Det. Sgt. Carroll caught sight of the inflatable boat with a rigid hull, commonly known as a RIB boat. It appeared to be brand new. The owner of a RIB himself, he was more than familiar with this type of craft. In fact, he was regarded as an expert. Some years previously he had single-handedly navigated his RIB on a complete circuit of Ireland to raise money for charity. He also noted the Land Rover Discovery parked in the laneway above the rocks and what he regarded as its distinctive English registration number M820 PPP. Standing at the front of the Land Rover were three men with Northern Ireland accents — Noel Morrison from Bradford Heights in Carrickfergus, Co. Antrim, Samuel Adams, from Abbeydale Park, Belfast (also known as Philip Adams) and Ian Symington from Quay Street, Carrickfergus. Morrison said he owned the boat and claimed he had bought it to race it. Det. Sgt. Carroll asked him if he subscribed to *RIB Magazine*. Morrison told him that he didn't, which struck the Garda detective as odd because the magazine was the only one in Europe that dealt specifically with RIB racing. Morrison also claimed ownership of the Land Rover. The Northern accents made the Gardaí think this was another IRA training camp they had stumbled upon. A Provo camp had been broken up nearby a few days earlier.

When asked what had happened the previous night, Morrison said the engine broke down and the boat drifted on to the rocks. He said he had given the boat to Jim Millar and Noel Johnston to 'go for a run'. As they walked down the grassy path towards the stranded boat on the rocks below, Symington chipped in to say he had been on board when the engine failed and the wind blew the boat on to the rocks. At the boat, Det. Sgt. Carroll was introduced to Noel Johnston, from Meadow Street, Ballymena. Johnston volunteered that he was 'driving' the boat when it got into difficulties with a broken engine. He said the boat had drifted for some time before eventually slamming up against the rocks.

It was at this time that Det. Sgt. Carroll got his first glimpse of the engine. He noted the damage to the propeller fins. This was the first thing that aroused his suspicions. 'They said that the engine cut out and the boat had drifted on to the rocks,' he recalled as we walked along the shoreline where they had run aground. 'But it was clear to be seen from the damage to the propeller that the boat hadn't drifted on to the rocks, that it was in actual fact driven on to the rocks and this was shown by the even and uniform damage to each of the three fins of the propeller.'

Det. Sgt. Carroll became even more suspicious when he looked into the boat and saw two five-gallon drums, each more than half filled with petrol, a gas cylinder with twin gas camping rings and a quantity of food including vacuum-packed rashers of bacon, dried noodles and some loaves of bread. There was also an orange life-jacket. Still, he kept his suspicions to himself as he continued talking to the four men, who were anxious to know how they could get the boat up on to dry land so they could take it away.

His curiosity aroused, Garda Carroll inwardly digested their story and quietly determined a course of action. He disputed their claim that the wind had blown them on to the rocks. As the owner of a similar boat, he was familiar with the weather and the waters. But still he kept his counsel. He devised a plan. He told them the engine would have to be removed in order to get the boat out of the water and clear of the rocks: 'I left them each with a task to do and I got their names and where they were from, discreetly from each of them. I then returned to my own motor transport which had a Garda radio on it and I did checks on each one of them as I got their names and addresses.' But while he was waiting for the results of his radio checks, he had to keep the men occupied without arousing their suspicions. In order to do this, he began a process of going back and forth between the rocks and his

Garda jeep in the pretence of needing particular tools to help remove the engine.

On one of these trips, Samuel Adams followed him. As Det. Sgt. Carroll returned from the jeep with another tool, Adams about-turned and walked back with him towards the boat. The Garda said he would like to take a photograph of the boat because it was so unusual to see a boat so high and dry and surrounded by rocks. Adams said he would rather not have a picture taken as he was already deeply embarrassed by what had happened. When Adams told Det. Sgt. Carroll he was on the boat the previous evening it surprised the police officer because the earlier conversations had indicated that Adams was not on the boat — yet another reason for suspicion.

Work on removing the engine continued. The four men said it would not be possible to remove the engine. But Det. Sgt. Carroll said he knew how to detach it from the RIB. They warned him the steering was jammed. Garda Carroll checked the steering mechanism connected to the outboard engine and the transom bracket. He noticed it was 'extremely bent' and that it had taken considerable force to bend this particular bracket. More evidence suggesting the men were not telling the truth and something else to add to his growing list of suspicions.

As they struggled with bolts holding the engine in place, there was yet another surprise for Det. Sgt. Carroll. Symington remarked that he was lucky to be alive. Why, asked Garda Carroll? 'I jumped into the water last night as we got washed up on to the rocks,' Symington replied. Det. Sgt. Carroll was stunned. He was becoming more and more convinced that whatever was going on the night before, it did not happen the way these four men described it. First only Johnston and Millar were on board . . . and at this stage there was no sign of a man called Millar. Then Adams and Symington had told him that they too were on board. But still he did not challenge the men about their contradictory stories.

Continuing to stall for time, Det. Sgt. Carroll kept the four men busy with tasks and it gave him and one of his police colleagues a chance to take a walk over the rocks and have a chat. In whispered tones, they agreed that the stories they have been given by the four men did not have the ring of truth. But then, even as they walked and talked quietly about their suspicions, they stumbled across yet another clue to the lack of veracity from the Northerners. There, hidden in rock pools, were a couple of bales of camouflage netting hidden away the previous night. Nearby they also discovered camping equipment, all-weather clothing and sleeping bags, along with some dried food and provisions. All hidden. Hand-held marine radios were also found concealed in the rocks. The clock was ticking on whether or not these men would have to be arrested.

More Gardaí arrived to help raise the stricken vessel from the rocks and transport it over hilly terrain to the vehicles. As Det. Sgt. Carroll returned once more to his jeep to check up on the names and addresses he'd passed on earlier over the radio, the fifth member of the boat gang arrived.

James Millar from Toome Road, Ballymena, was driving a Peugeot towing a boat trailer. It was another name for Garda Carroll to radio in. But before he did that, Millar told him that he had been on the boat the previous night. Det. Sgt. Carroll asked how many were on board. Millar repeated the original story given by Morrison, unaware of the slips made by Adams and Symington. 'Two of us,' said Millar, 'me and Noel Johnston.' Det. Sgt. Carroll was by now getting an adrenaline rush. Nothing these guys told him added up. What was going on? What were they really up to?

But now there was a problem. The Gardaí in Buncrana

informed Det. Sgt. Carroll that to speed up the checks on members of the boat gang, their dates of birth were needed. The detective returned to the five men and got their birth details — but by doing so he was sure he had alerted them to the fact that he was carrying out a background check. He asked another Garda colleague to discreetly search around the rocks where the netting and other equipment had been found. Then he rushed to his radio to pass on the new information. Waiting by his jeep was his superior, Inspector Jim Gallagher. They had a chat. Det. Sgt. Carroll explained his doubts about the stories the men had given him. Insp. Gallagher concurred. It simply did not add up.

Det. Sgt. Carroll had another idea. He got another Garda to check the providence of the boat. He suggested calling Red Bay Boats in Cushendall. He had noticed the name somewhere on the vessel. Garda Carroll wanted his colleague to find out if they had recently sold a Red Bay Storm Force Model 6.1 M with patrol type layout and a 150 GT Johnston outboard. It wasn't long before his colleague reported back that Red Bay Boats had indeed sold such a model in the past few weeks . . . to a Mr. A. Meegean & Company of Sky Hill, Dundalk. Not Noel Morrison, who right now was driving up the hill from the beach in his Land Rover Discovery towing the trailer with the boat on board. It was decision time.

Det. Sgt. Carroll got Morrison to stop. He asked the Carrickfergus man to confirm who owned the boat. Morrison repeated his claim that he did. When asked when and where he bought it, Morrison replied he got it from Red Bay Boats . . . from the manager there. Det. Sgt. Carroll asked him whose name he bought it in . . . and Morrison said his own. Now the Garda knew this was not the case. He told Morrison that he didn't believe him. Without hesitation Morrison said he had bought the boat in the name of A. Meegan from Belfast.

Colin Lees – the bankrupt, the conman and the drug runner.

Colin Lees' finest hour – the local boy made good stands beside Government Minister Richard Needham (right) at the opening of the shopping centre that Lees built in his hometown, Magherafelt, in 1991. (Pacemaker Press International)

'This really is one of the most important announcements of the century – not just for the north-west, but for the whole of this island.' John Hume MP and SDLP leader on 25 January 1991 describing Colin Lees' plan to set up a pulp mill in Derry producing wood chip to sell to Scandinavia. (© Chris Moore)

Det. Ch. Supt. Jimmy Molloy (centre) headed the police investigation of Lees, codenamed 'Operation Kilbreck'. He is seen here with Spanish police officers outside Lees' home in Spain. One of Molloy's officers – Sam Sittlington – is on the extreme right.

The 'money laundering anorak' Det. Const. John Horan (right) with a Spanish police officer outside Lees' home in Spain.

Archie McCorkindale on the remote Scottish island of North Uist, who says he found Colin Lees to be a 'fine man, a very nice man'. (© Chris Moore)

Garda officer Mick Carroll at Malin Head where he arrested five of Colin Lees' drug smuggling gang. (© Chris Moore)

ARREST ON SIGHT

NOEL PHILIP MORRISON
aka DAVID REID
DOB 6.5.63

Wanted on warrant for Drugs Offences

The wanted poster for Noel Morrison – one of Lees' friends who was arrested in Donegal but released before police realised he was there to meet the Plongeur Wisky *and help unload her cargo of cannabis. The photograph used was one taken at the time of his brief detention in Donegal. Morrison is still on the run.*

Colin Lees' criminal empire stretched right across the world and into the heart of the American economy in New York's Wall Street. (Rex Features)

Jonathan Lyons, the New York stockbroker, with his daughter. Lyons was
convicted of Mafia-related fraud on the American stock market and he was
a vital witness linking Mafia money laundering operations to Colin Lees'
American sidekick Derek Jones in Ballymena, Co. Antrim.

Dallas businessman and former district attorney Richard Worthy, who was fleeced of almost one million dollars by Colin Lees. (© Chris Moore)

Henry Khelm – former Head of Enforcement at the SEC (Securities and Exchange Commission) in New York who travelled to Northern Ireland to see the evidence unearthed at Derek Jones' home linking him to Mafia inspired stock fraud. (© Chris Moore)

The Ulster Bank in Ballymena where American Derek Jones opened a bank account with £55,000 (sterling). It was this act of folly that led police to step up their investigation of Colin Lees. (© Chris Moore)

The Plongeur Wisky *cost Colin Lees £55,000 (sterling) but when Irish customs officers found £17 million (sterling) worth of cannabis on board in Co. Clare it cost Lees a twelve-year jail sentence.*

Some of the bales of cannabis found on board the Plongeur Wisky –
in total the cannabis weighed just over one ton.

The bridge of the Plongeur Wisky *skippered by Donegal man
Kevin Lafferty on its journey from Gibraltar to Ireland.*

Living quarters on board the Plongeur Wisky.

A ton of cannabis was concealed on board the Plongeur Wisky.

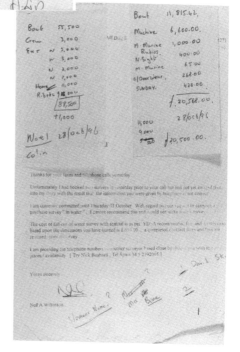

Colin Lees' handwritten fax confirming that 'David Reid' was going to purchase the Plongeur Wisky. Dame Hill Ltd was the 'paper' company set up to facilitate the deal for the drug boat.

DAME HILL LTD
Clifton House, Lower Fitzwilliam Street
Dublin 2
Telephone 00 3531 6613788
Fax 00 3531 6613200

Fax   00 3456 5664 1256.   23/Sept/1996

Mr NEIL A WILKINSON

ReF   Purchase of Boat From
                    Mr + Mrs BONET

Dear Sir,
        I have agreed Terms To Purchase
The boat Known as 'PLONGEUR WISKY' Subject
To Survey. Could You Please accept This Fax
As Confirmation To have an Inspection of The
boat Carried out As Soon as Possible
        I will be at Gibraltar Fri/SAT
and Perhaps You could have it Completed by
Then A Survey of Sea worthiness + Engines
Condition is of Main Concern. I will Finalise
Your Fee at The Week-End.
        If You wish To Contact me I will be
Mobile on 0802 29435   Regards

What police referred to as the 'Game Plan' – notes on the costs of the drug smuggling operation in Colin Lees' own handwriting. This was the positive proof of Lees' involvement as a drug runner.

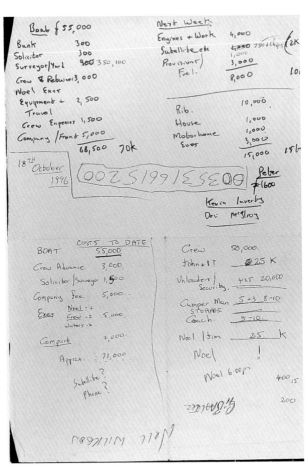

Another part of the 'Game Plan' found by police in the home of Lees' former bookkeeper – again Lees' handwriting going over the costs of the drug smuggling operation condemned him as the 'brains' of the whole enterprise.

Police found a receipt for work done to the Plongeur Wisky by a boatyard in Gibraltar in order to make it seaworthy for the drug run to Ireland.

No. 17348   Gibraltar 18th October 1996

. CO. LTD.

RECEIVED of D. Reid

the sum of Two thousand one hundred + forty nine pounds

Seventy one pence, in respect of

To Acc. 5026

£2149:71   For H. SHEPPARD & Co. Ltd.

?PORT
AR
4E: 77183/75148
15

:NT

		CREDIT	BALANCE
		100.00	-100.00
		1750.00	-1850.00
10/10/96 ADJ BB14	400.00		-1450.00
15/10/96 INV 27995	302.69		-1147.31
15/10/96 INV 27997	311.40		-835.91
15/10/96 INV 28010	34.49		-801.42
16/10/96 INV 28035	615.00		-186.42
16/10/96 INV 28036	1880.00		1693.58
16/10/96 ADJ BB15	100.00		1793.58
17/10/96 INV 28125	140.00		1933.58
17/10/96 INV 28126	202.63		2136.21
18/10/96 INV 28192	13.50		2149.71

| | TOTALS | 3999.71 | 1850.00 |

AMOUNT DUE
2149.71

CURRENT	1 MONTH	2 MONTHS	3 MONTHS	OVER 3
2149.71	0.00	0.00	0.00	0.00

INVOICE   No. 3669

RED BAY BOATS LTD.

COAST ROAD, CUSHENDALL, CO. ANTRIM
N. IRELAND BT44 0TE
Tel: 012667-71331 Fax: 012667-71474

H. MEEGHAN x Co

Builders of Speedboats, Fishing Boats and RIBS in GRP, Engine Stockists,
Ship Chandlers, Storage, Brokerage, Fishing Tackle, Boat Hire
OPEN 7 DAYS A WEEK

Skif High..

Dungacik

25th - Oct - 1996

QTY	DETAILS	AMOUNT	
	Export VAT NO IE65967234		
	NO VAT		
1	Red Bay Stormforce 6'1 A Series		
	c/w A Frame new lights sport		
	light VHF Radio		
	15ohp Johnston GT S NO R7498032		
1	Galvanized trailer	11660	07
1	Compass	55	32
1	Sport light	50	21
1	Battery	38	12
1	Gallon oil	11	70
	4.000		

V.A.T. Reg. No. 331 8135 80
TERMS and CONDITIONS / OVER
TITLE TO THE GOODS LISTED ABOVE DOES NOT PASS TO
THE PURCHASER UNTIL THIS ACCOUNT IS SETTLED IN FULL.
E & OE

£ 7815

Sub. Total	11815	42
V.A.T.	No VAT	
Invoice Total	11815	42

This receipt from a Co. Antrim boat builders was an essential part of the evidence against those involved in Lees' drug smuggling operation.

The gates of Maghaberry Prison in Co. Antrim where Colin Lees has been resident for the past six years. (Pacemaker Press International)

Turning to Symington, Det. Sgt. Carroll asked him where they were when the engine cut out the previous night. Symington said he hadn't been on the boat at all. He now claimed to be up on the shore watching the events at sea unfold. He was contradicting himself. The Garda then asked Johnston and Millar the same question: Where were you when the engine cut out? Johnston said he didn't know. Millar said they were around Magilligan Point. But how did you end up here? 'Blown round by the wind,' Millar claimed. But this answer only added to the Garda's suspicions because as a seafarer he knew the wind had been mainly westerly the previous night and this cove was to the north-west of Magilligan Point. He put this to Millar who laughed and walked away.

It really was decision time. Det. Sgt. Carroll didn't have a thing to pin on these men. He had his suspicions, but little else. In the eyes of the law at this point, there was nothing positive to suggest they had committed a crime. Yet, every fibre of instinct in Det. Sgt. Mick Carroll's body was screaming out to him that he had to stall to find out what these men had truly been up to. He had noticed a *Bartholomew's Touring Ireland* road map in the front of the Land Rover, which suggested these men did not know Donegal, or at least the Malin Head peninsula. No crime had been reported. All he had were these strong suspicions and his instinct. He just could not allow five men to drive off and then discover later some horrific crime. In his mind, they had been up to no good.

After a very brief chat with Insp. Gallagher, Det. Sgt. Carroll took the decision to arrest the five Co. Antrim men. It was 6.10 p.m. on 30 October 1996. They were to be held under Section 30 of the Offences Against the State Act, 1939, on suspicion of being members of an unlawful organisation, namely the IRA. They were cautioned and taken in a convoy of Garda vehicles to Burnfoot Garda Station for questioning.

With the five men in custody, Det. Sgt. Carroll waited for word from Buncrana about his suspects. He passed time by conducting a cursory search of the Land Rover. The map he had seen earlier was open at the section covering Donegal. He noticed two 'X' marks in blue ink — one at Inishtrahuall and the other at a point south-east of Ballymagarraghy. Now, something occurred to the detective sergeant. 'Looking at the position of the two 'X' marks,' he said, 'it was a clear indication that these men were intending to meet someone at sea. If I intended to meet somebody at sea in that area I would have chosen the same location in the Inishtrahuall Sound . . . between the island of Inishtrahuall and the mainland.' But, of course, it was still only suspicion and supposition on his part.

Meanwhile, news on the five men had come in from the Gardaí in Buncrana. They had run checks with their police counterparts in Northern Ireland. This was no IRA bust! The five men had loyalist connections! Det. Sgt. Carroll told me what he learned about his five suspects: 'It transpired that each of them had come to the notice of the police at previous stages in their life and that had made me even more suspicious . . . along with the fact that some of them had come into contact with the police in relation to firearms and explosives offences.' In fact, one of the five was a serial drug runner and informant for a Drugs Squad officer in Co. Antrim. But that information was most likely not passed on to the Gardaí because it would not be widely known to police officers in Northern Ireland. However, news of the informant's arrest in Donegal would almost certainly have been flagged up for the officer responsible for handling him.

Det. Sgt. Carroll interviewed his loyalist suspects but gained no new information. They wanted solicitors more than they wanted to talk. Symington, for example, had this to say after being cautioned:

'You have said that I don't have to say anything unless I wish to do so. I want to talk to my solicitor first.' He provided the name of his solicitor, stating that he was a friend, but Gardaí were unable to contact him.

When James Millar was brought into the interview room at Burnfoot Garda Station, he also was cautioned. He told his interviewers he had no idea where he had picked up the boat trailer, although he began to challenge the Gardaí about what they were writing down in their notes, as this section illustrates:

Question: Can you describe to me how you got to the place where the boat trailer was? By that, I mean directions by road turn-offs, etc . . .
Answer: I might show you to it if I get out. I might take you to it if I remember. There's a lot of roads there.
Question: Who told you where the trailer was?
Answer: I'm not saying. Wait till my solicitor comes. You are writing stuff down there that I'm not saying.

Millar was taken back to his cell after getting a hot meal. Before leaving the interview room, he refused to sign the notes of the interview.

Around midnight, Det. Sgt. Carroll left Burnfoot Garda Station to drive the Land Rover with the boat and trailer to Letterkenny Garda Station. There, he continued his search of the vehicle and found three mobile phones in the front. A fourth was fitted to the jeep. A number of receipts were of interest. He photocopied them and put the originals back in the vehicle. One of the receipts related to a purchase at a shop in London called Spy Catcher. It was for £6,400 and was marked 'paid in cash'. There was a receipt from Mullen Marine in Northern Ireland for

4xHHRT and six sleeping bags. It was for £1,000 and also was marked 'paid in cash'. He also found ferry tickets that told him they had recently travelled abroad.

Next day, 31 October, the questioning continued but with the same negative result. Lips were sealed in the interview rooms — even when a solicitor was produced for Millar. Before questioning began he told the officers he would like to speak to his solicitor. Millar was then told a solicitor had arrived and he was introduced. The Gardaí withdrew from the room to allow Millar to consult with the solicitor. When they returned, Millar said he wasn't impressed by the solicitor and asked if he had been a real solicitor — or a Garda dressed up. Later the same day, Millar was questioned again and warned that it was an offence to fail or refuse to supply an account of his movements if requested under Section 52 of the Offences Against the State Act. He made no reply. And so the interviews were terminated.

Once the men had been detained for forty-eight hours under the Offences Against the State Act they were released. They were set free, relieved to be going home . . . and they were relieved by the Gardaí of the Land Rover Discovery, the boat and the trailer that one of them, Noel Morrison, claimed as his own. Det. Sgt. Carroll said: 'We subsequently made a Police Property Application to the District Court in relation to the seizure of the Land Rover Discovery and the rigid hull inflatable boat and its engine and the ancillary equipment, which was also seized, and this was granted. The District Judge handed the Land Rover Discovery and the boat over to the Chief Superintendent based at Letterkenny for use in fighting crime.' As they left, the men asked the Gardaí to telephone them when they could return to get their belongings . . . the phone call was never made and there was no further contact with the five men. The Land Rover Discovery was painted in the colours of the Gardaí and patrolled the highways and byways of Donegal for a couple of years before being repainted for use in an undercover drugs bust south of Dublin. The RIB boat was given over to the Gardaí sub-aqua unit.

It wasn't until the five men had driven off that the true significance of their clandestine boat trip became clear. However, because of the diligence of Det. Sgt. Carroll, they would not escape justice entirely and the police investigating Colin Lees in Northern Ireland would soon have reason to celebrate Det. Carroll's vigilance. The five suspects had barely left Donegal when the second fortuitous breakthrough came for the Gardaí and, as a consequence, for the detectives investigating Lees in the North.

What happened was this. The day after their release, 1 November 1996, a 47-foot, six-berth motor cruiser limped into Kilrush Harbour in Co. Clare with engine trouble. A routine search of the vessel by Irish Customs Officers revealed a hidden cargo of cannabis . . . 1.7 tons of the stuff worth an estimated £17m on the streets. It didn't take long for Det. Sgt. Carroll to realise that the arrival of the *Plongeur Wisky* in Co. Clare was a vital piece of the jigsaw that had mystified him and his colleagues in Donegal during the previous forty-eight hours: 'I immediately realised what these men would have been doing up here. I believed that they were waiting for the *Plongeur Wisky* to come on to the coastline here in order to unload it using the RIB.'

The drugs find on the *Plongeur Wisky* brought the significance of the map into sharp focus. To Det. Sgt. Carroll it was clear that the mother ship, the *Plongeur Wisky*, was due to offload her cargo in Inishtrahuall Sound: 'If you were at sea, you would want to meet somebody within the view of two landmasses, and that is what a sound is really, a distance between the mainland and an island where you can see from the mainland to the island and it would have been an ideal location to meet and unload a boat.' And, incidentally, the *Plongeur Wisky* — like Noel Morrison's Land Rover Discovery, RIB and trailer — was seized by the State and eventually sold at auction for over £40,000.

But what was Colin Lees up to while all this activity was going on in the Republic of Ireland? With police forces in Scotland, Northern Ireland and now, albeit unwittingly, in the Republic of Ireland investigating crimes that involved him, he was busy operating another scam along with his friend Derek Jones . . . this time in England.

Lees and Jones had set up a company that became involved in the export of alcohol from Britain to the Republic of Ireland. It worked like this. Typically, a lorry would turn up at a bonded warehouse in London and remove a consignment of alcohol. Securing delivery of the goods was dependent on completing Customs and Excise duty forms that had to be returned once the alcohol had reached its destination — i.e. another bonded warehouse in the Republic. But before the lorry returned to Ireland, it would stop off along the M6 in somewhere like Manchester and the cargo, mostly of vodka, would be sold off for cash. The Customs forms would be completed bearing a false stamp for a bonded warehouse in Dublin and were mailed from Dublin by one of Lees' and Jones' contacts. The police investigation discovered that Lees, Jones and others were responsible for falsifying the documents. By this means they defrauded the British government of around £2m in duty and VAT. This scam began operating the same month the five men were arrested in Donegal and continued until the following June, by which time it was under surveillance by HM Customs and the police.

While Lees was earning cash as a drink smuggler, police in the Republic of Ireland were busy tracing the origins of the *Plongeur Wisky*. They were about to discover a vital piece of information that would accelerate Operation Kilbreck on to an even higher level. Gardaí traced payment for the boat to recent transactions involving bank accounts in Gibraltar, Dublin and Ballymena, to accounts held by an American citizen, Derek Jones.

Gardaí in Dublin made a routine call to the police Economic Crime Bureau in the North. They simply wanted to ask if there was any interest in the Gibraltar cash transactions of an individual called Derek Jones. 'Does the name Derek Jones mean anything to anyone in your office?' the Garda inquired. As it happened, the name meant nothing to the person who had taken the call, so he shouted around the room: 'Anyone here interested in a man called Derek Jones?' Det. Const. Horan knew the name well. 'Yeah, me,' he called out. The mystery over the £50,000 and £5,500 payments out of Derek Jones' accounts was about to be resolved. It seemed certain that Derek Jones' money was used to purchase the drug running ship the *Plongeur Wisky*.

Since they'd begun looking at Jones' bank accounts in March 1996, Det. Ch. Supt. Jimmy Molloy's team had been busy trying to establish the reason for the money transfers to Gibraltar when the Gardaí called. That telephone call greatly excited the police in Belfast because it offered a solution to one of the multitude of puzzling transactions centred on Jones' bank activities.

'Within weeks of finding out about the payments to bank accounts in Gibraltar, lo and behold the *Plongeur Wisky* comes ashore at Kilrush in Co. Clare, with nearly two tons of cannabis on board,' Det. Const. Horan remembered. 'So in effect, it appeared that Mr Jones had bought the *Plongeur Wisky* which was loaded up with cannabis, I would assume in North Africa, and then was sent to the United Kingdom . . . albeit that it was captured in the Republic of Ireland. My own gut feeling is that the cannabis was for the UK market.'

It wasn't long after the telephone call from the Gardaí that Jimmy Molloy and John Horan were heading down to Dublin for a meeting with the Gardaí. Operation Kilbreck was going up a gear or two! The scale of the drug smuggling operation was staggering. Det. Ch. Supt. Jimmy Molloy tried to put it in perspective: 'It was surprising because if you look at 17 million pounds worth of drugs, which can be purchased for probably in around three hundred thousand pounds; you've almost 16 and a half million pounds profit. And if you take that down to a joint, you're talking about 12 million joints for a country the size of Ireland, and that's roughly about three to four joints for every person on this island, North and South.'

Det. Const. John Horan briefed his Dublin colleagues about the ongoing investigation into Derek Jones and Colin Lees. Together the two forces could put together a picture of criminality leading up to the drug smuggling shipment that ended up in Kilrush Harbour. Undoubtedly this was a major breakthrough. Once back in Belfast, Det. Ch. Supt. Jimmy Molloy held a briefing with his officers. The decision was made to concentrate on Derek Jones. It was too early to make an arrest — there would be time enough for that later, once more intelligence and evidence was secured.

From the very earliest observations of Jones' bank activities which had begun in the seven months prior to the events in Donegal and Clare, the police were convinced that they had tapped into a major money laundering operation. They also believed they were dealing with someone who was using a technique known in money laundering circles as 'smurphing'. This is where the launderer sets up a multiplicity of accounts and moves the same money from one account to another to another to another until, he hopes, the audit trail has become so confusing that the investigators give up. Apparently the term 'smurphing' has its origins in that the people used to open the multiplicity of accounts all over the globe are referred to as 'smurphs'. In other words, patsies or idiots.

Detectives in Northern Ireland had also quickly established that their money laundering suspect lived well. After arriving in Northern Ireland, Jones lived at a plush hotel on the outskirts of Ballymena. He apparently survived on coffee and Chinese take-aways. Jones made a style statement by driving around in an old Rolls Royce and he had membership of a number of prominent clubs in London — the Pall Mall for example. But he rarely visited them. He just wanted to be able to say that he was in membership of these exclusive clubs. He left the hotel to take up residence at The Willows in Ballymena. Police discovered that the house there was in the name of Lees' common-law wife — but it was in reality purchased for Jones by Lees.

More importantly in terms of their investigation, the police quickly learned that Jones ran a number of companies. They discovered that Jones owned five firms — two haulage companies in Co. Antrim; a public house in Belfast; a furniture business; and a bogus airtime company. The real owner, the sleeping partner in these companies, was bankrupt and disqualified from being a company director. It was, of course, Colin Lees.

As Det. Const. Horan told me, the more they delved into the activities and background of Derek Jones, the more they learned about his relationship with Lees: 'Once we began the investigation into Mr Jones it became apparent he was an associate of Colin Lees, because within the companies that he had set up in Northern Ireland Colin Lees' common-law wife Zara Lees was working. So it was very obvious that Colin was the man behind the scenes to us. As a result of that we then widened our remit to have a look at Mr Lees as well as Mr Jones, and then inevitably our enquiries led us on to other people, and other offences.'

And whilst they were continuing their investigations, with the help of HM Customs, they learned of Lees' and Jones' drink smuggling operation. They also learned that Lees had, in spite of his bankruptcy and disqualification from being a company director, interests in a number of companies in England. The profile on Lees and Jones was building quite rapidly. Surveillance had become a key element of the investigation as officers involved in Operation Kilbreck attempted to follow the money trail centred on Jones' bank accounts. Operation Kilbreck was also growing in stature.

Under Det. Ch. Supt. Jimmy Molloy's leadership, the challenge to his team of detectives was to find out whose money was passing through the multitude of bank accounts held in Derek Jones' name. But given the events in Donegal and Clare, there were two main areas of priority: first, to establish more detail about the purchase of the drug running motor cruiser and the smaller RIB boat; and second, to find out more about Jonathan Lyons, whose name so frequently appeared on bank transactions linked to Jones.

First, let's look at what detectives discovered when they followed up on the five individuals from Co. Antrim who were arrested in Donegal and the paper trail created by the sale of the *Plongeur Wisky* in Gibraltar. A couple of officers were detailed to travel to the British colony and speak to the former owners, Serge and Angelique Bonet, while others began digging around in to the associations of what had quickly become known in police circles as 'the Donegal Five'.

With the assistance of the Royal Gibraltar Police, detectives visited the previous owners of the *Plongeur Wisky*. By this time, the Bonets were living in France, but a member of their family still lived at Governor's Street in Gibraltar. Before travelling to the British colony, the police had to be satisfied about the status of the Bonets. A wrong move at this stage could provide Jones

144

and Lees with vital information about the development of their investigation. So the police sought assurance that the Bonets were honest brokers in the deal for the *Plongeur Wisky*. Having got that assurance two detectives set off for Gibraltar.

There, the Bonets welcomed them. The boat, they were told, had originally been registered at Nantes in France. The Northern Irish visitors were shown a bill of sale for the motor cruiser dated 16 October 1996 that had been faxed between the two parties. The purchaser was listed as David Reid of Dame Hill Ltd, Clifton House, Lower Fitzwilliam Street in Dublin. The document was witnessed. One witness was named as Olivier Bonet. But the other witness was more than interesting to the police. He was described as 'Kevin Lafferty, skipper from Manchester in England'. Interesting because the skipper of the *Plongeur Wisky* arrested in Co. Clare was one Kevin Lafferty . . . who came from the Malin Head district of Co. Donegal.

Det. Sgt. Mick Carroll had meanwhile been doing some homework on the mobile phones found in the confiscated Land Rover Discovery . . . with fascinating results: 'Checks in relation to these mobile phones showed contact with the *Plunger Whiskey* [sic].' This was one of the key factors in the successful prosecution of Kevin Lafferty in Dublin Central Criminal Court. He was jailed for six years for his role in smuggling the huge drugs cargo.

The receipts found in the Land Rover by Det. Sgt. Carroll also provided the police in Northern Ireland with a number of important leads to follow. They visited Mullen Marine, a company based at Kinnego Marina, Oxford Island, just outside Lurgan in Co. Armagh. Mullen Marine had sold a Bombardier Sea-Doo Speedster with trailer for 'export' to A. Meegan Enterprises Ltd, of Skey Hill, Dundela, Dundalk, on 6 August 1996. The £11,064 price paid was marked as 'Nett sterling — ex VAT'. That detail was provided on invoice number 0051 — although the word 'invoice' had been scored out. But the police found that invoice number 0052, and dated the same day, was for £5,000 paid by a Mr Noel Morrison, of Bradford Heights, Carrickfergus, for other equipment . . . the same individual detained by Det. Sgt. Carroll at Malin Head. The police net was widening as their lines of inquiry led them in a number of different directions and to a number of different individuals who had not thus far featured in their investigation.

Of course, the police travelled to Cushendall — a small picturesque town on the North Antrim coast where the RIB seized in Co. Donegal had been built. At Red Bay Boats Ltd, the police saw the sales invoice made out to A. Meegean & Co., and this time the address was given as Sky Hill, Dundalk, not Skey Hill. The invoice was for a Red Bay Storm Force 6.1; 4-seater with galvanised trailer; compass; spotlight; VHF radio and 150 hp Johnston GT engine. Again, there was no VAT charged, presumably because it was for 'export'. The total purchase price was £11,815.42. The date was 25 October 1996. On the same day, the police discovered during their visit to Mullen Marine, that Noel Morrison had returned to buy six sleeping bags for £180 and four HURT for £820 — another £1,000 investment in what was going to be an enormously profitable transaction. Obviously, there was a last minute rush to get everything ready for the rendezvous with the *Plongeur Wisky* on 29 October. Slowly the jigsaw was nearing completion.

Meanwhile, back in Gibraltar, the police were getting their first glimpse of a series of communications between the Bonets and the Dublin buyer of their boat. To clinch the deal, on 16 September 1996, David Reid increased his offer to the Bonets. On Dame Hill Ltd headed paper he sent a typed fax which read:

Dear Miss Bonnee [sic], Following our conversation yesterday, I am willing to increase my offer of £52,500 to £55,000. I travelled down to Marbella, Fungerola and Benemenda [sic]. I have seen three boats and left offers on the three, so if you could please come back to me with an answer, as soon as possible. I am currently travelling at present and will contact you tomorrow, as I will not be in the office all week. If you accept my offer, I can transfer 10% deposit within 4 days, the balance subject to surveyor and solicitors, will be paid six days thereafter. You can contact me on my mobile 0802 299385. Kind regards . . . David Reid.

The new offer was acceptable. An agreement, dated 18 September 1996, was signed by both Bonets and faxed to Dame Hill in Dublin for signature by David Reid. The contract stipulates a deposit of £5,500 with the balance of £50,000 to be paid by 10 October 1996.

Returning the completed contract by fax to Mrs Bonet under the letterhead of Dame Hill Ltd, David Reid includes a handwritten note which states:

F.T.A. of Mrs Bonet: Dear Sirs, I enclose agreement signed as requested. Please note amendment to Number 5. [The French couple had written the word 'surety' instead of 'survey'.] I will transfer deposit of £5,500 to your account as requested tomorrow. It is not necessary to mail original as I will be in Gibraltar Fri/Sat this week to finalise everything and we can complete contract. I will instruct surveyor today by fax. Could you please speak to him and if possible have survey carried out before my arrival. I hope to test the boat with my skipper over the weekend if this is also acceptable your husband/son would be available.

This fax is dated 23 September. From their scrutiny of the Jones bank accounts, the police already had in their possession the precise details relating to payment for the boat. On 23 September, Derek Jones instructed the Ulster Bank in Ballymena to make an electronic payment of £5,500 to the Bonets' account with Barclays Bank in Gibraltar. The police recovered documents showing that the Ulster Bank International in Linenhall Street, Belfast, made the transfer. They also have the documents showing the £5,500 turning up in the Bonet's account on 26 September. The police note that the balance of £50,000 is paid out of Jones' account with the Ulster Bank in Lower Baggot Street, Dublin . . . arriving in the Bonet's savings account on 4 October 1996. The full significance of the fax documents between the Bonets and Dame Hill in Dublin would not become clear to the police until much later. In the meantime, they continued their investigation quietly and without fuss in order to maintain secrecy about their interest in Jones and Lees.

Pressing on with their inquiries into the 'Donegal Five', the police made another significant discovery. Det. Const. Horan explained: 'Five individuals, all associates of Colin Lees, were detained in Donegal acting suspiciously. Unfortunately for them, just after they were arrested the *Plongeur Wisky* comes ashore in Co. Clare and it's being skippered by a guy called Kevin Lafferty, who's actually from the very area of Donegal where these gentlemen were detained. I said unfortunate for them because it became obvious that the boat wasn't intended to come into Clare, it was actually intended to go round to Donegal and its cargo of drugs was going to be split up and loaded on to the RIB boat, and brought into Donegal, and I think then into the United Kingdom through Northern Ireland. Their bad luck at being detained in Donegal meant if we could establish evidence to link them to the drugs shipments, we could make arrests.' The 'Donegal Five' were, from this point on, living on borrowed time.

Their arrests gave detectives involved in Operation Kilbreck their first hint of Colin Lees' involvement in the drugs trade. As far as they were concerned there was no discernible pattern to Lees and drug smuggling. As Det. Const. Horan put it: 'It wasn't a specific network in the sense of it wasn't the Kray brothers sort of organisation. Lees almost had the ability to sub-contract his work if you like; if he needed a driver, he was able to get a driver, if he needed a guy with an expertise in drugs importation, well then he went and got him. You know, there were shifting alliances perhaps. There was never one gang that operated all the time together.'

By the summer of 1997, the police were getting ready to pounce. Det. Ch. Supt. Jimmy Molloy had his troops prepare for a major arrest and raid operation. But by then at least ten police forces in Britain were ready to join this impressive operation.

The investigation had grown rapidly as more intelligence and evidence was gathered. Operation Kilbreck now involved an ever-growing number of law enforcement agencies throughout Britain and Europe. There was a determination to bring Jones and Lees to justice. Here is a list of the agencies that became part of Operation Kilbreck:

- Gardaí — involved in every aspect of the investigation, particularly in relation to the drug smuggling, money laundering and drink smuggling;
- Northern Constabulary — Inverness police investigating the Lees Group Scotland;

- Lancashire Police — surveillance on a Blackpool address used by a company owned by Lees in relation to the drink smuggling;
- Greater Manchester Police — investigating the sale of the smuggled alcohol in their area;
- Northampton Police — examining the bogus airtime company being run by Jones and Lees;
- City of London Police — also investigating the bogus airtime company;
- Avon and Somerset Police — helped identify assets owned by Lees such as new business venture Severn Side Commercial in Bristol, set up by Lees under the name of Colm Maguire. It was involved in re-spraying trucks and vehicles for leasing or sale;
- National Crime Squad — full involvement in the investigation;
- Royal Gibraltar Police — involved in the full investigation particularly in tracing the origins of the *Plongeur Wisky* and the movement of cash;
- Police de Internationale — assisted with interviews in Spain and with the 'proceeds of crime' aspect of the investigation relating to a house bought in Tortosa, south of Barcelona, by Lees;
- Strathclyde Police — involved in tracing the Spanish property deal;
- Surrey Police — assistance with bank account transactions;
- Jersey Police — money transactions;
- Essex Police — money transactions;
- Isle of Man Police — information on Wharton Trading Ltd and bank accounts;

- Irish Customs and Excise/HM Customs — full involvement in the investigation with particular reference to the drug and drink smuggling.

This was an impressive array of talent. Every weapon available in the armoury of international policing appeared to be targeted against Colin Lees and Derek Jones. The police in Northern Ireland clearly intended to take prisoners.

The chosen day was 10 June 1997. The arrest and raid operation took meticulous planning. The element of surprise was imperative, so each raid was timed to take place at 6 a.m. throughout Britain and Ireland. Colin Lees was not arrested at this time. But Derek Jones was taken into custody and the raid on his home provided so many vital leads that it would take the police operation into another period of acceleration . . . another journey of discovery.

A 40-foot articulated truck was required to remove all the paperwork found in Jones' home. Now in the weeks and months and year ahead the police would finally resolve the issues surrounding the money transactions involving Jones and the mystery man in the United States — Jonathan Lyons. New horizons beckoned . . . along with new challenges and new friends in law enforcement!

7 Pleading the Fifth!

'A Meyers Pollock Robbins stockbroker is the first person to plead guilty in one of the US Government's biggest cases alleging organised crime influence in the securities industry. Jonathan Lyons, who headed the New Hyde Park, NY, office of now-defunct Meyers Pollock, pleaded guilty to one count of conspiracy to commit securities fraud and wire fraud. Later three reputed members of New York's Mafia pleaded guilty to extortion in what has become the biggest prosecution of the mob's infiltration of Wall Street. Rosario Gangi, a.k.a. 'Rossi', alleged capo in the Genovese crime family; Frank 'Curly' Lino, alleged capo in the Bonanno family; and Gene Lombardo, alleged Bonanno associate, pleaded guilty to security fraud and extortion conspiracy charges. John 'Boobie' Cerasani, a reputed Bonanno soldier, pleaded guilty to an extortion conspiracy charge. Ernest Motsykulashvili,

*a.k.a. 'Mike the Russian', an alleged Genovese soldier, is set
to plead guilty next week to extortion conspiracy charges . . .'*

Extracts from American newspaper coverage of a
court case involving nineteen people, stockbrokers and
Mafia gang members, accused of fraud and manipulating
stock prices for personal gain.

❧⸱❧

As detectives on Operation Kilbreck continued to build their case, the United States Constitution became an issue on both sides of the Atlantic.

First it was raised at Strandtown RUC station in East Belfast, where Derek Jones, following his arrest on 10 June 1997, considered it an obstacle.

The extent of the documents seized during the raid that day at his home — around half a million of them in all — kept the police occupied in shifts for over a year. The volume of material to be sifted through, analysed and researched was phenomenal. Every week detectives would be deployed to the storeroom where Jones' papers were held to search out new leads or to find answers to old ones. This was a major undertaking.

And while the police were busy searching through this paper mountain, Jones was busy preparing himself in his prison cell. It was soon filled with books on the law and a mass of paperwork relating to his detention. He was becoming what in slang is commonly referred to as a 'barrack room lawyer'.

Although born in England, Jones had long since taken American citizenship. Det. Const. Horan found him a fascinating character — a charming man who was always polite and considerate. Cigarettes had given him a deep, hoarse tone. 'He was always thanking me for the professional manner in which I conducted my business with him,' recalled Det. Const. Horan. 'He was a rogue, but a very likeable rogue — bright and intelligent. He had the perfect attributes of the 'con' man. Most good white-collar criminals have good personalities because it's their stock in trade — they're selling themselves. I found Derek Jones very affable, very pleasant, very mannerly. There's certainly nothing of the thug about him. And he was very, very plausible. I wouldn't say he was a pleasure to interview, maybe that's not the right word, but he certainly didn't cause any grief during interviews. But a very clever man who admitted nothing. It was easy to understand how people could be taken in by his easy-going manner and his undoubted wit. But at the end of the day I was there to do a job — to produce evidence that would secure a conviction and halt his criminal activity, at least for a while.'

But Jones had a major fear — that whatever he said during these interviews with the police in Northern Ireland had the potential to get him into trouble back in the United States. This totally overlooked the fact that he had already come to the attention of the authorities in the States because his name cropped up in the investigation there into the fraudulent stock trading of Jonathan Lyons.

So, in spite of his 'streetwise' nature, Jones had a major difficulty in accepting that he, as an American citizen, was not entitled to 'plead the fifth' whilst in custody in Northern Ireland. The Fifth Amendment of the United States Constitution protects a citizen's right to silence in circumstances where they might otherwise incriminate themselves. It has no standing in United Kingdom law. And that was the position Det. Const. Horan increasingly found himself having to adopt during a series of verbal skirmishes

with Jones and his solicitor . . . as this brief extract from one of
their many taped interviews illustrates:

Horan: Mr Jones, you're in here in relation to offences to
use the common parlance of money laundering, in effect
the concealment of some proceeds of criminal conduct. For
that offence I must caution you that you do not have to say
anything, but I must caution you that if you do not mention
when questioned something which you later rely on in
court, it may harm your defence; if you do say anything it
may be given in evidence. Do you understand the caution?

Jones: I understand the caution.

Horan: Specifically we wish to talk to you about your
relationship with a Mr Jonathan Lyons of New York. We
have information that Mr Lyons has been indicted in New
York on offences of racketeering relative to the Genovese
and Bonanno crime families, which are two Mafia crime
families, and from our examination of documents seized
from you we have established that you have been sending
substantial sums of money to Mr Lyons in New York.
Could I ask you first of all what is your relationship with
Mr Lyons?

Jones' solicitor: Just if I could just preface Mr Jones'
response to clarify some issues that cause us some very
fundamental concern regarding the nature of the proposed
interview here today. And I think it is important that we
clarify at this stage that the offences which you seek to
interview Mr Jones today about — do they pertain to any
issues, matters, alleged offences alleged to have been committed outside the territory of jurisdiction of the United
Kingdom?

Horan: No. Specifically they don't pertain to any offences committed outside Northern Ireland.

Solicitor: Arising from that then, at this stage in your investigation do you have sufficient evidence with which to charge Mr Jones with the alleged offences under investigation and the subject of this particular interview?

Horan: We won't know that until after the interview.

Solicitor: Mr Jones' concerns are . . . he would describe them to be fundamental and they pertain to his legal rights against self-incrimination, his rights to silence, and in America the Fifth Amendment . . . plead the Fifth Amendment . . . his rights not to incriminate himself, his rights to exercise his rights to silence, and it is Mr Jones' view and indeed it is my view as his lawyer that the subject of this interview involves constitutional matters upon which Mr Jones will wish to seek the constitutional advice of attorneys in America to ensure that he does not incriminate himself or tend to prejudice himself by the giving of any answers on taped interview here today upon which the American authorities, the FBI, or the CIA or whatever the relevant police authorities are in American jurisdictions may seek then to levy charges on dittum for trial in America. These constitutional matters therefore make us make the application to you today that the nature of this interview be committed to written questions and answers upon which Mr Jones will then take a constitutional advice and will then consider his responses and undertake to return here at a later date subject to your own convenience in order to furnish detailed and constructive responses to detailed and structured questions. You'd appreciate that my concerns are that you are intimately involved from the outset of this investigation. I think anybody would agree that it's a very complex investigation and certainly I am aware that some five hundred thousand documents belonging to Mr Jones have been held at Knocknagony Police Station for the purposes of this investigation and it's my concern that documents may be presented to Mr Jones this morning which he hasn't had access to for the last year. He will be a year on remand on 10 June 1998, he hasn't had access to his documents albeit for a very short period of time when he was complying with his High Court orders to repatriate assets in other jurisdictions. But with . . . of accounting to you on tape-recorded answers here today about the operation of his accounts in Dublin for example . . . for the subject of this interview he would require those documents to be made available to him in exhibit format photocopied, made available to him to allow him to properly analyse and assess those documents and account to you in tape-recorded further interview for the appropriate responses regarding the movement of monies in or out of those accounts. You'd appreciate that not having access to those documents for over a year has caused him some prejudice.

Horan: Well, first of all I don't accept that not getting access to his documents for a year has caused him any prejudice relative to the questions that I intend to put to him today. That's the first point I'll make, second point I'll make is his constitutional rights under the Fifth Amendment are of absolutely no concern to me in the investigation of crime within this jurisdiction. So I do not intend putting the questions in written format. He may consult any constitutional lawyer he wishes; that's a matter for himself. I am investigating offences committed in

157

Northern Ireland and relative to Northern Ireland and I intend to conduct that interview in accordance with the rules as laid down under the Police and Criminal Evidence Act, which are the only rules of evidence that I have any concern with . . . rules, conduct, procedures that I have any concern with. I'm only interested in offences committed within the jurisdiction of Northern Ireland and I intend investigating those offences now today, and I intend conducting that investigation by means of a question and answer session with Mr Jones. He can exercise whatever right he wishes, the Fifth Amendment has no legal authority in the United Kingdom and he is not cautioned under the Fifth Amendment so I intend conducting the interview exactly in accordance with our own rules; remind him about the caution and it's not a Fifth Amendment right that you do not have to say anything, but I must caution that you if you do not mention when questioned something which you later rely on in court it may harm your defence; if you do say anything, it may be given in evidence. That is the caution in the UK, it has no relevance to the United States and it may be that one of your concerns are the things that you may say here may be entered into evidence in the jurisdiction of the United States. That is a matter for your lawyers in the United States to have it disbarred . . .

Of course by the time this conversation took place, the police had been busy elsewhere. Following Derek Jones' audit trail had already taken Det. Ch. Supt. Jimmy Molloy and Det. Const. Horan to the United States. Information uncovered from among the half million documents not only assisted the police in Northern Ireland but was of considerable evidential value to the authorities in the United States, who were at the time busy prosecuting a case of stock fraud involving the Mafia.

A large number of documents referring to 'Regulation S' were the key for officers of the law on both sides of the Atlantic. Remember we established earlier that the American authorities regarded Jones and his landlady Carol Martino as 'experts' in 'Regulation S' — a piece of badly drafted legislation governing the sale of US stock to investors living outside the United States.

In order to establish the significance of these 'Regulation S' documents, Det. Const. Horan rang a contact in London, the head of security at the Stock Exchange as it happened. It was recommended that he get in touch with the Securities Exchange Commission (SEC) in New York — the watchdog for the American stock market with teeth to conduct and initiate investigations when suspicions are aroused. But before contacting New York, Det. Const. Horan rang the SEC's market surveillance group in Washington DC. John Horan was not aware that his call would spark great excitement in the United States and bring about a turn of events that would solve riddles on both sides of the Atlantic. Just as the telephone call from the Gardaí about the Gibraltar payments had rekindled a line of inquiry for Det. Const. John Horan in Belfast, his call to the SEC had a similar impact. The SEC's market surveillance group immediately called their New York office. It was November 1997.

Henry Klehm was Head of Enforcement for the SEC in New York at the time. When I caught up with him in January 2000, he had switched jobs and had taken up the post of Head of Regulation for the Prudential. Thirty-five floors above Wall Street and the financial district of New York overlooking the Hudson River and the twin towers of the World Trade Centre, he told me about the buzz of excitement when news of the call from Northern

Ireland reached his office: 'Jonathan Lyons was initially charged in the fall of 1996, and while those cases were in pre-trial discovery here in the United States I received a call from the SEC's market surveillance group in Washington DC, who in turn had received a call from Det. Const. John Horan of the RUC, suggesting that they might have come across some documents that might be of interest in our investigation of Lyons and others.'

Literally within minutes of hearing about what he termed 'this odd connection', his office was talking by phone to Det. Const. Horan in Belfast. 'He identified that a fella named Derek Jones had been arrested over there and that a number of records had been seized from Mr Jones' premises. There were about eighty boxes, or ninety boxes, many of which contained stockbrokers' records involving accounts in the United States, Canada and elsewhere. The name Jonathan Lyons was prominent in many of those records.'

John Horan asked if anyone from the SEC would be interested in visiting Belfast to view the evidence. Of course there was an interest! Soon Henry Klehm was on his way to Northern Ireland along with two other SEC attorneys and a senior prosecutor from the US Department of Justice. 'Other members of law enforcement from the United States, like the FBI, joined us as well,' said Henry Klehm, 'to review those records.'

Tired after the transatlantic flight, the US delegation grabbed forty winks at their hotel before turning up at Knocknagoney headquarters of the RUC's Financial Investigation Unit. One glimpse of the documents in a warehouse there and they suddenly realised the enormity of the task ahead of them.

Refreshed from their sleep, they set to work, as Henry Klehm recalled: 'We then set to reviewing the records on a page-by-page basis, which took almost four or five full days for the team of four of us plus two other members of the law enforcement that were there. But we knew within a matter of an hour or two of starting to look at the records that what the RUC had come across was really the other half of a jigsaw puzzle involving Lyons' fraudulent stock dealings in the United States and Canada and ultimately in the Republic of Ireland, Northern Ireland and I think in London as well.'

But the real significance of Derek Jones' well-maintained record of transactions was immediately apparent to Henry Klehm: 'Early on we realised these records were the kinds of things we usually didn't get in our investigations. Number one because these records were generally from brokerage firms outside the United States. And number two, these records were pretty complete and it was unusual for us to get records that complete all in one place at one time. Normally in an investigation like this it would probably take us two, three . . . even five years, to get these records by going to the different brokerage firms around the world.'

So Jones' meticulously preserved paper trail provided the US authorities with chapter and verse on exactly how Lyons had been laundering the proceeds of his illegal stock market activities in America. They now had a perfect record of transactions showing how Lyons went through a brokerage firm in Canada, then into the Republic of Ireland where they were controlled by Jones, and then on to London before being transferred back to bank accounts in Florida where Jones' company Consolidated General was located. Once in Florida, the cash was dispersed to other accounts. The US authorities easily established that Lyons used the laundered cash to pay his bills. Sometimes Lyons would have Jones pay personal bills directly from Jones' bank accounts in Europe. This was a textbook illustration of sophisticated international money laundering.

Naturally, the US delegation was delighted with this development because it had another added significance for them, as Henry Klehm explained: 'We were able to bring back some of the evidence and as a result the prosecutors working the case were able to convince Mr Lyons that it was ultimately in his best interests to co-operate with the United States government, and to plead guilty to some criminal charges that were very serious here in the States. And we were able then, at that point to make Mr Lyons available as a witness to the RUC in connection with their prosecution of Mr Jones.'

Operation Kilbreck had come a long way from its origins in Ballymena. The money trail that began in the 'Bible Belt' had now led RUC detectives to accounts in Dublin, England, across Europe to Canada and eventually to Wall Street in New York, the financial heart of the US economy. It was here they were now about to meet a bent New York stockbroker with Mafia connections to more fully understand the links to Jones and ultimately, to Colin Lees as well. Det. Const. Horan said he had to pinch himself to make sure he wasn't dreaming: 'It was a case of having to make sure I was awake and wasn't on some fantasy island because it was absolutely astonishing. I mean, two New York Mafia families linked to Ballymena, not even . . . there's nothing wrong with Ballymena . . . but not even to the city of Belfast, but the small rural town of Ballymena in North Antrim. It was astonishing.'

The police in Northern Ireland needed international assistance to help advance this investigation, and very soon they were in regular contact with a wide range of law enforcement officers throughout the Americas. Very soon they were getting help from:

- Royal Canadian Mounted Police — assistance with details of stock deals used by Jones and Lyons to launder cash;

162

- West Palm Beach Police, Florida — helped in producing details about Derek Jones;
- New York Police — crucial assistance in relation to Wall Street fraud and help with access to Jonathan Lyons, the bent stockbroker;
- FBI, US Attorney's Office and Drug Enforcement Agency — assisted in all aspects of the investigation of money laundering, the Florida scam and provided vital background information on Jones;
- Securities and Exchange Commission, New York — helped with the money laundering and Mafia links;
- Internal Revenue Service — flew four agents to Northern Ireland during the investigation to help police — two from California, one from Germany and one from London.

But before John Horan could feast his eyes on Jonathan Lyons, there was the small matter of Lyons seeking assurances that his co-operation with the RUC would not result in further charges in the United States. The Fifth Amendment was an issue in New York too. In other words, Lyons wanted the same kind of guarantee being sought by Derek Jones back in Belfast . . . except he was actually in the United States where he did have the right to plead the Fifth Amendment. He had rights, and negotiations commenced about how both sides could achieve a result to their satisfaction.

The situation was resolved. This is how it was done. Henry Klehm again: 'Because of the way the constitutional privileges here in the United States work against self-incrimination, in order to obtain evidence from Mr Lyons and to get a full statement from him, Mr Lyons had to be given or his attorney requested on his behalf that essentially he be given immunity for giving a statement to the US government and to the RUC in connection with this. The Department of Justice agreed with that request, at the RUC's request, and granted him immunity for giving those statements. So effectively those statements couldn't be used against him here in the United States, as direct evidence. But the RUC would be able to use those as part of their case in Northern Ireland.'

'It is called a 'Queen-for-a-day' arrangement,' said Det. Const. Horan. 'Lyons had to tell us everything he knew. That was his obligation in return for immunity from prosecution in the States. If he was later found out to be telling untruths, then he could be prosecuted. So it was in his interests to make a completely clean breast of it all.'

Jonathan Dru Lyons had it all: a Ferrari, a leased Mercedes-Benz, two snowmobiles, two personal watercraft . . . and a dozen former employers, fifteen customer complaints and two indictments for securities fraud. That's how one American newspaper reporter began a feature on the nature of securities fraud under the headline, 'A License to Cheat You . . .' Reporter Susan Harrigan, writing for Newsday Inc., continued:

Documents show that the Brookville stockbroker, indicted in November in an alleged mob-related stock manipulation scheme, is a classic example of what the industry calls 'a repeat offender' — a major embarrassment for regulators trying to crack down on small-stock fraud.

Lyons and brokers like him have left a nationwide trail of aggrieved customers, some of them elderly people with little financial sophistication, who say they were persuaded to invest their life savings in highly risky stocks and bonds and wound up losing tens or even hundreds of thousands of dollars.

Lyons was able to keep going and going even though the first person who complained about him, a pharmacist in his sixties, went out of his way to warn regulators. 'It was my civic duty,' the pharmacist, who didn't want his name used, said recently. 'I couldn't see him coming after some poor widow.'

The pharmacist's dealings with Lyons cost him dearly — to the tune of $271,000, he said. Paying off the debt he incurred has kept him from retiring or helping with his grandchildren's educations, he said. The broker, now thirty-six, apparently lived well. In the past he has leased a white Rolls Royce, a BMW and a Lincoln Town Car. By all accounts, Lyons is a superb salesman and a likable person. He is 'very sweet, very appealing, very attractive,' said the wife of one man who filed a complaint against Lyons, alleging he made more than $143,000 worth of unauthorised trades. The case was settled for an undisclosed sum. 'He never gets mad,' said Manhattan attorney Thomas Lynch, who represented the pharmacist in a successful arbitration case against Lyons. 'As much as I knew about him, I liked him.'

Brokers like Lyons managed to hang on to their licenses and hop from one firm to another despite long histories of complaints, including unauthorised trading, concealing information and failing to sell when ordered to by customers. They are estimated to represent 5% of the nation's 560,000 brokers. But many regulators think they are behind much of a recent increase in complaints about small-stock fraud. Complaints of securities fraud in New York had doubled during the past two years.

Born on 21 December 1961, Lyons was raised in Great Neck, New York. He was a bright and very capable student, graduating from high school in 1980 and then enrolling as a pre-medical school major at the University of Miami. But after two years he returned to New York to continue his studies. He didn't settle and moved soon afterwards to join a medical school in St Lucia in the Caribbean. He lasted only six months there and gave up education without any qualifications.

Back in New York, Lyons passed Securities Brokers Licensing Examinations at the fourth attempt. That was in 1984 and it gave him the opportunity to become a stockbroker, after spending some years working for reputable New York securities companies. For a time he was partner in a brokerage firm before a disagreement with his partner. His next venture was investment banking. Married with three children, Lyons had no major criminal convictions, although he was now facing serious charges.

Casting an eye down the names on the indictment at the US District Court in New York demonstrates the kind of problems Lyons was facing. It reads like the cast list for a Godfather film. People like Rosario Gangi, a.k.a. 'Rossi'; Ernest Motsykulashvili, a.k.a. 'Mike the Russian'; Frank Lino, a.k.a. 'Curly'; John Cerasani, a.k.a. 'Boobie'; and Ernest Montevecchi, a.k.a. 'Butch' or 'Green Eyes', appear on the same charge sheets as Jonathan Lyons, stockbroker — outwardly at least, a figure of respect.

Mafia hoods muscling in on the Wall Street action had been a major challenge to law enforcement in the United States. They bribed and threatened brokers. Stories emerged of threats of violence, intimidation and coercion. The charge sheets seldom mentioned acts of actual violence, but in New York there has been violence.

Business Week magazine complained that the police did not take seriously an incident of violent intimidation. They reported an event that happened around 3 p.m. on 25 September 1996. According to the story three men appeared on the twenty-eighth floor of a Manhattan office complex and went into the office of a stock dealer. They were burly. 'Like lumberjacks,' said one eye-witness. A gun was clearly visible from the belt of one of the men.

The magazine quotes from the police report of the incident: 'At that point they asked the victim what he was trading in. Then they slapped him in the head and stated again, "What the fuck are you trading in?" Then he slapped the victim in the head again. A witness recalls one of the men saying: "Don't fuck with our stock." The stock: Crystal Broadcasting Inc. After the men left, Sharpe Capital Inc stopped trading in Crystal Broadcasting.' That's how the police report described the incident. *Business Week* said that, to the police, the incident described above was about as serious as a scuffle over a parking space. A police source told the magazine that the assault, categorised as a low-grade misdemeanour at best, is considered closed and is not being investigated because the victim was not seriously hurt, no gun was displayed — even though one was clearly observed by eyewitnesses. The police even said the perpetrators were unknown. But *Business Week* quotes a disgruntled eyewitness who said the police did nothing to ascertain their identities, such as examine security camera surveillance.

The point of this story is that it illustrates just how far violent, gun-toting thugs are prepared to go to assert their influence in the heartland of the US economy, Wall Street. With billions of dollars to launder, the Mafia set about finding ways of using Wall Street. One method they used was to put up stock for sale that had no value at all. They invented companies with obscure products and used their dirty money to buy heavily on the open stock market. The fact that they were buying large amounts of these bogus companies meant the stock value rose and attracted the attention of others. This is known as 'ramping' the value of the stock and the bogus companies.

One such company was Biotech Immune — a bogus drug company. The Mafia set about cold-calling the 'mom-and-pop' investors — retired individuals who were looking for means of improving the value of their savings. Once the Mafia had built up sufficient stock value, they would sell and get the clean money, leaving the poor investors with a load of worthless stock in a bogus company. For example, if the stock was floated at $16 and the stock market activity got the price up to $24, the Mafia would sell at $24. Thus they laundered their dirty money at a profit. On Black Wednesday a few years ago, the SEC in New York noticed that the only companies that didn't lose out were the bogus companies set up and run by the Mafia!

The mob forced their way into stock market fraud by putting the squeeze on brokers by either offering them financial induce-ments or in some cases drugs. As Henry Klehm explained, it was a mixture of greed and the prospect that the penalties for white collar crime carried less severe sentences: 'During a period of eight or nine years it's estimated that organised crime was generating anywhere between a hundred million and some estimates have gone up to close to a billion dollars. Well, often times members of organised crime did kind of a calculus and figured out that because of the way sentences work here in the US criminal justice system, that it was a lower risk operation for them to get involved in the stock market as opposed to other traditional organised crime activities and in some instances they did it as an add on to their other activities.'

In Jonathan Lyons' case, the mob had targeted the stock of an Arizona health club company, HealthTech. Then they paid off brokers of New York based Meyers Pollock to overstate assets and hype the stock. When the stock peaked, the mobsters sold quickly at a 'healthy' profit and the remaining stock collapsed. At one point, apparently, HealthTech owner Gordon Hall balked at the arrangement and a mobster threatened to knife him in the throat. As it happened, Gordon Hall was subsequently arrested along with another HealthTech official after it was discovered the pair had gifted tens of thousands of shares to gangsters.

Jonathan Lyons ran the New Hyde Park office of Meyers Pollock. He agreed with the mobsters to hire 'crews' of brokers who would manipulate HealthTech stock and in return Lyons' brokerage firm would receive commissions plus additional compensation. The 'crew' of brokers used what's known as 'boiler room' tactics — that is, they called numerous customers misrepresenting the value of HealthTech assets by as much as 800% and pressurised them to buy.

Lyons got into trouble with the Genovese crime family when he used brokers who were not controlled by them. A dispute arose and the Genovese associates threatened Lyons and others involved at his brokerage. Lyons went to the Bonanno family to seek help. The two families then had what's called a 'sit-down' at which they determined a resolution.

After Lyons was charged, his lawyer said: 'If you read the charges, the allegation is that he was victimised by mobsters. He was extorted. His consent was induced by fear of violence.' That may have been true, but Lyons was caught red-handed by the FBI at another scam.

Henry Klehm told me the FBI set up an undercover operation to try to establish the modus operandi of the Mafia on Wall Street. It was code-named Operation Thorcon: 'Operation Thorcon was one of the first long-term undercover investigations that the FBI mounted into the low-priced security markets. Over a number of months an FBI controlled brokerage firm was established. Agents were given fictitious identities as stockbrokers and got involved in accepting bribes for selling stocks controlled by people on an undisclosed basis to customers. And in that operation they ultimately, in the fall of 1996, arrested over forty people in New York. A number of cases were brought by the SEC at the same time — involving some of the same people, for that kind of activity. Mr Lyons came up in the Thorcon investigation as someone who had offered and sold stock to undercover FBI agents in exchange for kickbacks, and that's how he first came to the attention of law enforcement here.'

Rob Kasami is the FBI's Chief of Security Fraud in New York. He explained why it was necessary to go to such extraordinary lengths to protect Wall Street from the Mafia: 'In general you have seen in recent years more frequent use of wiretaps and undercover operations in securities fraud and other white collar criminal investigations. As a result of those devices we've been able to gather evidence regarding, not only organised crime influence in the markets but all sorts of different groups that are engaged in fraud. So we've brought more of the investigative devices that were traditionally used in narcotics and organised crime and investigation like that, and brought them to bear on white collar criminal investigations.'

This then was the man brought face to face with Det. Ch. Supt. Jimmy Molloy and Det. Const. John Horan in the US Attorney's Office at St Andrew's Plaza in New York early in 1998. The two policemen were not alone in the room with Lyons. There was a considerable line-up of heavyweight law enforcement and government representatives. Lyons' lawyer, Howard Sirota, was present along with a number of US government representatives: Robert Sternthal, SEC; Anthony Zampogna, SEC; Bruce Ohr, Asst. US Attorney; and Supervisory Special Agent D. True Brown. There was one other visitor from Northern Ireland, Even

170

Bell, Restraint and Confiscation Section, DPP, Royal Courts of Justice, Belfast.

Lyons said he was introduced to Derek Jones through Carol Martino. Martino told Lyons that she and Jones had a working relationship. According to Martino, Jones was an individual who could hide money offshore. Martino implied that she had been involved in an enormous number of transactions with Jones, including providing offshore accounts for Martino's use. By using these accounts Martino could avoid the United States tax laws. Jones used an account in the name of Consolidated General to move stocks and cash.

Lyons told the Northern Ireland detectives: 'Carol told me Derek could assist me in forming offshore companies etc. I felt he could assist me in other ways also. Derek had a corporation called Consolidated General. He was the signatory and he held the corporate seal. Derek agreed to my using Consolidated General for some of my illegal deals.'

Both men used the same stockbroker in Toronto — a man who had no idea that he was helping Jones and Lyons to make illegal deals. Lyons said Derek allowed him to buy and sell shares through Consolidated General's account. Money from such deals went directly to Derek and he forwarded it to Lyons in New York through a number of different recipients. Lyons said: 'Derek was permitted by me to keep a percentage of the money I earned illegally. This percentage varied between 5% and 10%, on occasion rising to 15%. There were no hard and fast rules about what he kept for himself.'

Jones' value to Lyons was that he had access to overseas accounts. Lyons was also able to use Jones as a means of marketing to his customers who wanted to falsely push up the price of shares. Mafia-inspired price hikes could produce profits payable to

171

Lyons through Jones' offshore accounts. In that way they avoided detection from regulatory authorities. In other words, Jones provided Lyons with a haven to hide the receipts of his, and the Mafia's, illegal activity.

Lyons said Jones opened an account with a brokerage firm that he, Lyons, had owned — J.J. Morgan. But Lyons resigned after a dispute with one of J.J. Morgan's associates, at about the time Derek Jones told Lyons he was going to Ireland on holiday. This is what Lyons said: 'During Derek's time in Florida I spoke to him very frequently. During one conversation Derek told me he was going on vacation to Ireland. I had two contact numbers for him. One at a castle called Galgorm Castle and one at a pub. I spoke to Derek at the pub most days. Derek did not return from his vacation. He stayed in Northern Ireland. Despite the fact that Derek was now in Northern Ireland we continued to use his Consolidated General account with Midland Walwyn to trade illegally, and the proceeds from these deals now went to a bank account held by Derek in Dublin. From this bank account he sent me money periodically, keeping as usual a percentage for himself.'

Lyons identified a number of documents brought from Northern Ireland. Most related to money transactions, although a couple of letters were also produced. Lyons coolly told how he and Jones profited from shares in a company called Princeton American . . . without having to do any work.

Lyons' story went as follows: 'The chief executive officer of Princeton American was a man called Dale Eymon. Dale Eymon employed me to employ brokers to sell the stock and by so doing to drive up the price of the stock. As a reward for doing this I was given shares in Princeton American. In order to obtain more shares I told Eymon that Derek Jones had the ability to contact money managers in Europe who would further bolster the price of the shares and therefore he should give Derek some of the shares.' Eymon agreed. All the shares from Eymon were held in Lyons' name and in the names of corporations Lyons owned or in the name of Consolidated General.

'Over a period of time I received a large amount of stock from Eymon,' Lyons recalled. 'Neither Derek nor I had any intention of doing what Dale Eymon wanted. We sold the stock he gave us and kept the money. Dale Eymon subsequently discovered we had fed him a line of bullshit and was angry. He could do nothing about it, however.' Jones took a cut from the cash raised in the sale of Princeton American shares held in Consolidated General's account in Dublin.

Lyons told police about a number of ways Jones sent him cash from the profits of his Regulation 'S' stock deals. Funds were sent from Jones through American Express Traveller's Cheques and through bank draft cheques. Another method was for the cash to be paid into Lyons' lawyer's account. He identified for the Northern Ireland police officers $130,000 that represented the proceeds of the sale of Princeton American stock. Other payments to arrive in his lawyer's account were for $160,000; $70,000; $68,000 and $35,000.

Back in Belfast, Jones was not so forthcoming. Effectively, he was still playing his 'Fifth Amendment' card!

Derek Jones: Are you saying that the person you're asking about is indicted at the moment?
Det. Const. John Horan: Yes, Jonathan Lyons is indicted...
Jones: ... for racketeering?
Horan: Yes. But I have ... the FBI have not expressed an interest in talking to you. But that's not, that is as of today but that may change by tomorrow.

Jones: You mentioned once before they missed me by minutes or something . . .

Horan: Yeah. I would say they missed you by minutes . . . I mean that the last indication to me and Paul's [**Jones lawyer**] picked up on it, the last indication to me was that they've no interest in you. Now, the reality of it is, no interest as at three o'clock on the 28th isn't the same as no interest, period.

Solicitor: I don't want to keep labouring the point here and I'll say it for the last time just to rehash for the benefit of this tape. Mr Jones wants to co-operate with the RUC in their investigations, right. He has co-operated in the interviews to date in relation to matters on which he has been charged. He does have concerns that if he co-operates any further with his interviews without having had the benefit of American constitutional lawyers' advice regarding self-incrimination that he could prejudice himself upon his return . . .

And so Jones' interviews went back and forth on the issue of the 'Fifth Amendment'. As a consequence, he was circumspect in his answers to specific questions relating to specific documents regarding specific money transfers involving Lyons. He was still adopting his 'Fifth' attitude.

Horan: The next one with a credit advice is 21 November 1996, coming into D. Jones Consolidated General and the ordering customer is Midland Walwyn again, and it is with respect to an incoming payment for 100,000 US Dollars. Do you wish to pass any comment on that?

Jones: I refer to the previous answer.

Horan: The next one is dated 17 November 1995, no, I won't address that one, I think that is a payment for one of your credit cards; it is not related to my investigation. The next one is beneficiary Consolidated General, 23 April 1996, and is coming in from the Great Southern Bank and it is for the amount of 41,477 dollars 41 cents. Is there any comment you wish to pass on that?

Jones: No.

Horan: The next one is a debit dated 29 November 1996, ordered by you and the payment is to go to Yale Capital Advisor Incorporated for the attention of Alan Brooks and the account is with Citibank West Port . . . It is the amount of 58,500 US dollars. Is there anything you wish to say about that?

Jones: No.

Horan: The next one is 23 February 1997. It's in the amount of 15,700 US dollars and the beneficiary, it is coming from your bank account in Dublin, and the beneficiary is Homes of Distinction LLC, Citibank Wall Street, New York, if I could ask you to look at that and if you wish to comment on it?

Jones: No.

Horan: I will now ask you to comment on a credit advice which is an incoming payment into your bank account, this is from Midland Walwyn again, dated 21 October 1996, and it is in the sum of 164,600 dollars.

Jones: How much is it?

Horan: 164,600 dollars.

Jones: And in Canada?

Horan: Yes, the same Midland Walwyn.

Jones: And there is no reference like Lyons or anything?

Horan: No, this is incoming to your bank — it's credit, you see.

Lyons received other payments from Jones via his wife's bank account — one for $190,000 and another for $40,000 he was able to recall. The latter payment was made on 11 October 1996. During questioning about the money transfers into accounts in the name of Ellen Lyons, Jones was vague to say the least.

Horan: Do you know Ellen Lyons?
Jones: Same answer I previously gave.
Horan: If I could tell you that from our enquiries, Ellen Lyons is the wife of Jonathan Lyons, is there anything you wish to say about that?
Jones: Same answer.
Horan: This is actually a customer copy from an Ulster Bank foreign draft, and it's from the Boucher Road branch at Belfast. It's a foreign draft in favour of Ellen Lyons, drawn in the USA — account holder D.J. Jones, 778 Shore Road, Belfast, signed by, we would say, you. Draft number 49027, booking reference 603325 and it's in the sum of $40,000. Is there any comment you would wish to pass on that?
Jones: What date was that?
Horan: Here you are . . . have a look at that.
Jones: Same answer I previously gave.

In New York, Lyons continued to help the Northern Ireland police officers. A payment of $154,621 was sent by Derek Jones in respect of a Mafia-inspired scam that Lyons orchestrated to boost the value of shares in a company called Empire Capital. Lyons had received 300,000 shares as his reward for this operation, and he told Det. Ch. Supt. Molloy and Det. Const. Horan: 'This, of course, was illegal and I have pleaded guilty of crimes in respect of this illegal activity.'

In another transaction, Lyons wrote to Jones to instruct him to send $25,000 to a company he had used to re-design his home! But again Jones refused to answer directly.

Horan: Here is a handwritten fax, they are originating faxes not identified, but if I could read the first one to you, it says: Derek please make bank cheque payable to, and the cheque is written in American manner c-h-e-c-k, payable to Simmons Design Group for 25,000 dollars. No personal cheques — only bank cheques and other bank cheques made payable, and another bank cheque made payable to American Express for the balance, please, to Ellen Lyons, 155 Foxgrove Drive, Brookville, New York. Phone ********, thanks, and the signature is missing from that. Ellen Lyons and that address, that is the address of Jonathon Lyons and Ellen Lyons is his wife, have you paid anything to American Express on behalf of Jonathon Lyons?

Jones: I refer to the question I previously answered. Is there a fax number on top of the page?

Horan: Is there? No, that is just the number of faxes that have been sent from that machine, I think. It is not legible; it just gives you the dates in American style. That could be the time it arrived here, anything you want to say about that?

Jones: I have no comment on the dates.

Horan: This one is dated 12 February 1997. Derek, from the 45,000 dollars you received please deduct 2,000 dollars for the outstanding debit and wire 23,000 to Citibank, 111 Wall Street, New York, Homes with Distinction LLC, 20,000 dollars to Simmons design group, which is the same group, but again there is no signature on it, anything you wish to comment on that?

Jones: No, thank you.

With *his* 'Fifth Amendment' rights protected in New York, Lyons was singing like a bird. In concluding his statement Lyons said: 'I have no idea what legitimate trading Derek did through Consolidated General. Any trading that I did or he did on my behalf, however, was illegal and any money which he sent to me directly or indirectly was generated with his full knowledge and co-operation from illegal activity on the stock markets.'

But Lyons wasn't done yet. He had one other piece of information that would assist the police in their case against Colin Lees. Lyons said his former partner at J.J. Morgan, Kenny Ohr, had put together a consulting agreement with Colin Lees. Of course, as with Jones, who was also a paid consultant, there was no consultancy work to be done. It was simply a word used to disguise money laundering.

Ohr and Lyons dealt with Lees through Derek Jones. Lyons stated that he never met Lees. Lyons does not believe that Ohr has ever met Lees. Documentation relating to J.J. Morgan's dealings in the stock of the company, Pacific Financial, would reflect their dealings with Lees. The consulting agreement in the name of Lees was another method used by Lyons and Ohr to launder their profits from manipulating the stock of Pacific Financial.

Lyons told the police he would most often contact Jones by telephone at a pub in Ireland. This was the Loughside Inn on the Shore Road in Belfast. As we will learn later, Jones fronted the pub for Colin Lees as yet another means of laundering their money. According to Lyons, he last contacted Jones at the pub asking him to wire him $5,800. During this conversation, Jones told Lyons about his interest in starting a trucking company. This final conversation took place some time between mid-May and mid-June of 1997. After the FBI had arrested Lyons, he tried to place a call to Jones at the pub in Ireland to tell him. Someone at the pub told him that Jones had been arrested. Lyons was given a telephone number for Jones' solicitor. The solicitor told Lyons that Jones had been arrested in connection with the trafficking of marijuana into Ireland.

The trip to New York had been thoroughly worthwhile for Molloy and Horan. They left with a statement from Lyons that would be crucial evidence against Jones back in Northern Ireland. They also returned with a more precise understanding of how Jones was laundering money. They returned to the mountain of documents that told the story, fully aware by now that Jones was shifting millions around the globe: 'Derek Jones was acting for and on behalf of Colin Lees here in the UK and for and on behalf of Jonathon Lyons in the United States. And we're talking millions; we're talking about millions. When we arrested Derek Jones we brought it to an end, and of course obviously with Lyons being arrested in the United States it also killed it at that end as well. But we were at the two million dollar figure at that time, and I have no doubt that had the operation not been brought to an end it would still be ongoing today.'

Back home, the Northern Ireland police renewed their efforts to discover more about the companies Jones and Lees were running. They realised that the extensive contacts built up internationally by Jones made him an essential figure in helping Lees hide the proceeds of his criminal activity.

As Det. Const. Horan put it: 'It was Jones' expertise in the laundering of the money that allowed Lees to do as much crime as he did. And it's a web; you can't separate the two enterprises — the New York enterprise and the Northern Ireland enterprise. Now whether Colin Lees knew Mr Lyons personally I don't know, but what I have no doubt is that he knew that Derek Jones knew the right people in the United States to move money.'

And he added: 'Here you have Jonathan Lyons, ostensibly an honest businessman; also you have Colin Lees and Derek Jones, both ostensibly honest businessmen. Yet all three are involved in laundering money in New York and in Ballymena. Some reports I have read suggest that 10% of the world's income is derived from organised crime. It's quite clear from the Lees case that organised crime had reached its tentacles into the very heart of Northern Ireland.'

Colin Lees was not arrested on 10 June 1997 when Operation Kilbreck conducted raids throughout England and Ireland — North and South. He enjoyed his freedom for another four months. Through Jones he could keep up to date with the police line of questioning.

Lees was finally picked up for questioning in October 1997. The police had good reason to arrest him at this time . . . something had turned up during a search of the home of a woman who had once kept Colin Lees' books — two A4 envelopes that Lees had apparently asked the woman to keep safe for him.

Written on the envelopes was the name 'Dame Hill'. What detectives found inside was to prove devastating for the bankrupt Lees. Once again, Operation Kilbreck was to receive an unexpected boost . . . one that would finally nail Lees and others as drug smugglers. As it happened, he had been under suspicion for some years, but proof had eluded the police until now!

8 The Game Plan

'. . . there was a handwritten document, giving details of the crew, their expenses and travel times etc. It was very significant because this was recorded in the handwriting of Lees himself. It was the final nail in the coffin for Colin Lees in that it meant our investigation could now bring about his prosecution as a drug runner. This was his drug smuggling game plan.'

Det. Ch. Supt. Jimmy Molloy, formerly of the RUC and Police Service of Northern Ireland, commenting on the outcome of Operation Kilbreck.

❖

The front door of the terraced house in Blackpool smashed open. Upstairs Colin Lees, Noel Morrison and Samuel Adams shuddered in their sleep.

Moments later police officers from the Lancashire Constabulary, accompanied by members of the RUC, were bounding up the stairs.

Above them in separate bedrooms, Lees, Morrison and Adams were suddenly fully alert. So too were two women staying in the house — Debbie Gabriel, a niece of Lees' common-law wife Zara, who had moved to England to do secretarial work for Lees, and Carol Dunkley, who was Adams' girlfriend.

It was 6 a.m. on 10 June 1997 and Operation Kilbreck was under way here at Riley Avenue in Lytham St Annes, near Blackpool, and at twenty-two other locations in Britain and Ireland.

Neighbours in this sedate coastal town were unaccustomed to dawn police raids on this scale. They were shocked; not as shocked as Morrison and Lees perhaps, but nevertheless shaken by the loud intrusion. The local golf links is considered good enough to host the Open Championship and it is regarded as a town for retired or 'made' individuals — not a place to have its peace shattered by burly uniformed police officers conducting raids on a couple of Irish suspects!

Meanwhile, Lees, Morrison and Adams, having been aroused from their slumbers, were introduced to the various officers now standing in their bedrooms and crawling all over the house searching for clues into drug smuggling, money laundering, duty evasion on alcohol and the proceeds of a £23m fraud. Morrison, Lees and Adams were shown the search warrant and it was explained to them what was taking place.

Adams and Morrison might initially have believed this raid was in some way connected to their arrests in Donegal the previous October. Shortly after his release by the Gardaí, Morrison had decided to make himself scarce in Northern Ireland. He moved to

England where he sold furniture under one of the various aliases he used, David Wright. But although the police were fascinated to find him living under the same roof as Lees in Lancashire, Operation Kilbreck was not yet ready to arrest the 'Donegal Five'. It would not be long though before they would make that move.

For his part, Lees had at this time been spending his weeks in England — working at a haulage company ostensibly owned by his friend Jones and going home to Zara and his family at weekends. The reality was that he and Jones were running their drink smuggling scam, among a range of other illicit money-making operations. To Lees, England offered him a greater opportunity to continue trading as a company director at a time when he would have found it almost impossible to function at home because he was an undischarged bankrupt and was disbarred from being a director.

The search continued for some time. Documents were bagged and tagged. In a briefcase the police found cash — a large amount of cash — around £90,000 to be exact.

Remarkably, Lees, Morrison and Adams were not arrested. The £90,000 was confiscated. There was no reasonable explanation forthcoming as to how it had been acquired. So it was taken into police custody pending a reasonable case being presented by one of the three about its provenance. The cash remains in police custody to this day.

The police also found a passport application in the name of Andrew Hankin. There was no one by that name in the house. But detectives decided to take it away to check. The police also recovered an interesting piece of information from Lees' wallet — a telephone number for someone called Dessie McIlroy. They said nothing at the time, but they realised that this was one of the crew on board the *Plongeur Wisky* when it was boarded at Kilrush eight months earlier.

But the fact that Lees, Morrison and Adams were not arrested is most intriguing — as it was even to some of the police who were part of Operation Kilbreck. Officers with years of experience know that often there are compelling reasons not to effect arrests when on search operations. It can mean insufficient evidence at the moment of the raid . . . or it can mean that outside influences have prevailed in favour of one or more of the targets of the particular operation. And in Northern Ireland, during thirty years of violent conflict, more often than not it meant that someone was being protected from within the law because of his or her value to that particular branch of policing.

'The fact that none of them was arrested was puzzling to some of us,' said one officer who was part of the Operation Kilbreck team. 'Previous experience has taught us that there is usually some ulterior motive. Every search operation had to be approved by the Special Branch. And over the years this meant that on some occasions, by the time we arrived for a search, the subject had mysteriously disappeared. This we knew was Special Branch's method of protecting a source. Of course, there were other instances when we would be permitted to conduct the search but would be told not to make any arrests. Again we knew this to mean that a Special Branch source was being protected. So in the Blackpool raids, we made our own assumptions.'

The dawn raid undoubtedly helped Noel Morrison make up his mind about his future sleeping arrangements! Next time the police went looking for him, he had disappeared. A wanted poster was subsequently issued and Morrison is still at large. It's thought he moved to Spain for a time to co-exist along the Costa del Sol with a group of exiled loyalist paramilitary drug runners. Nowadays, the police reckon he divides his time between England and Spain, although they have yet been unable to track him down.

He is still suspected of being deeply involved in drug running.

Lees, meanwhile, was allowed to enjoy another four months of freedom as the police began a detailed study of the documents found in the twenty-three raids they conducted. Of course, the 40-foot lorry load removed from Jones' home presented the biggest challenge, but it was essential to match up whatever was found there with other documents. 'This was an enormous jigsaw,' said Det. Const. Horan, 'and we now had a considerable number of the pieces. Our job was to begin to match up those pieces to create a much fuller picture of what exactly Jones and Lees had been up to. Making this happen was time-consuming but enormously satisfying when you made connections.'

The police began to develop a profile of Jones and Lees. The decision to arrest Jones and leave Lees free was taken deliberately, in order to keep an eye on the bankrupt businessman. There was a hope that extra surveillance on Lees would be fruitful, especially if he was in any way 'spooked' by the arrest and detention of his business partner along with a number of his other associates.

When the breakthrough came against Colin Lees, it came from a most unexpected source. Half a million documents removed from Jones' Ballymena home obviously had much to give up to the police . . . but the crucial and damning evidence that would eventually condemn Lees as part of the drug smuggling conspiracy came from the raid on the Lisburn, Co. Antrim, home of Norma Elder, a woman who had been employed by Lees and Jones as a bookkeeper. Her home was one of many targeted for the Operation Kilbreck raids on 10 June. She was arrested, questioned and was initially charged with money laundering offences and with inducing others to import the £17m haul of cannabis. Later, all charges against her were withdrawn. It became clear that she was simply following orders from Lees and Jones.

She had typed up faxes. She had run errands. She had been at Lees' beck and call at an office above the Loughside Inn, formerly the Tudor Lodge, on Belfast's Shore Road. The pub had been bought in the summer of 1995 as the perfect cover to launder the proceeds of crime. It was purchased in such a manner that Lees' interest in it was difficult to detect. Det. Ch. Insp. Jimmy Molloy explained: 'Criminals who are involved in the likes of drug offences or smuggling tobacco and alcohol have to have some way of disposing of their money, because they must get it back into the banking system. A pub is purely a cash-driven business, so therefore it's easy to dispose of your cash through a legitimate business and get it back into the banking world, or financial world again. Then it becomes clean money and it conceals the proceeds of the criminal activity.'

The Loughside Inn became the headquarters of Jones' money laundering operations and the place where, as it turned out, Lees planned the £17m shipment of Moroccan hashish on the boat he bought in Gibraltar. With no experience of running a bar, Lees and Jones sought some professional help to put together their business plan in order to impress a local brewery into investing. In other words they needed a 'patsy'. The man they chose was Jonathan Murphy, a perfectly respectable businessman who had experience of running a chain of bars in England and who was the secretary-manager of the plush Fitzwilliam Tennis Club in Dublin — a job he lost when his home was raided as part of Operation Kilbreck and he was arrested.

Later, Murphy was tried and convicted for helping an undischarged bankrupt. He managed to avoid jail and was fined £6,000. But he deeply regretted the day and hour he ever agreed to help Lees and Jones with the Loughside Inn. 'We have suffered a lot,' he told me. 'I was destroyed for four years and it was only my own stupidity that got me into business with this man. A lot of people have been destroyed by Lees along the way. That guy can't have breakfast without committing a crime!'

According to Jonathan Murphy, Lees and Jones asked him to sign forms giving his personal guarantee to the business, but he refused. 'They went ahead and forged my signature,' he said. Murphy said the pub was a good business when they bought it, but it was never given a chance by Lees and Jones.

Murphy claimed the dubious pub owners owed money to loyalists and he further claimed that that was the reason the pub was eventually torched by the paramilitaries. It wasn't until the police came calling at his home at 6 a.m. on 10 June 1997, that Murphy learned about the truth of why Lees and Jones had wanted to own the bar in the first place. But, by then of course, it was too late.

Detectives on Operation Kilbreck soon found out what really went on in the tiny offices on the top floor of the Loughside Inn. Now they were about to become very busy studying the two A4 sized envelopes marked 'Dame Hill' found among other paperwork in the bookkeeper's house. Inside the envelopes were the documents that told the story Colin Lees tried to bury the day he handed them over for safe-keeping at the Loughside Inn to Norma Elder. He mistakenly thought that if the police came after him they would never think of looking in the bookkeeper's home. Taken back to the headquarters of Operation Kilbreck, the envelopes were logged and bagged for evidential purposes. Then one of the investigation team came across them as he began sifting through the many bundles of documents laid out in offices of the Financial Investigation Unit at Knocknagoney RUC station.

Before midnight on 10 June 1997, police officers involved in leading the investigation and the planning of that morning's dawn raids were celebrating yet another vital piece in the enormous jigsaw they were trying to piece together from the enormous haul of documents.

The 'Dame Hill' envelopes contained the key to unlocking the identity of the mastermind behind the failed drug smuggling operation at Malin Head and Kilrush. There, in Lees' own handwriting, were the 'accounts' for the entire operation . . . from the purchase of the boat in Gibraltar to the cost of the equipment found hidden in Donegal. What was christened the 'Game Plan' was contained on the reverse side of an A4 sheet of Dame Hill headed paper and on two yellow post-its found attached to a written engineering survey into the sea-worthiness of the *Plongeur Wisky*. They made fascinating reading and presented the investigators with the challenge of matching up the figures to the costs they had been able to establish.

This is what the detective saw when he first cast his eyes on the doodles of an as yet unidentified individual. The page had been folded in half, then half again. In the top left corner, a number of costs were listed: Boat £55,000; bank 300; solicitor 300, Surveyor/Yard 900, which was stroked out and followed by 350, 100; Crew and retrievers 3,000. Then under 'Noel exe +' was written: Equipment 2,500; Travel, with space left blank; Crew expenses 1,500; Company/Front 5,000. Underneath was the total of 68,500. To the right of this figure was written '70k.'

The police knew the *Plongeur Wisky* had cost £55,000 because they had been busy tracing the bank payments and talking to the previous owners. They had recovered paperwork from the boat itself and, of course, from Jones' home. They had tracked down the payments from Jones' bank. They discovered that in order to make the £5,500 deposit payment they could not write a cheque because there were insufficient funds in the account. So they had to rustle up the cash and get one of the office girls to rush down to the bank before closing to get funds into the account so that the bank could make the electronic transaction into the Bonets' account. And they also noticed that on the day of the big payment of £50,000 to the Bonets, a payment of £37,000 had come into the account. Mafia money perhaps . . . and it was used to fund the boat purchase. Detectives speculated as to whether or not the Mafia knew that some of their cash was used to help put a drug deal together.

The *Plongeur Wisky* also provided the police with a copy of the bill of sale. So the figure £55,000 stood out when they looked at the doodles. And, of course, the name of the Dublin company Dame Hill Ltd featured in their inquiries because of the paper trail they had followed during the negotiation and purchase of the *Plongeur Wisky*.

In the same pen and on the top right corner was written: — Next week — Engines + work 4,000; satellite etc 1,000, which was stroked out and followed by 750+ chips and then in brackets 2k. Continuing underneath he had written: Provisions/fuel 3,000 to give a grand total of 8,000. To the right this figure was rounded off to '10k.'

Directly underneath these figures further expenses were being identified and totted up: Rib 10,000; house 1,000; motor home 1,000; exes 3,000, which represented a total of 15,000. Beneath these figures he had written: 'Peter £1,600. Kevin Laverty [sic: Lafferty]. Desi McIlroy.' This particular section really excited the team of detectives because here were the names of the skipper of the *Plongeur Wisky* and one of his mates, Dessie McIlroy. Both men — and a third found on the boat — were by this stage in custody in the Republic of Ireland charged with importation and possession of 1.7 tonnes of cannabis. So whoever wrote this note appeared to know the crew of the drug smuggling boat.

All this information was on the top half of page that had been folded in two. Below the fold there was even more fascinating data as the writer explored once again the costs of the whole enterprise. This time a different pen had been used . . . but some of the figures were familiar! He was obviously going over and over the figures, calculating the costs of the enterprise that was going to make him, and others around him, very rich.

Under the heading: 'Costs to date', the writer again went through what cash had already been laid out to make the drug shipment work. He had written: Boat 55,000; Crew advance 3,000; Solicitor/Surveyor 1,500; Company fee 5,000; Exes: Noel 2 . . . Crew 2 . . . Workers 2: 5,000; Comput 2,000. Underneath he had added it up to come to a total of 71,000. Beneath these figures the writer noted: 'Satellite? Phone?'

On the bottom right of the page he continued working out the costs with the following figures: Crew 50,000; John + 1 — 25k; Unloaders/security 4 times 5 — 20,000; Camper van (storage) 5+3 — 8-10; Coach 5-10; Noel/Jim 25k. For the police, this was a joy to behold. One of the officers said he reckoned the writing was that of Colin Lees — he had noticed the strangely childlike writing on other documents that were being sifted through. Documents discovered, for example, in possession of the Bonets in Gibraltar — paperwork relating to the sale of the boat, handwritten faxes sent and received at the Loughside Inn from and to the Dublin office of Dame Hill Ltd. The reference to '5+3 — 8-10', was thought by detectives to refer to the number of bales of cannabis that could be transported by the camper van and the coach.

The police could not believe their luck. Det. Const. Horan regarded this discovery as of great importance: 'What we had here were the accounts for the drug deal. It had major significance. Colin Lees has very distinctive handwriting. Now I'm not an expert in handwriting but we did get an expert in handwriting to examine the documents, and he was able to say that the handwriting on the documents was the handwriting of Colin Lees. So yes, it really was of major significance.'

More of what the police regarded as Lees' handwriting appeared on two yellow post-its. Here again, the figures had been written down with the clear intention of establishing the cost of bringing in 1.7 tonnes of Moroccan hashish. This is what appears on one of the post-its: Boat 55,500; Crew 3,000; Exs 3,000; 3,000, 2,000; 2,000; Home 11,000; Rib etc 9,000. This was totalled up to 88,500. And immediately underneath was written '+1,000.' Beneath this figure was written: 'Noel/Colin — 28/Oct/96.'

Colin? Noel? The same 'Noel' detained briefly by the Gardaí in Donegal? Large sections of the jigsaw were beginning to fall into place. The police were becoming more and more excited as they continued reading through the Dame Hill envelopes.

The second yellow post-it gave yet more figures: Boat 11,815-42; Machine 6,600-00; M. Marine Radios 1,000-00; N. Sight 400; M. Marine 65-00; O/Door Wear 268-00; Sunday 420-00. This added up to '£20,568-00.' Directly underneath it stated 28/Oct/96 and had the following notations: '11,000; 9,000.' A figure of 5,000 was scored out and replaced by '500'. This section added up to '£20,500-00.'

This post-it really had the Operation Kilbreck team celebrating as wildly as a Manchester United striker might when scoring the winning goal against Liverpool in an FA Cup final. By now the police in the Republic and in the North had gathered a number of receipts from the boat and Noel Morrison's confiscated Land Rover Discovery.

For example, they had a copy of the receipt for the purchase of the RIB boat at Red Bay Boats in Cushendall . . . and, guess what, it showed that it cost £11,815-42! It got better and better as they checked down the list on the second post-it. For they also had receipts from Mullen Marine for £1,000; another for £267-46 from The Gun Shop in Portglenone for 'outdoor wear' which consisted of camouflage netting, shoes, coal, rucksack and so on. In addition, on this receipt was a separate transaction for £65 for a life jacket. The case against Colin Lees as a drug runner was becoming more and more watertight . . . unlike the vessel in which he had bankrolled his future prosperity.

The head of Operation Kilbreck, Det. Ch. Supt. Jimmy Molloy, was delighted and saw 'the Game Plan' documents as important: 'As part of Operation Kilbreck we carried out twenty-three searches across the United Kingdom and the Republic of Ireland. During the course of these searches we uncovered a series of documents that gave us even more detail about the purchase of the *Plongeur Wisky*, the boat that was found to have £17m worth of cannabis resin on board. But more importantly, there was a handwritten document, giving details of the crew, their expenses and travel times, etc. It was very significant because this was recorded in the handwriting of Lees himself. It was the final nail in the coffin for Colin Lees in that it meant our investigation could now bring about his prosecution as a drug runner. This was his drug smuggling game plan.'

The police continued to study 'the Game Plan' and to follow up leads it provided, but still did not move to arrest Lees, believing that much good intelligence could be gathered as they watched him squirm uncomfortably. Lees continued to lead the good life — eating well during his business weeks in England and enjoying the company of a variety of ladies of the night. Many of his friends were still in custody and facing some tough questioning from police officers who daily grew in confidence as more and more pieces of the jigsaw fitted into place.

Inside the envelopes detectives also found receipts from a boat-yard in Gibraltar that had been responsible for sea trials for the *Plongeur Wisky* after they had spent a great deal of time making sure it was seaworthy and providing the boat with larger fuel tanks so that it could make the long journey to Northern Ireland with its illicit cargo. In all, the work cost over £2,000 and the police found receipts for cash from H. Sheppard & Co. Ltd signed by the boat's skipper, Kevin Lafferty.

Meanwhile, careful checks on other paperwork revealed a business profile that showed Lees in control of a number of companies in Northern Ireland and Britain. Obviously, as a bankrupt, Lees could not hold any directorships but it did not stop him from buying up companies using the name of his sidekick Derek Jones as a front.

Researching for this book, I spoke to Co. Antrim auctioneer Stafford Lynn, who told me about one particular piece of business he did with Lees. The bankrupt businessman wanted to buy the rolling stock of a haulage company that had been liquidated. Bold as brass, Lees openly admitted to Stafford Lynn that he was bankrupt and unable to hold a company directorship but then proceeded to go ahead and negotiate a price for the assets of the haulage company. He then told the auctioneer that his partner, Derek Jones, would complete the deal so as to disguise Lees' interest in not only the transaction but the business as well. Stafford Lynn did not want to identify the family concerned because of the pain they suffered after doing business with Lees. Stafford Lynn said they had been paid, but according to a police source, the problem for this highly respected family was that Lees and Jones scammed them for the cash. It was not an untypical means of doing business for these two particular conmen.

Increasingly, the police found that all the companies owned by Lees did very little genuine business. 'They were bogus companies,' said one officer who did not want to be identified. 'They produced nothing, sold nothing and were set up purely to conceal the profits they made from criminal activity. They were a means to an end and the end was to launder their dirty money.'

The list of companies was impressive only if you did not look beyond the surface. Among the various companies owned by Lees and Jones were Alexander Hunter & Sons, road hauliers; Pony Express Ireland Ltd, a cut price telephone service based on an American idea; International Traction Services Ltd, another road haulage company based in Blackpool; Dame Hill Ltd in Dublin; Leisure Trading Ltd — the company running the Loughside Inn in Belfast. There were other company interests in Bristol, Southport and Blackpool.

Lees moved frequently between Northern Ireland and England, keen to look after his 'business interests' in Bristol and Blackpool. Eventually the police decided it was time to bring him in for questioning as well. Lees was apprehended exactly four months after the initial arrests as he returned to Northern Ireland on a flight from Manchester. It was 10 October when he was intercepted at Belfast International Airport.

When Lees was arrested the police seized his wallet. Inside they found a collection of hookers' calling cards lifted from public telephone boxes commonly found in a number of English cities. When they were returning the wallet, minus the cash and everything else they needed, to Zara, one of the cops made a point of watching as she checked the contents and found the cards. She stormed out of the police station. When she next got to see Lees, it was noted that there was a row about the hookers' cards. Lees told her the cops had planted the cards and she believed that . . . eventually.

Of course, by now the police had a substantial file on Lees, Jones and their joint 'business' ventures. There was a lot to talk about. Unlike Jones, Lees talked to his interviewers. It's just that in spite of his sometimes verbose answers, he gave little away. In fact, he spent a lot of time trying to twist and turn things to his advantage. He was arrogant enough to believe that his skills as a bullshitter and a confidence trickster would be sufficiently agile to dodge tough questions and to keep the police confused and bewildered. But with the documents and the intelligence gathered from surveillance, the police could see through his act.

Top of their list of priorities when it came to quizzing the former champion of industry and champion of the race track, were his handwritten 'doodles' about the £17m drug haul found on the *Plongeur Wisky*. And detectives were keen to question Lees about the handwritten faxes sent to Gibraltar during the negotiation and purchase of the *Plongeur Wisky*. Most particularly, they were anxious to establish if Lees was the owner. Was he the David Reid who clearly signed for ownership?

First he was gently probed about what he knew about the *Plongeur Wisky*. The following is an extract from one of many hours of taped interviews conducted by detectives involved in the Operation Kilbreck investigation:

Det. Const. Horan: Mr Lees, you are in here for questioning in relation to conspiracy in the United Kingdom to import drugs into another jurisdiction, in this particular case the Republic of Ireland. And for that particular offence I must caution you that you do not have to say anything, but I must caution you that if you do not mention when questioned something which you later rely on in court it may harm your defence. If you do say anything it may be given in evidence. Do you understand?
Lees: Yes.

Horan: Mr Lees, have you heard of a boat *The Plunger of Whiskey?*

Lees: Yes.

Horan: What do you know about the *Plongeur Wisky?*

Lees: I was aware that my boss Derek Jones was arrested and charged under a similar sort of charge to what you have put to me today regarding this boat.

Horan: What's your knowledge of the *Plongeur Wisky?*

Lees: Very little.

Horan: Well, tell me what you do know.

Lees: That it was a boat that was caught with drugs apparently in the South of Ireland.

Horan: No, I mean what's your knowledge in relation to Derek Jones's involvement with the boat and your involvement with the boat?

Lees: Very, very little.

Horan: What is it?

Lees: The boat apparently was registered to a company which Derek owned.

Horan: No. What involvement had you in the purchase of the boat, I'm asking?

Lees: None.

Horan: None, you had no relationship with the boat at all?

Lees: No relationship with the boat at all.

Horan: Did you know he was buying a boat?

Lees: I was not aware that he was buying a boat.

Horan: And you didn't issue any instructions to him to buy a boat?

Lees: I wouldn't be in a position to buy a boat.

Horan: I didn't ask you that, I asked you did you issue any instructions to him to buy a boat?

196

Lees: No.
Horan: Do you know anybody called David Reid?
Lees: No.
Horan: Do you yourself use the name David Reid?
Lees: No.
Horan: Do you use any name other than Colin Lees?
Lees: On occasions. Yeah.
Horan: What other name do you use?
Lees: Various.

Lees told Det. Const. Horan that one of the aliases he used, the one he could remember at that moment, was Peter Murphy. But there apparently were so many he could not recall them all. He also volunteered to the interviewing officers: 'On a few occasions, most of my people I do business with know my problems, can accept it but on some occasions it's difficult in a fresh situation, particularly in the North of Ireland where my name was flashed around the media and week after week and year after year, on previous problems, it became well nigh impossible to make a living you know in the simplest sort of names.'

When Horan asked Lees about David Reid and whether or not he, Lees, had had any dealings in the purchase of the boat in Gibraltar, it was in the certain knowledge that Lees had written some of the faxes that arrived with the Bonets in Gibraltar with 'David Reid's' signature at the bottom. The police had also by this stage found Lees' fingerprints on a number of key faxes.

Horan then momentarily switched subjects. He asked Lees if he could tell him what he did for a living.

Horan: What's your actual occupation?
Lees: I work for Derek Jones.

Horan: In what capacity?

Lees: I was his Assistant Business Consultant, whatever.

Horan: And how much did he pay you for that?

Lees: It depended, but on average it was say about £1,500 a month.

Horan: Net?

Lees: Yes.

Horan: And were you given expenses as well?

Lees: Yes.

Horan: And how much were you given in expenses a month?

Lees: Depended on the nature of the expenses, what I was doing, you know. If it was just travel, whatever the cost of the travel was or if it was something important like a dinner or something . . .

Horan: Derek Jones's business is haulage, is that correct?

Lees: Two haulage companies, he had a pub in Belfast as you're aware and over the last six or nine months he was looking heavily into England to look at new business set-ups there.

Horan: Has he diversified into Europe?

Lees: Has he diversified into Europe? Yes, we talked about one or two things abroad, yes.

This line of questioning was an attempt to get Lees to admit that he actually called the shots, not Jones, and that Jones was simply a front for all the businesses because Lees as a bankrupt was barred from holding directorships. But Lees had obviously decided he was going to admit nothing of any consequence. He told officers he was unable to travel because his passports had been taken from him. It was time to switch back to the Dublin company

Dame Hill and his relationship with the bookkeeper, but only after a brief return to the question of aliases. The key to the boat purchase in Gibraltar was David Reid. The police wanted to know who David Reid was . . . they already knew it was a false name.

Horan: Well, OK. You've never used the alias David Reid; you've never had any connection with the *Plongeur Wisky?*
Lees: No.
Horan; Well, basically what you're saying there is you've used aliases or assumed names for business reasons, isn't that right?
Lees: That's correct.
Horan: Have you ever used it when you have been involved in any illegal activity where you wanted to hide your identity, have you ever used the name in that fashion?
Lees: No.
Horan: As you'll appreciate, from the police's point of view, that would be something we would be looking at if somebody was using an alias or using it for a reason. You've given us your reason, we might think that somebody's trying to hide their criminal activity. I'm asking have you ever used an alias in those circumstances?
Lees: No.
Horan: To hide criminal activity? You're shaking your head.
Lees: That's no.
Horan: It's definitely no.
Lees: Yes, definitely no.
Horan: What do you know about the company Dame Hill?
Lees: What do I currently know about it?
Horan: No, what is your historical knowledge of the company Dame Hill?

Lees: Well, historical I suppose is up to a minute ago.

Horan: Well, all right then, let me put it to you like this. Did you know the company was being formed?

Lees: Dame Hill, no.

Horan: Did you have anything to do with the formation of the company?

Lees: No.

Horan: Prior to 10 June, which was the day that Derek Jones was arrested, had you any knowledge of Dame Hill?

Lees: No.

Horan: What is your relationship with Norma Elder?

Lees: She was a bookkeeper for Derek.

Horan: Was she a bookkeeper for you?

Lees: No, she worked with me, directly with me.

Horan: Did she work in a subordinate position to you?

Lees: Yes.

Horan: So you could give her instructions?

Lees: Yes.

Horan: But you knew nothing about Dame Hill?

Lees: Well I knew there was a file in the office. I'm trying to think, you asked me the question on 10 June?

Horan: Prior to 10 June.

Lees: Oh, prior to 10 June I was aware there had been a company in amongst twenty or thirty other companies and I had seen a file on it, yes.

Horan: Have you met people known or have you ever had any conversation with or correspondence with people known as Serge and Angelique Bonet?

Lees: No.

Horan: Do either of those names mean anything to you?

Lees: No.

The police had established that Jones had set up Dame Hill Ltd. It cost IR£340 and he paid by Visa. Dame Hill was bought 'off the shelf' at a company's shop in Dublin's Lower Fitzwilliam Street and came into existence on 10 July 1996 . . . just a few months before the drug shipment was due to leave Gibraltar. Throughout its life, the company used the address of the company's shop. It appeared on all the company's letterheads, which, as police were to discover, were generated on a word processor in the office above the Loughside Inn.

The police were slowly building up to the big questions about what they had been calling 'the Game Plan'. Lees was clearly not prepared to volunteer any information. He was still hoping that he could bluff his way as he had done for years with bank managers, leasing companies, his own staff and those unfortunate enough to have regretted ever meeting him once they realised they had been suckered into a scam that either left them short of hard-earned cash or deeply humiliated that their good name had been dragged into the gutter by Lees.

Lees told police he could not remember having given Norma Elder any envelopes for safekeeping. He did recall cleaning out the office above the pub when he and Jones wanted to move out of the Belfast office. Lees told his interviewers that he moved into the office of Hunter's haulage company at Templepatrick in Co. Antrim while Jones operated out of the Ballymena office in the courtyard at Galgorm Castle Golf Club. He couldn't remember the date of these moves but thought it was around Christmas 1996 or January 1997. It was time for the police to focus the questioning very clearly on the Dame Hill envelopes found in Norma Elder's house. In order to ensure the documents did not degrade pending the trial, the police photographic department prepared an album of photographs of these vital pieces of evidence. So

201

during questioning, Lees did not actually see the originals, he saw only the police pictures.

Horan: Quite simply the allegation is that you gave to Norma Elder to conceal a file which was marked Dame Hill, which held all the documents relative to the *Plongeur Wisky* and the drug deal.

Lees: What drug deal? I wasn't involved in any drug deal.

Horan: Right. I am now going to produce to you exhibit SH1. Exhibit SH1 is a working copy, an album of photographs of a number of documents which were taken from the Dame Hill file. The reason that it is in photographic form is for ease of reference for ourselves. The original documents are in our possession. I now show to you the first photograph in that album. It is marked Dame Hill. It is bigger than an A4-sized brown envelope and written on it is Dame Hill and underneath that David in brackets. Do you recognise that envelope?

Lees: No.

Horan: Do you recognise the writing on that envelope?

Lees: No.

Horan: I'm now showing you a rear view of the same envelope and written on it is the name Sheppards and beneath it an international telephone number. Do you recognise the writing on that envelope?

Lees: It could be mine, I'm not sure.

Horan: Why would you have written the name Sheppards and an international phone number on the back of an envelope marked Dame Hill?

Lees: I've no idea but maybe if we could look at the whole file you could see why.

Horan: You have no idea?

Lees: No.

Horan: What we're going to do here, Mr Lees, is, we're going to do this brick by brick. OK? Sheppards were the marine engineers who did work on the *Plongeur Wisky* prior to its setting sail from Gibraltar. You say it could be your writing. We have one of the foremost experts in handwriting in the world who will say: yes it is definitely your writing.

Lees: Well, I don't write the best and sometimes it's . . .

Horan: Your writing is very distinctive, I think you'd agree.

Lees: You could say that, I'm not so sure. It's not very good.

Lees was shown photograph copies of handwritten faxes relating to the purchase of the *Plongeur Wisky* . . . and his excuse was that he simply worked in Derek Jones' office and often dictated faxes for people with whom Jones was doing business. He could not remember every detail of every fax he wrote or dictated. He could only remember something about Dame Hill because there was a folder held in the office by that name. The more he talked, the more difficult questions he raised in the minds of his inquisitors.

There was much to-ing and fro-ing in the office above the pub, Lees told detectives. He was trying to say he could not recall who was doing what or when. Asked to explain this, Lees introduced new names.

Horan: How many people were in this office?

Lees: Well, I know it had something to do with our friends O'Kane and Kelly who were using the office at the time.

Horan: They were taking to do with Dame Hill?

Lees: Well, Kelly was involved and had spoken to Derek on quite a few occasions.

Horan: Which Kelly's this?

Lees: Thomas Kelly.

Horan: You mentioned there about the goings on with Dame Hill. What goings on were there to be precise?

Lees: Well, I knew there was something had been going on with Dame Hill. I remember Kelly had come in and O'Kane were in and spoke to Derek and bits and pieces but I wasn't directly involved with it. I think I can recall leaving money at one time which had to be collected by someone in the office.

Horan: Who left money?

Lees: One of the two of them, I can't remember, I think it was Kelly, you know.

Horan: Who is Thomas Kelly?

Lees: A guy who we tried to do business with last year.

Horan: And where's he from?

Lees: I think he's originally from London or Bristol.

Horan: Describe him to me.

Lees: About six-foot; well built.

Horan: Age?

Lees: About forties, you know.

Horan: And how did you come to be associated with him?

Lees: I met him through James O'Kane, you know.

Try as they might, the police were unable to trace any Thomas Kelly and concluded that this was one of Lees' aliases . . . or a figment of his vivid imagination, dreamed up to try to spread the area of blame and confusion. As it happens they were later to get confirmation that Lees did indeed use this name as an alias. It was time to go back on the offensive relating to the identity of David Reid — apparently an 'employee' of Dame Hill in Dublin.

Horan: Who works for Dame Hill Ltd? Who's David Reid working for Dame Hill Ltd?

Lees: I don't think anybody works for Dame Hill Ltd. I just think it was one of Derek's many companies which he formed.

Horan: What sort of business did it carry out?

Lees: I couldn't honestly say. I wasn't aware that it had carried out any business at all. Derek had businesses all over the world. Hundreds of them, you know.

Horan: The mobile number on this is 0802-299385. Do you recognise that mobile number?

Lees: It looks like a mobile that was used around the business, yeah.

Horan: By whom?

Lees: I don't know.

Horan: You're living in a common-law relationship with Caroline Zara Lees. Isn't that correct?

Lees: That's correct.

Horan: That number is allocated to Caroline Zara Lees.

Lees: Yes, this is the phone that you interviewed her about then.

Horan: Do you have any knowledge of that phone?

Lees: Yes, Zara took that phone out for me a long time, I don't know, when was it taken out, you would know?

Horan: She took it out for you. Why?

Lees: Because I can't get credit worthiness, because I'm a bankrupt . . . undischarged. I used the phone for some months and then it was used around the rest of the business.

Horan: Why would somebody called David Reid give your phone number?

Lees: It wouldn't be my phone number.

Horan: Well, whose phone number was it? It was taken out for you.

Lees: Well, I discussed this with Zara; she took the phone out to me because I broke my phone. I used it for a very short period of time.

Horan: How short a period, Colin, did you use it for?

Lees: I can't recall but I'm sure . . .

The significance of the questions about the mobile phone was that the phone with this particular number was used in Donegal by Noel Morrison to make contact with Kevin Lafferty on board the *Plongeur Wisky*. In addition, in a fax to the Bonets in Gibraltar, 'David Reid' offered this same number as a point of contact with him. The fax was handwritten by Lees but signed by 'David Reid', alias Noel Morrison.

Horan: Photograph number 55, which will be given in its original format, the exhibit marking RM20 is a handwritten note on Dame Hill headed notepaper dated 23 September 1996 for the attention of Mrs Bonet. 'Dear Sirs, I enclose agreement signed as requested. Please note amendment to number five. I will transfer deposit £5,500 to your account as requested tomorrow. It is not necessary to mail original as I will be in Gibraltar Friday Saturday this week to finalise everything. We can complete contract. I will instruct surveyor today by fax. Could you please speak to him and if possible have survey carried out before my arrival. I hope to test the boat with my skipper over the weekend, if this is also acceptable' — there's a scoring out — 'your husband/son would be available. Will call you shortly.'

and then its signed 'David Reid'. Do you recognise that document, Mr Lees?

Lees: I don't recall it, no.

Horan: But it is in your handwriting?

Lees: It appears to be, yeah.

Horan: You accept that's your handwriting?

Lees: I can't be sure but it looks like it, yes.

Horan: Do you wish to give me any explanation as to why you have handwritten a letter signed David Reid to the Bonets about the purchase of the *Plongeur Wisky*?

Lees: The point I'm trying to make here, I mean, if someone came in to me and said hey would you draft me a fax and send it for me, I would be good at that. I work in the office, that was my job you know and that's obviously what happened.

Horan: You just can't recollect that that's what happened there. You were acting on instructions from a David Reid. Who's David Reid, Mr Lees?

Lees: Pardon?

Horan: Who's David Reid?

Lees: David Reid must have been the name that Kelly or some of the people who were involved in the . . . you know.

Horan: Do you think so, Mr Lees?

Lees: I do think so, yeah.

Horan: Yeah, you forgot, you said you did not know anybody connected with any company belonging to Derek Jones or yourself called David Reid.

Lees: I don't.

Horan: Well then, if you didn't know anybody called David Reid, why did you draft a fax for the signature of David Reid?

Lees: I can't recall who asked me to do that at this moment of time but I'm sure . . . .

Horan: In the normal course of events, are you in the habit of drafting faxes for non-existent people for the purchase of boats which are going to be used to transport enormous amounts of cannabis into United Kingdom waters?

Lees: All I've, someone's come in and asked me to draft a fax. I haven't signed it you know, that's all I've done.

Horan: You were asked quite specifically a couple of questions ago did you have anything to do with the Bonets. Did you have anything to do with Gibraltar?

Lees: I don't recall anything about Bonets or Gibraltar. Someone came in and asked me to send a fax. I sent a fax.

Horan: Excuse me, that is your writing. That was not dictated to you. Are you saying you wrote this down at someone else's dictation?

Lees: Yes.

Horan: You are?

Lees: Well, I must have.

Horan: Whose dictation?

Lees: I don't recall.

Horan: Why?

Lees: Because I just don't remember who asked me.

Horan: Colin, you're not an idiot; you're not a fool.

Lees: I'm not and I think in the fullness of this interview I'll recall, I'll know exactly the circumstances but it's like a lot of things I was involved in, I wasn't personal and people asked me to do things . . .

Lees was finding it more and more difficult to come up with any plausible explanation as to why his handwriting appeared on so many fax documents relating to the purchase of the boat that was found to have 1.7 tons of cannabis on board when it was searched at Kilrush Harbour in Co. Clare.

What Lees did not know at this stage, was just how much the police knew of the operation to buy the boat, secure the drugs at an estimated cost of around £510,000 and transport the shipment back to Ireland. By tracking down all the details of the mobile phones that had been recovered in Donegal and aboard the *Plongeur Wisky*, the police were able to establish that they had all been bought by International Traction Services Ltd and were signed for by Derek Jones.

They had also established that Lees and Jones had been in telephone contact with the drug-laden boat as it made its way from Gibraltar to Ireland. Of course, the *Plongeur Wisky* was not equipped to make such long sea journeys and in order to make it possible, the new owners needed to make adjustments. As the police established on a visit to Gibraltar, larger fuel tanks were fitted by H. Sheppard & Co at their marina, boatyard and chandlery at Waterport, Gibraltar. The *Plongeur Wisky* account held at their chandlery is in the name of 'D. Reid'. On 4 October 1996, two payments were made to Sheppards — one for £100 (receipt number 17338) and a second for £1,750 (receipt number 17340).

But details about alterations to the boat were not the only information gleaned by detectives on their trip to Gibraltar. For example, they discovered that on 3 October, Noel Morrison checked in at the Caleta Palace Hotel at Catalan Bay. His hotel bill showed he made two cash payments on the day he arrived; each for £60. Then on 4 October, evidently still flush with cash in spite of handing over nearly £2,000 to the boatyard owners, he paid the hotel £300 in cash. He remained there as a guest until 11 October.

On 17 October, Noel Morrison turned up at Malaga Airport to collect a hire car. It was a three-day hire and it appears the car, a

Peugeot 106, had been pre-booked on 2 October. There's no evidence of a credit card number being used — it appears this was a cash-based agreement. The day following the collection of the car, the final payments were made to Sheppards in Gibraltar. Another £2,149.71 was also handed over in cash to settle the balance. Cash was used so that there would be no telltale credit card transactions for the police to follow should they ever become involved in an investigation.

In the Land Rover Discovery seized in Donegal, other vital clues were found . . . for example, the Gardaí found flight tickets showing travel from London Heathrow to Malaga and finally to Madrid. The return to Heathrow is marked 'VOID'. The ticket issued by Iberia Airlines in London was in the name of a 'Mr P. Norris' who was travelling to Malaga on 17 October and then on to Madrid from Malaga on 21 October.

But the police also found another one-way ticket in the name of Noel Morrison issued by First Choice for an Air 2000 charter flight to Belfast on 20 October 1996. Also found in the Land Rover was a business card for a Mr Soodi Abdeljailil from Tangiers with a Moroccan connection.

So the police had a fairly clear picture of how the whole drug smuggling operation had been run in the weeks immediately prior to the events in Donegal and Kilrush. Armed with this information, they decided it was time to make a major push with Lees about the discovery of the Game Plan. Lees' only 'game plan' in the interview room was to play as dumb as ever when faced with very damning, self-incriminating evidence.

Horan: I'll go back to photograph 69 which will be RM23, it's the same document but this time it's with the original post-its on it. These original post-its — there are two in number, each about four inches by two inches — and they set out in essence in your handwriting a number of instructions or calculations. I'll deal first of all with the one to the right-hand side of RM23 and it says boat and then the numerals 111,815.24, then the next one is machine 6600, the next one M. Marine 1000, the next one radios, the next one night sight 400, the next one M. Marines 65 pounds, the next one outdoor wear — it's O/door wear, I'm assuming that's outdoor wear — £268, the next one is sundry £420: it's then totalled. There's then the date, 28 October '96 and then there's a sum of 20,500 underneath that. To the left underneath the handwriting is 11,000, 9,000 and figure scored out is 500. That's in your handwriting — can you explain what that is to me?

Lees: Well, looks like someone's been telling me to tally what's been spent or what it was costing or something.

Horan: You don't remember what you were doing the tally for?

Lees: No, I don't honestly, no.

Horan: The left-hand post-it, which again is in your handwriting — the first comment is boat 55,000, your handwriting, 50,500, which happens to be the cost of the *Plongeur Wisky*.

Lees: Mm hmm.

Horan: Crew 3,000, X [times] whatever that means I don't know, 3,000, then there's a number of 3,000's on the way down, then number there's home 11,000, rib etc 9,000 with a total of 88,500 plus 1,000. Can you explain what that means? It's in your handwriting.

Lees: Well, it must have been that they've wanted to keep a record of what it was costing them or something.

Horan: You just wrote it all down for them?

Lees: Well at . . . at the end of the day they were in my office, they were working in my office.

Horan: Who's Noel, Colin?

Lees: I don't know.

Horan: Do you know anybody called Noel?

Lees: I do, yes.

Horan: Who do you know called Noel?

Lees: I know Noel Morrison. He's my friend.

Horan: Is he?

Lees: Yes.

Horan: Were you surprised to hear, Mr Lees, that these figures correspond to expenses outlaid by Noel Morrison, James Millar, Samuel Adams . . . what do you call the other two individuals? Millar, Adams, Morrison, Symington, and who's that other clown who's inside at the minute for drugs? McIlfee? **[Noel Johnston is the name that Horan could not remember.]** No, no, um. Anyway, it refers to the expenses of five persons who were caught off the coast of Donegal in and around the time that the *Plongeur Wisky* was captured in Kilrush, including Mr Morrison, your associate, and four others, one of whom is currently on remand for drug offences. Do you wish to pass any comment on that?

Lees: Noel and I are very good friends — we do lots of business deals together.

Horan: I'll bet you do . . . I'll bet you do. The point is this — would you write something like that down and be totally oblivious to what you're writing down?

Lees: No, not at all.

Horan: No, of course you wouldn't. You have to if somebody's calling something out to you, 'write this down' or whatever; you're sitting, you know what's being written down, you're not just writing down 10,000 — what does that 10,000 relate to? Write it down so you know what's being written down there.

Lees: If Noel came to me and said 'I want to . . .'

Horan: You just . . . you just did what you were told, Mr Lees?

Lees: No, I did not do what I was told. Noel says to me I want to do this; I want to do that; plenty of times. You'll see all over my file figures that I've done with Noel in dealings, you know.

Horan: Well, it just so happens that a lot of these documents which we have shown you are in your handwriting all the time. It just so happens people happen to be coming along to tell you . . .

Lees: I was sitting in the office, that was my job.

Horan: Why don't they do it themselves?

Lees: What?

Horan: Why don't they do it themselves?

Lees: Well, Noel's not the sort of guy would write faxes and you would know that, you know . . .

Horan: Why?

Lees: He's . . . he's not a good writer he, he . . .

Horan: Gotta be better than you?

Lees: Well, he would actually be worse, you know. If he came in to me and asked me to do a fax I would do it, you know.

Horan: And this guy Kelly can't write either?

Lees: Well, Kelly is a very flash gentleman with a lot of dough; but he doesn't seem to do much work, you know.

Horan: And O'Kane? He can't write?

213

Lees: Indeed he can write all right, you know.

Horan: Why doesn't he do it himself?

Lees: What?

Horan: Why doesn't he do it himself?

Lees: I don't know why I did it; I just said if he asked me to do it I would do it.

Horan: Just an accommodating sort of guy, Mr Lees?

Lees: Well, I try very hard.

Horan: There are a number of other documents in relation to Dame Hill Ltd. A handwritten one — sorry, I beg your pardon, a type-written one re: the survey of the *Plongeur Wisky* addressed to 'Dear Mr and Mrs Bonet' and so on and so forth with kind regards, it's pp'd for David Reid — do you recognise that signature?

Lees: No.

Horan: Is an employee of yours Debbie Gabriel?

Lees: Yes.

Horan: Is that her signature?

Lees: I don't know, I don't think so.

Horan: This document RM24. The next document, which is photograph 71, it's the same document as previously . . . no, it's not. I beg your pardon, it's a document this time addressed from Dame Hill to Mr Wilkinson and attached to it is another post-it. The post-its being those little yellow slightly gummed pieces of paper that have become so common now, and written on it, in your handwriting, is the name Sheppards, underneath that Brian Pizarro, underneath that, arranged tomorrow cost £90; £130 plus anti-fowling, which I'm assuming is some method of cleaning engines.

Lees: Mmmm . . .

Horan: What's that about?

Lees: It must be a phone call I took or something, stuck a note in the file, you know.

Horan: You took a phone call and stuck a note in the file?

Lees: I don't know, I'm assuming it's something like that — why else would I have written it down, you know.

Whilst visiting Sheppards boatyard, the police collected another couple of clues to help them place another piece of the jigsaw. It appears that some of the cash advanced to Sheppards was used as a means of getting money to the skipper of the *Plongeur Wisky*, Kevin Lafferty — the Donegal man who was to be responsible for guiding the boat from Gibraltar to Ireland. He obviously had living expenses whilst waiting for the work on the boat to be completed. With the mobile phone links between Lafferty and the other phones issued to International Traction Services Ltd, the police wanted to know a little more about these connections. Aside from the traces on the telephone calls from Lees' and Jones' phones to the drug boat, there was something else the police had found to connect the bankrupt businessman to the Donegal skipper of the *Plongeur Wisky*. It was time to spring this surprise on Lees. It was yet another opportunity for Lees to display his only defence . . . that someone else did it and ran away!

Horan: Photograph 48 is an invoice. Sorry, I beg your pardon; a letter from Sheppards of Gibraltar, H. Sheppard & Company Ltd, Waterport, Gibraltar, dated 9 October 1996 and it says 'received from H. Sheppard and Company Ltd four hundred pounds' — the four hundred pounds written in words — 'in cash from account SO26 Plongeur Wisky', then there's a number 6168 and underneath that 101096 in the name the legend Kevin Lafferty, Skipper, and then it's signed by Kevin Lafferty. Have you ever seen that piece of paper before?

Lees: No.

Horan: Do you know anybody named Kevin Lafferty?

Lees: I do now, yes.

Horan: Did you then know anybody called Kevin Lafferty?

Lees: No.

Horan: Where do you know Kevin Lafferty from now?

Lees: I understand subsequent to the . . . he was the skipper in charge of this boat.

Horan: And you've only since heard of him?

Lees: Yes.

Lees: Never heard of him before?

Lees: No.

Horan: Did you ever have any contact with a Kevin Lafferty at any stage?

Lees: No.

Horan: Do you know any sort of guy called Kevin Lafferty?

Lees: I don't think so. No.

Horan: Would you have written anywhere in a diary or a piece of paper the phone number of Kevin Lafferty?

Lees: No, not unless someone had instructed me to do it.

Horan: Aw, Colin, come on, I have seen it in your personal diary here. Surely you have a mind of your own and you think . . .

Lees: A phone number that I phoned that Derek would have given me to contact these ones in.

Horan: I thought it was your own personal . . .

Lees: I don't know . . .

Horan: Your pocket diary. Would you have Kevin Lafferty's phone number in your pocket diary for any reason that you can think of?

Lees: Is that ah, ah, a recent statement is that?

Horan: No, no, no, I'm not going into all that, no . . . you say you don't know a Kevin Lafferty.

Lees: I don't know.

Horan: Right, so what reason will you have a phone number of Kevin Lafferty in your phone book if you don't know him?

Lees: I really shouldn't have, no.

Horan: Not unless somebody else told you to write it in your book?

Lees: Och no; I mean there's people I deal with who say I'll take so and so's number like that, you know.

Horan: There are a number of other documents from Sheppards including a receipt signed by Kevin Lafferty who you don't know, so I'm not going to, ah, I'm not going to, I'm not going to go through them since he has no knowledge of these Sheppard documents. Does Noel Morrison use the alias David Reid?

Lees: He would use an alias on occasion, yes.

Horan: Is David Reid the alias he uses?

Lees: Could be.

Horan: Could be?

Lees: Could be, yes.

Horan: Well is it or isn't it?

Lees: He's got his own problems and he uses an alias.

Horan: I'm asking you, Mr Lees, have you ever heard Noel Morrison use the alias David Reid?

Lees: I think so, yes.

So at last, some sort of recognition from Lees that he knew David Reid — the man he so vehemently denied knowing earlier in the interviews with detectives. Now, he acknowledges that David Reid is Noel Morrison. A breakthrough of sorts, the police thought. Time to press on with questions about the Game Plan. Confronted with his own handwriting giving details relating to the drugs operations in both Gibraltar and Donegal, surely Lees would finally be compelled to put his hands up and admit it was a 'fair cop'! No chance. He was still in his 'a big boy did it and ran away' frame of mind. Or, in other words, he was just following orders! It's becoming increasingly difficult for Det. Const. John Horan to avoid being sarcastic when he hears some of the responses from the millionaire bankrupt.

Horan: I'll now take you to document 19; photograph 19, which is in your handwriting, it's on A4-shaped paper, it's been folded a number of ways and it will be getting exhibit marking RM27. It's not a draft fax. It is I would say a game plan for the *Plongeur Wisky* and I'll go through it with you. Your handwriting, do you accept that's your handwriting?

Lees: I think so, yes.

Horan: Boat 55,000 pounds, bank 300, solicitor 300, surveyor/yard 350, then there's comma 100, I'm assuming that's not 350,000, crew plus retainers 3,000, Noel expenses equipment plus 2,500, travel crew expenses 1,500, company front 5,000, total 68,500 pounds, and it's been rounded up to 70,000 pounds — why would you have written that down?

Lees: I don't know, it must have been a budget for Mr Kelly or O'Kane, you know.

Horan: You just made it out for him?

Lees: No, I mean I did work for them on occasion — you

see piles of stuff in that office where I've worked for them.

Horan: Absolutely. Next week underlined engines and work 4,000, satellite etc 750 plus chips (2,000), provisions and fuels, provisions 1,000, fuels 3,000, total of 8,000 pounds. Why would you have written that down?

Lees: I must have been . . . been putting together a budget for sorting the boat out, you know.

Horan: Underneath that RIB 10,000 pounds, house 1,000 pounds, motor home 1,000 pounds, expenses 3,000 pounds, a total of 15,000 pounds, that all refers to the capture of those four guys, five guys off the coast of Donegal — can you tell me why you'd written that down?

Lees: It must have been something to do with Noel and . . . and his RIB, I'm not sure.

Horan: But it's all part of the same thing. What about Noel and his RIB?

Lees: What about it? I think he's trying to get it back, you know.

Horan: Do they have a paddling pool in Maghaberry? *[prison]* You've also written the name Kevin Lafferty and Desi McIlroy.

Lees: Mmmm . . .

Horan: Why have you written those two names?

Lees: I must have been given them at the time.

Horan: Who gave you them? Both of those were captured; both those persons were captured on the *Plongeur Wisky* in Clare. Now think hard — why would you have written that down?

Lees: I'm telling you if I was doing something I was doing it on behalf of some of the people who were, um, organised in trying to purchase that boat and it wasn't me. If it was

O'Kane or Kelly, um, they might have turned round and said 'right put a deal together', I don't know. I don't, I don't even recall, to be absolutely honest, and when Derek was arrested I scratched my head big time to try and remember what the circumstances had been, you know.

Horan: So after Derek was arrested you remembered all this?

Lees: After Derek was arrested I remembered what had happened and I . . .

Horan: Well, how come you sat there in this interview not forty-five minutes ago and said you knew nothing about it.

Lees: Because it was like as I've said to you; I'd gone on . . . there was other deals were going; there's things I didn't put into them, there's things that were in — until you see the file how do you know?

Horan: You're a businessman, you're a busy man, you've all these business dealings . . .

Lees: I'm not that busy.

Horan: . . . going on in your head, right. But I mean it's not every day of the week you're dealing with, um, boats, boat equipment, writing stuff down about ah . . .

Lees: I wouldn't know anything about it if it hit me on the head.

Horan: No, right, okay, fair enough, but you're . . . this document here shows that you were writing it down and you had knowledge . . . you must have had some knowledge . . . some knowledge?

Lees: I do now that I've seen what, what . . .

Horan: That's what we're here to ask you — what exactly is your knowledge, Colin? I mean you're conveniently not remembering.

Lees: I'm not.

But he was! Conveniently choosing not to remember, that is. The police were more determined than ever to use the Game Plan to help secure a conviction for drug smuggling against Lees. His own handwriting had put him in the frame as having played a major role in organising the whole drug smuggling operation. Without this, the case against Lees would have remained entirely circumstantial, but with these documents they had tangible evidence that Lees was the mastermind of the whole drug shipment. Questioning Lees was like trying to draw hen's teeth, according to John Horan. But he had to keep going, had to touch every base. Now Horan decided to pursue Lees on the question of the 'unloaders' mentioned in the handwritten Game Plan notes.

Horan: Right. Let me ask you this then . . . you're now running the haulage business on behalf of Derek Jones in essence?
Lees: There's no one else.
Horan: Right. Do you employ any people in the yard other than the drivers?
Lees: Currently no.
Horan: Have you ever employed in your capacity as a director of a company anybody involved in labouring unloading goods?
Lees: Yes.
Horan: Have you ever in your time as a company director employed people for security?
Lees: What sort of security?
Horan: Well, closing and opening the gates.
Lees: Ah yes, yes, yes.
Horan: If you're employing a guy to unload a lorry, one job, you've got a load coming in and think I'm gonna have to . . . what would you pay him?

221

Lees: What sort of a job?

Horan: Well, you've a 40-foot trailer arrives into the yard, your drivers are all away and you think 'I need a guy, this is a one off, I'll ring Pete — he's on the dole, he could do with an extra few shillings. Pete, bring along three of your mates, we've got a load coming in, I want to unload it.' OK, it's a 40-foot trailer, I don't know what, let's say bottles of Coke on palettes, right? I want to unload it — what would you pay him for that one job?

Lees: Depends on the load, wouldn't it?

Horan: Well, alright; what's the upper, what's the most you'd pay him for unloading a 40-foot trailer in a day?

Lees *solicitor:* Sorry I, um, wait a minute — I'm missing the significance of this at all.

Horan: I'll come to the significance of it.

Lees: Alright, if it was with a forklift it could be a fiver or if it was as they say in the trade it could be a handball job it could be 500, I don't know.

Horan: Right. You have written down on this document crew 50,000 pounds. That's quite an expensive crew. John plus one 25,000, I don't know what that is. Or is that John plus I. Plus I that could be yeah, no you wouldn't put John plus I. Would you? . . . Unloaders security 4x5 20,000 pounds. Why you were sitting writing all this out on somebody's instruction and it doesn't occur to you to say 'Jeez I could get you 4 boys who'd do that for 20 quid each'?

Lees: I'm not too sure that that's got anything to do with a boat, you know.

Horan: Well what sort of thing would you say was worth unloading for 5,000 pounds per person?

Lees: I don't know what that . . .

Horan: Have to be a high risk, wouldn't it? What's the highest risk? Something that you're gonna face fourteen years in prison for? It's quite a high risk. Drugs spring to mind.

Lees: Well, everything's drugs for you but I have never had anything to do with drugs in my life.

Horan: I would say everything's drugs for you. Remember John Ferguson?

Lees: Yes.

Horan: I interviewed John Ferguson, Mr Lees, and while it can't be used against you it's twelve fourteen John Ferguson told me that every halfpenny he got to buy drugs with, you gave him, OK.

Lees: Well, that's not true.

Horan: Well, of course not, and I can't use it against you. But let's not play silly games, OK?

Lees: I'm not playing silly games.

John Ferguson had drug convictions. Lees admitted knowing him and he also admitted to police that he knew other felons, such as Paddy Farrell, the notorious millionaire Newry drug smuggler who was shot dead by his mistress, before she turned the gun on herself. And of course he knew the drug dealers and loyalist terrorists who had travelled to Donegal to unload the drug shipment on to the RIB boat. What he may not have known is that one of the 'Donegal Five' was actually an informant for the RUC's Drug Squad. As it happens, this was one bit of business that he neglected to inform his handlers about!

Lees' involvement in the drug trade had long been suspected by police officers in the RUC Drug Squad, but until this moment there was no definitive proof of his activities. The 'tout' who was among the five in Donegal had told his handlers that Lees and a Liverpool man known as 'Rocky' had brought millions of E-tabs into Northern Ireland as well as tons of cocaine. Most of the drugs were smuggled in vehicles specially adapted by a Co. Antrim garage owner with specially built false compartments on buses and lorries. One bus was stopped at Dover with 17 kilos of coke, 100,000 E-tabs and 400 kilos of cannabis. The bus had travelled to the continent empty and returned empty — yet the springs were clearly carrying a substantial load. A Newtownabbey man was arrested and later convicted.

The 'tout' also informed police that there were eighteen major importations of drugs by Lees and others. All came through Liverpool — from Amsterdam, Spain or Belgium. The Liverpool man took his cut and the rest was distributed to the other 'investors' who financed the deal. Between Manchester and Liverpool they used a huge shed to divide up the drugs shipment into three vans. Once a large man with ginger hair was spotted subsequently on a boat trip to Scotland.

Even worse for Lees was the fact that his good friend Paddy Farrell had been a Special Branch informer for around twenty years. Because of his work with 'the Branch' he was able to conduct his drug business virtually unmolested or untroubled. It was Farrell who apparently collected all the money to finance the drug runs to Amsterdam with the Liverpool syndicate. The late Ciaran Smith, who was murdered by terrorists, was in this category. And John Gilligan in Dublin was said to be involved in putting up a huge amount of money as well.

Through these various informants, the RUC Drug Squad got onto another notorious drug smuggler who operated in the Newry area along with Farrell. Speedy Fagan, who was later shot dead in a drug feud, was known to trade drugs, and the RUC informed the Gardaí about this involvement. My sources tell me the Gardaí subsequently recruited Fagan as a 'tout'. Watching Fagan, the Gardaí learned that he would meet customers in the Fairways Hotel in Dundalk and, after collecting the cash, he would direct them to a pub further down the Dublin road. The drugs were hidden in a cornfield beside the pub. Eventually, the Gardaí followed Fagan and saw him in Gilligan's warehouse and hit it in a raid, recovering a disappointing 25 kilos of coke.

According to my police sources, Fagan was killed because of 200 kilos stolen in a car in Dundalk. Fagan was into gambling and women. He bought women cars so that he could get into their knickers. He had £30,000 in cash on him when shot dead. And on the day he was killed, he had £25,000 on a pony and trap racing along the dual carriageway between Newry and Warrenpoint.

My police sources also tell me that most drug deaths relate to the paramilitary involvement in the drug trade. The deaths are regarded as 'just business'. The dealers have run their course and have no value any longer to the paramilitaries — Brendan Campbell, Bear Courtney and Ed McCoy. By killing these hard men the paramilitaries were able to take control of the business. And as Special Branch had taken control of all informants, including those of the Drug Squad, it meant that certain informants against the paramilitaries would be permitted to get away with a certain amount of 'business'.

So by the time the police found themselves in a position to question Lees about drugs, they knew quite a bit. Lees admitted to them that he knew the late Paddy Farrell as someone he did business deals with quite regularly. His admission came during questioning that touched on his friendship with Tony Meaghan.

Horan: I would argue it's not yours but that's . . . Do you know anybody called Anthony Meaghan?

Lees: I do, yes.

Horan: Where do you know him from?

Lees: He was involved in the business with me in 1993.

Horan: Do you have any contact with him now?

Lees: Sometimes, yeah.

Horan: Tell me this, do you know Paddy Farrell?

Lees: I do, yes.

Horan: Friend of yours?

Lees: Um, I knew him, I did some business with him.

But while he appeared to be willing to admit his business dealings and friendships with known terrorists (Noel Morrison) and drug dealers (Paddy Farrell), Lees will not tell police anything that would help them find Thomas Kelly, the mystery man who had, according to Lees, dictated to Lees some of the faxes relating to the purchase of the *Plongeur Wisky*. In some instances, Lees refers to a 'Tom Kelly' or a 'Mr Kelly', and during questioning he tried to say he was simply an errand boy following the orders of this Mr Kelly. But when asked where Mr Kelly could be contacted in order to confirm this or at least to ease the guilt on himself, Lees was vague and couldn't remember much about him.

But there was someone who did recall Mr Kelly very clearly indeed. Yet another nail was about to be driven into the coffin of Lees' criminal empire! Remember one of the women found in the house in Lytham St Anne's? Debbie Gabriel was about to provide police with a very important statement . . . but even when confronted with what she had to say, Lees refused to be fazed.

But there's no doubt it was almost as damning for Lees as the Game Plan. Here was someone who had worked alongside Lees, someone who had witnessed many letters and telephone calls, and who had spoken to many of Lees' so-called business acquaintances.

What she had to say was devastating. It solved some of the mysteries about Lees' criminal life. It's a statement worth repeating in some detail.

Debbie Gabriel told police that whilst she was a student at the University of Ulster, Jordanstown, doing a BA Honours in business studies during the 1995/96 academic year, she began part-time work at weekends in the Loughside Inn, Shore Road, in Belfast. She explained: 'I got this job through my aunt Zara who uses the surname Lees because she lives with Colin Lees at 12 Ardmoneen Court, Magherafelt, Co. Londonderry.' When Debbie finished her studies in 1996, her aunt offered her full-time employment at the pub doing office administration work — typing and answering the telephone. The 'typing' involved working on two word processors in the small office and, as far as Debbie Gabriel was aware, the offer of full-time employment came from 'Colin Lees through my aunt Zara'.

She then told police officers: 'As far as I know, the Loughside Inn was owned by Colin Lees and another man called Derek Jones. Routine matters were dealt with on a day-to-day basis by Norma Elder, the bookkeeper. Matters relating to finance were usually overseen by Colin Lees. Derek Jones also played a role in the business finances but Colin usually had the final say. From time to time my aunt Zara also helped out in the office. There was also a YTP person who would have done menial office tasks. During my time at the Loughside Inn one of the directors was a person called Nicky Bass. Nicky tried to make a success of the pub but after a period of time she became disheartened and left.'

She said Colin Lees asked her 'at least once a day' to either type up letters on an existing letterhead or draft up new ones. She remembered some of the letterheads Lees requested her to create as: 'Dame Hill with a Dublin address; International Traction

Services at Unit 8b, Waterfront Marine Industrial Estate, Lytham St Anne's; Alexander Hunter & Sons of 57 Hollybank, Ballyclare; The Loughside Inn, Shore Road, Belfast; Moira Direct Furnishings of Moira; Market One International Ltd of Maggs House, Bristol, and also one for the same company at Hogan House, Hogan Place, Canal Street, Dublin. There was another one from Market One International with an address in Stockport. There was also one called Clifton Transport with an address in Bristol and also with an address again in Hogan House in Dublin. There was another one called Shinerock Insurance Services and another one called Ancore (Encore) Export Ltd. Another one I recall was a company called Henninger Island Ltd with an address at Lower Fitzwilliam Street, Dublin. Another one I recall was Emlin Transport which I think was at the Southport address.'

According to Debbie Gabriel, when Lees wished to send a letter from one of the above companies he would write a draft letter out on a blank letterhead and pass it to her to type. She would then give him the printed letter. Then she or Norma Elder would fax some of Lees' letters at his request.

'I can recall specific occasions when I sent Henninger letters and Market One International letters to Hogan House in Dublin,' she said, before going on to reveal details of the drink scam being operated by Jones and Lees. 'They were always marked for the attention of a girl called Rita. I recall these letters always related to deliveries of spirits to a bonded warehouse in Dublin. I didn't think there was anything wrong with any of this as my understanding of a bonded warehouse was a place where a large quantity of drink was stored. The typed name of the sender at the foot of any letters I was asked to type would be typed on by me after typing the letter and the name would have been that as written by Colin Lees on the manuscript. Colin Lees called himself various names; for example when he wrote as Henninger he used the name Jonathan Murphy. I know this as I have heard him on the telephone referring to himself as Jonathan. Also on one occasion I travelled with Colin to the Easter furniture sale in Dublin. He was involved in a furniture business with a man known as Sidney Howard. Before going to the sale Colin Lees knew that Sidney Howard knew him as Jonathan Murphy and I was to refer to him as Jonathan Murphy and not Colin Lees. He also used the name Liam Simpson in signing Market One International letters. Another name he used, usually in connection with signing letters from Tristan Transport, was Thomas Kelly. I never met anyone called Jonathan Murphy, Liam Simpson or Thomas Kelly. Another businessman associated with Colin Lees came to the Loughside pub on several occasions. His name was James O'Kane, a brother of one of the drivers of Alexander Hunter & Sons Haulage Company, which was operated by Derek Jones and Colin Lees.'

Here, at last, the police had confirmation that Lees used a variety of false names, including the mysterious Thomas Kelly. It was poetry to the ears of the police officers who had endured hours of listening to the arrant nonsense of the bankrupt millionaire. Debbie went on to talk about how she had counted large sums of cash at the Loughside Inn for Lees. This cash represented the proceeds of the illicit sale of wine and spirits.

Debbie told the police that she knew about the large quantities of wines and spirits Lees was selling because of the amounts of money that were received in payment. She recalled one occasion when she had reason to check up on the available stock. She said Lees stored wines and spirits at the Loughside Inn and also at Alexander Hunter's yard at Hollybank Road, in Ballyclare. She said: 'I know this because Colin Lees asked me on one occasion to advise him on how many cases were left. I counted the ones at

Loughside and dispatched some to Hollybank. I can't remember the exact number of cases but in total it was somewhere in the region of 300 to 400 cases.'

In January 1997 Lees offered Debbie a job in Croydon, near London. She accepted. Lees was setting up an insurance brokerage. Once again, Debbie's work involved typing letters. She recalled one letter in particular which was addressed to Noel Morrison. 'It was,' she told police, 'drafted in manuscript by Colin Lees. I can't recall the full content of the letter but it was instructing Noel to be Les Loader and YTP who was known as Philip Adams. Noel Morrison was a friend of Colin Lees who was involved in a furniture business with Moira Direct Furnishings. Philip Adams I believe was a friend of Noel's, who in turn became a friend of Colin's and worked at Market One International Ltd. Before I moved to work in Croydon, Colin Lees instructed me to delete any Henninger correspondence that was on the computers in the Loughside Inn. I can recall that he seemed concerned about this as he subsequently asked me on a number of occasions if I had definitely deleted every-thing. After a couple of months working in Croydon the insurance business collapsed and I went back home to Northern Ireland.'

But it wasn't long before Lees offered Debbie another job in England. In April 1997 he wanted her to continue secretarial work at the Lytham St Anne's offices of International Traction Services. The office was based at the Waterfront Marine Industrial Estate. It was clear to Debbie that the company was run by Lees as part of Alexander Hunter & Son. This, of course, was at variance with Lees' stated position on these companies. Debbie's office was at the top of the building and, although small, there was just about enough space for two desks and a filing cabinet. There were two other small offices — one used by Lees, who shared it with Noel Morrison and Philip Samuel Adams. Sometimes James O'Kane would also use Lees' office. By this stage Debbie had downloaded all the letterheads on to two floppy discs that she nicknamed 'Doodles One and Doodles Two'. Doodles, she explained to the interviewing detectives, was her nickname. The letterheads had travelled with her to Croydon and then on to Lytham St Anne's, where new ones were added to the discs.

At first she was employed by International Traction Services at the Lytham St Anne's warehouse, but as time progressed she was asked to do more and more word processing on Market One International letterheads. Colin Lees always dictated letters to her or provided handwritten drafts. On rare occasions James O'Kane would have asked her to process letters on Market One International Ltd paper. And strangely enough, on these rare occasions James O'Kane would have used the name Thomas Kelly or James Kelly. Debbie also told the police that during the three months that she worked at the warehouse, between April and June 1997, 'there wasn't a lot of evidence of the movement of freight'.

She described seeing cases of vodka on wooden pallets in the warehouse, and in an open area overlooking the warehouse there was a table with various samples of beers, wines and spirits. According to Debbie, Lees and James O'Kane were the only people who seemed to bother with the samples. The only other use made of the warehouse was for the storage of used cars — another business Colin Lees was involved in with Noel Morrison.

Debbie Gabriel was providing useful information about Lees and his so-called businesses. She remembered getting business cards printed for Lees from a local printing company. Lees told her what he wanted to put on the business cards, which were then printed out on the computer before taking it to the printing company. Lees then gave his approval after seeing a sample card. She went on to explain: 'These cards were for the company Market

One International Ltd. The cards Colin Lees requested were to bear the name Liam Simpson and the cards for James O'Kane were to be in James O'Kane's own name. Colin Lees also requested the design of invoice books which would be used for Market One International. These subsequently were never printed.'

Zara's niece also provided an insight into life at 19a Riley Avenue: 'Noel Morrison, Philip [Samuel] Adams also stayed there. Colin Lees also stayed there from time to time. Colin Lees and the other two would have what I would call business meetings in the house at 19a Riley Avenue, St Anne's, but I was never included in these — in fact, on occasions when I entered a room the conversation that was going on would cease immediately.' No doubt they did not want to let Debbie know of their scheme to import £17m worth of cannabis.

In May 1997, she said Colin Lees invited her to attend a wine trade fair in London. Debbie travelled to London on 21 May 1997 and met Colin Lees there. At the trade fair they registered — Lees was using the name Liam Simpson and used his newly printed Market One International Ltd business cards. The information was recorded on a computer and the police were later able to check with the organisers of the trade fair and recover details and evidence for the drink scam case against Lees and Jones.

She even recalled signing a letter to Her Majesty's Customs and Excise in Bristol on behalf of 'J. Kelly, director'. The letter bore the heading Way Early Ltd and quoted a VAT number. When police showed her a copy of the letter she told them: 'Colin Lees gave me a manuscript draft which I produced and which I signed on his behalf and on his instruction. I can confirm the signature's mine but can't recall why I pp'd the letter.'

Lees listened patiently as the entire statement was read aloud by Det. Const. Horan. When he had finished, the police officer said to Lees that it was obvious from the young woman's statement that he, Colin Lees, ran the companies she mentioned.

Lees: I did not run those companies.

Horan: You did not run those companies, so what Debbie Gabriel states is inaccurate?

Lees: No, I think you have taken Debbie Gabriel, a secretary with a limited knowledge who worked for me stating totally out of perspective.

Horan: You think so?

Lees: I know so.

Horan: Is what she's saying accurate?

Lees: No, nor would she be in a position to know. It's like you putting the fear of God into a young girl and asking those specific questions.

Horan: Do you feel that's what's happened?

Lees: I think that's what you have done, yeah.

Horan: I didn't take that statement, but nice thought.

Lees was ready for trial. In fact, he had a number of trials to face on charges relating to the evasion of nearly £2m duty on alcohol; fraud of £23m; money laundering and importing £17m worth of cannabis.

9 The Legalities of Justice

'He was never listed, even as a witness. We couldn't even get him as a witness because the Crown decided that he was not going to appear. My lawyers were of the opinion that he should have been brought across here from Northern Ireland.'

Malcolm Baillie, who ran Lees Group Scotland with his son Stuart, reflecting on the fact that Lees was not brought before the Scottish courts alongside the two Baillies on fraud charges.

❖

Colin Lees might have been in custody for less than forty-eight hours, but the Operation Kilbreck detectives thought he was just about ready to charge with the drug shipment. The arrests of Derek Jones and others four months earlier had enabled them to build up their case against Lees and, having witnessed his performance in the interview rooms, they were confident of a successful prosecution.

So, by the end of questioning on the second day the police prepared to charge him with drug running. Having made their intentions known, Lees' solicitor sought a break in the interview during which he advised Lees not to answer any further questions. It was just before 8 p.m. on 11 October 1997 when the interview resumed.

Horan: This is the continuation of an interrupted interview. The time is 19.48 by the interview room clock. I was going to ask you some questions. Your solicitor has already made representation in relation to those questions. The first thing I'm going to say to you is we questioned you in relation to your . . . or we mentioned that you may have been in possession of the phone number of a Kevin Lafferty. If I can now say to you that found in your property was the phone number, actually found in your wallet on the 10th June, was the phone number of a Dessie McIlroy, who was also detained on the *Plongeur Wisky*. Do you wish to offer any explanation for that?

Lees: No, on the advice of my solicitor I can't make any comment, any further comment on that.

Horan: You also said that Noel Morrison uses the alias David Reid. Then you said in your interview that Kelly dictated to you faxes which you produced and which were personalised David Reid. Are you saying that Noel Morrison and Thomas Kelly are one and the same person?

Lees: Again, on the advice of my solicitor I can't answer that.

Horan: You mentioned in the interview, and I didn't give you an opportunity to expand on it, that you used a number

235

of aliases and they were used primarily to prevent people pre-judging you in relation to your business dealings and that you said you had a whole lot of people who would be prepared to back up the fact that after they got to know you they then were prepared . . . you then were prepared to give your real name, and the business relationship developed from that. Could you tell me who those people were so that we can check that?

Lees: On my solicitor's advice I can't answer any more questions.

Horan: You also said that the things that went on in the company and the office and discussions about the boat to which you were not really privy to and I didn't really ask you to clarify who else was in the office at the time, what the size of the office was, in other words, how many people work in the office and why you weren't involved in these discussions, bearing in mind that you're the financial advisor to Mr Jones.

Lees: Again I can't answer that question.

Horan: OK, is there anything else you want to say, Mr Lees, in relation to your previous interviews?

Lees: No, I don't think so.

Horan: Mr Lees, normally we charge you off tape but since you're here and since we have the charge sheet, I think we'll just charge you now. OK. Those questions were purely to clear up some ambiguity; you were always going to be charged. I must tell you, you are charged with the offences shown below. You do not have to say anything, but I must caution you that if you do not mention now something which you later rely on in court it may harm your defense, if you do say anything it may be given in evidence. You are charged that you on a date unknown between the 1st day of September 1996 and the 2nd day of November 1996 at Belfast in the County Court Division of Belfast assisted in or induced the commission of an offence at County Clare in the Republic of Ireland, namely the unlawful possession with intent to supply controlled drugs, an offence punishable under the provisions of a corresponding law in force in the Republic of Ireland contrary to Section 20 of the Misuse of Drugs Act 1971. Have you anything to say in answer to that charge?

Lees: Not guilty.

Horan: You are further charged that you on a date unknown between the 1st day of September 1996 and the 2nd day of November 1996 at Belfast in the County Court Division of Belfast assisted in or induced the commission of an offence at County Clare in the Republic of Ireland, namely the unlawful importation of controlled drugs, an offence punishable under the provision of a corresponding law enforced in the Republic of Ireland contrary to Section 20 of the Misuse of Drugs Act 1971. Have you anything to say in answer to that charge?

Lees: Not guilty.

Horan: The time of charge is 19.53 on the interview clock. My watch reads 19.50. The time of the charge is 19.50 on the 11th.

What was unique about the prosecution of the *Plongeur Wisky* case was that it was the first time that the State had used Section 20 of the Misuse of Drugs Act. 'Under Section 20 they could bring Lees to book in the United Kingdom for an offence that was actually committed outside the jurisdiction — in this case the

237

Republic,' said Det. Const. Horan. 'It meant the prosecution had to prove that Lees has induced an act outside the United Kingdom that contravened the laws not only in this State but in the other as well. A Garda officer came to court with a copy of a certificate signed by the Republic's Justice Minister, David Andrews, which stated that it was an offence to import drugs into the Republic.'

So Colin Lees was set for trial. But no one could have guessed just how much trouble lay ahead as Lees received legal aid to contest his guilt at the expense of the taxpayer — even though millions he had fleeced from his £23m fraud were still unaccounted for. And just as he had arrogantly believed in the interview room that he could hoodwink the police, he now believed he could hoodwink the judicial system as well. Before justice could be dispensed, Lees would create judicial havoc over the next three years by first pleading guilty to all charges, then seeking the court's permission to change those pleas — a move which necessitated a new trial just as he was about to be sentenced and a move which in the process almost ruined the career of a highly regarded and respected barrister. Not that it mattered much to Lees, who arrogantly rode roughshod over a system of justice designed to protect the innocent until proven guilty. All along Lees knew he was far removed from innocence and was guilty as charged. It was yet another example of how he was happy to stick his nose into the trough to make extensive use of other people's money. And when finally convicted, Lees enjoyed the protection of the court from having his life of crime reported in the media — an issue which had ramifications for press freedom and which was unsuccessfully challenged in court by one broadcaster, the BBC.

Lees made his debut in the dock on the drug trafficking charges on 14 October 1997. Det. Const. Horan told the magistrate that Lees had replied 'not guilty' when charged. The detective said there was a strong objection to bail and added: 'We have information to suggest that the person behind the importation is the defendant, Colin Lees.' Lees' solicitor, Brendan Kearney, objected to the court hearing any more allegations on the grounds that there had not been an application for bail. That, he explained, would be made later in the High Court. But Lees' days of freedom were over and he remained in custody right through to the end.

But, of course, by the time Lees made his first courtroom appearance, many others caught up in his criminal conspiracies were already before the courts in three jurisdictions — Northern Ireland, the Republic of Ireland and Scotland. Indeed, the Dublin courts had already dispensed justice to the crew of the *Plongeur Wisky* — skipper Kevin Lafferty from Donegal, Dessie McElroy from Ballymena and Andrew Kelly from Aston in Birmingham. Lafferty had been given a six-year jail sentence on 22 April. And the boat itself, the *Plongeur Wisky*, had been sold on behalf of the Revenue Commissioners for IR£45,000 in June 1997 — four days before the Operation Kilbreck raids and four months before Lees' arrest.

What is more remarkable perhaps is that the Scottish fraud investigation headed by Det. Insp. Angus Chisholm of the Inverness Constabulary reported in the spring of 1993, and yet it was not until 16 November 1998 that the trial reached the High Court in Edinburgh. In the absence of any explanation for this extensive delay it is perhaps worth considering that the Scottish authorities — aware of the ongoing investigations in Northern Ireland into Colin Lees — agreed to a process whereby the trials would in effect be 'choreographed'. Either way, the accused in Scotland, Malcolm Baillie and his son Stuart, were unimpressed by the fact that Lees was not brought before the Scottish court to face the allegations of £13m fraud. It turned out to be the longest trial in the history of the High Court in Edinburgh. From the comfort of his prison cell, Lees observed from afar the results of his handiwork in Scotland — no doubt thankful that he was not to be involved in the case, not even as a witness.

Malcolm Baillie and his son Stuart had been arrested in Birmingham on Wednesday, 29 January 1997. Next day they were charged at Inverness Sheriff Court where the Scottish public prosecutor said the sum involved in the alleged fraud was almost £13m. Both men were granted bail. But it was a move that cost Stuart Baillie dearly.

For while the Baillies watched five years go by since the collapse of the Lees Group Scotland with debts of over £8m and since they had last been interviewed by police in the spring of 1992, Stuart Baillie had moved to the west coast of Ireland and had become the managing director of the State's largest fish-farming company, Gaelic Seafoods (Ireland) Ltd. While angry creditors in Scotland were fruitlessly campaigning to get their money back and while the police were examining a fraud of almost £13m, Stuart Baillie had teamed up with one of the wealthiest men in Ireland to establish Gaelic Seafoods. In 1995, the company took over the bulk of ESB salmon farming — the fish-farming subsidiary of cigarette company P.J. Carroll. In an amazing turn of events, Stuart Baillie and Gaelic Seafoods had returned to Scotland to purchase the remnants of the Lees Group from the receivers, Ernst & Young. Now, Gaelic Seafoods was the market leader in Ireland — with a managing director in trouble with the law. Stuart Baillie was obliged to step aside 'voluntarily and temporarily pending the resolution of the judicial process'.

Once in Edinburgh, the court accepted medical evidence that Malcolm Baillie was — at seventy-one years of age — too ill to withstand the stresses and strains of the trial. He was excused from the dock, leaving his 39-year-old son there alone. For six months the court listened to the evidence against Stuart Baillie — most of it contained in the sixteen cases of documents positioned at the front of the courtroom. During 101 days the jurors listened to a story that must have seemed at times to have more in common with a spy novel than a criminal case. Judge Robin McEwan described the trial as 'unique'.

The court was told that what began as a ruse to foil IRA bombers led to a string of frauds involving bogus leases for heavy industrial plant and equipment. The court also heard that a key figure in setting up the operation was working for the intelligence service MI6 and that at one early business meeting a revolver was left on the table at Baillie's Inverness home. It was the secret agent who was responsible for introducing Malcolm Baillie to Colin Lees. In court, the MI6 agent was not identified by name.

But according to the Baillies, and police sources and solicitors involved in the Scottish trial, it was a reference to Chris Nicholson, the man who denied involvement with MI6. But then he also said that even if he was the MI6 man he was not likely to admit it to me. What is clear, however, from talking to the Baillies is that Nicholson offered to assist in Malcolm's defence if the court would agree to him giving evidence anonymously and from behind a screen. The Baillies' solicitors apparently went through some strange arrangements in order to meet Nicholson. According to Malcolm and Renee Baillie, their solicitors were given to clearly understand that Lees had close links to the security services in Northern Ireland and that Nicholson was one of those close links as an MI6 agent.

Malcolm Baillie told me about the offer of help from Nicholson: 'He certainly contacted my solicitor and offered to give evidence on my behalf and that was on the Friday before the court was due to open and he claimed that he would only do it behind a screen or with a written statement. The Crown checked it out because they were of the opinion that you often get cranks doing these things to stop or postpone things. They checked him out and they found that it was bona fide and I declined his offer of coming to give evidence because by that time I didn't trust him.'

The prosecutor told the court that Stuart Baillie used his position as a director of Marine Structures, the Lees Group Scotland and a string of subsidiaries in fish farming, construction and forestry to front the fraudulent scheme. It was said he obtained cash from finance companies pretending it was for plant and equipment which was put up as security. But the same equipment was used in more than one deal, some was worth only a fraction of its alleged value and sometimes none was actually supplied at all. Brokers were told of business which simply did not exist — such as a claimed £2.7m contract to supply telegraph poles to the Syrian government.

Advocate depute Alan Dewar, prosecuting, said that without the millions flowing in from the bogus leasing deals, the companies would not have survived. He explained that in the beginning many of the purchases were said to have been supplied by the Plant Corporation Ireland — a Colin Lees company that was later exposed as a sham. But, he continued, Stuart Baillie became tired of the cut going to Lees for doing nothing. A copycat operation was set up, registered as the Nationwide Plant Corporation. But it was 'a complete sham' established to generate false invoices. No figure was ever given as to how much Stuart Baillie benefited personally but the court did hear of American Express bills totalling £23,000 being paid.

Stuart Baillie did not give evidence but he presented a defence that it was Colin Lees who had benefited from the fraudulent activity. Baillie's defence team made the case that Baillie had been

242

used as a 'patsy' to front up companies which Lees wanted to use in Scotland to continue the kind of fraud he had begun back home in Northern Ireland. The prosecution said that whatever the jurors thought of Lees, there was sufficient evidence to indicate that Stuart Baillie was doing his own deals. The defence countered that Lees would fly over to Inverness from time to time in his private plane or helicopter — which was also subject of leasing deals.

But the defence could not call Colin Lees to testify. This angered Malcolm Baillie, who told me: 'He was never listed, even as a witness. We couldn't even get him as a witness because the Crown decided that he was not going to appear. My lawyers were of the opinion that he should have been brought across here from Northern Ireland.'

More than seventy witnesses were called to give testimony. It was reported in the *West Highland Free Press* on 25 June 1999, that 'the closing speeches lasted longer than many High Court trials'. The jury deliberated for three days and cleared Baillie of some offences, but on majority verdicts they found him guilty of offences with a face value of almost £8m.

The defence advocate Robert Henderson QC insisted that throughout, Stuart Baillie had been no more than an accessory, acting under orders from the real perpetrator of the frauds, Colin Lees. He also informed the court that Baillie had not gained anything as a result and the cost to him of being forced to resign his company directorships following his arrest came to £200,000. Further, Henderson told the court, since the investigations began in 1991, Baillie — who had never been in trouble before — had led a blameless life. He had already suffered by having the matter hanging over his head. 'No purpose whatsoever will be served by sending this man to prison years and years after the offences,' Henderson said in court.

Those pleas for leniency were backed by testimonials from business associates, including a former president of the Irish accountants' professional association and a member of the Dáil for the Galway area. Judge McEwan, acknowledging 'the most eloquent plea in mitigation I have ever heard,' went on to say that a jail sentence was inevitable, given the jury's verdict. He added: 'The sum they have found you guilty of is enormous, almost £8m, and I would be failing in my duty if I took a lenient view of that.'

Judge McEwan said the leasing companies who were the victims of these frauds were claiming capital allowances, so ultimately anyone paying tax was a loser. No evidence was given during the trial about how far the finance houses were left out of pocket, and the defence argued that they were not interested because they had already made their profit 'up-front'. The judge praised the jury, describing the eight men and seven women as 'very special'. He added: 'It is a matter of considerable pride that we have kept all fifteen of you on board for all this time, which is not easy.' The judge said it was open to him to excuse the fifteen jurors for life. But he wasn't going to do that. He concluded his remarks to the jurors by saying: 'I do not think that would be appropriate, if only because you are possibly the most experienced jurors in Scotland and Scotland is ever likely to see. I am going to excuse you for ten years. It does not mean you are disqualified, merely that if cited again you are entitled to be excused if you so wish.'

There was to be no escape hatch for the accused. On 7 July 1999, Judge McEwan gave Stuart Baillie a five-year jail term. He was granted bail pending an appeal and returned to Ireland to try to pick up the pieces of his shattered career — something he managed to do in spite of a string of anonymous letters and telephone calls to his various employers informing them of his Scottish conviction.

While Stuart Baillie was still enjoying his freedom in Dublin, one hundred miles north, Colin Lees had begun making regular appearances in court from his prison cell. Of course, he wasn't alone. A string of others were also before the courts including his sidekick Derek Jones, three of the 'Donegal Five' and a couple of others on the periphery of his business empire. The effect of this series of separate trials was that reporting restrictions were placed on the trials for fear that it could prejudice the other trials by influencing the juries. So for most of his time in prison, few details emerged about the extent of Lees' criminal past. He was a blessed man in this respect. And it could be argued that he tried to protect that position, to maintain the infuriating and frustrating silence surrounding his worst excesses. Nevertheless, the Belfast courts were kept busy.

- On 12 April 1999 Lees made his first important court appearance to plead guilty to a total of forty-seven charges involving theft and fraud of £23m from his own company as well as a string of lending institutions.
- On 7 September 1999 he appeared again to plead guilty to involvement in the £2m drinks scam he operated with Derek Jones.
- Just two days later Lees' co-accused, Jones, went on trial on the drinks scam charges. The trial ended on 29 September with his acquittal on eight charges, while the jury was hung on eleven others.
- Next day, 30 September, Lees pleads guilty to involvement in the drug smuggling operation. Lees' admissions, together with the fact that he was awaiting sentence for the theft and fraud charges and the drinks scam, was reported in the media.

- On 10 October, Jones went on trial for the drug smuggling and was finally acquitted by jury on 27 October. But a reporting ban on coverage of the Jones case was enforced by the then trial judge Mr Justice Higgins on the grounds that Jones faced trial on other charges of money laundering for the Mafia and a retrial on the drinks scam.

- On 6 December 1999 Jones appeared before Mr Justice Higgins to admit two charges relating to the drinks scam and to laundering Mafia money — and to laundering money with Lees. Jones was given four years imprisonment on the drink charges and five years on the money laundering. As the sentences were suspended, he walked free from court and returned to Florida in the United States. Reporting of the case was banned because of the money laundering charges to be dealt with in the Lees case.

- On 20 December 1999 the proverbial shit hit the fan in the Crown Court. Lees was distraught when he learned that his American pal had walked free and had been acquitted of the drugs charges. He clearly felt that Jones being cleared of the drugs charges by a jury suggested that he too could be cleared . . . except, of course, by this stage he had admitted the drugs charges in court. Now he turned his anger on his legal team. He sacked them, leaving experienced and highly respected barrister Eugene Grant to stand up in court and explain to the trial judge that he would no longer be representing his client, who now wished to change his legal team and apply to the High Court to set aside his guilty pleas and to again plead not guilty. Reporting restrictions remained in place throughout all this, because of the prospect of four jury trials in the Lees cases.

As Lees prepared to go into battle on all fronts, the fallout of his actions and the subsequent legal ramifications were — behind the scenes — slowly beginning to unfold. But few knew exactly what was going on. The rumours ended only when Mr Justice Higgins ruled on the Lees application to vacate his guilty pleas. What he had to say in his judgement on 18 February 2000 was revealing in that it confirmed much of what the public have long suspected or known about the 'horse trading' that takes place in the corridors of judicial power. At the centre of the dispute between Lees and his legal team were the events on 12 April 1999 — the day Lees pleaded guilty in court to fraud charges. Mr Justice Higgins began by referring briefly to the sequence of events leading up to the hearing he was conducting:

> At the opening of the Crown Court in January Mr Grant applied for the case which was ready to proceed to be adjourned until April. This application was acceded to and the trial was fixed for 12 April 1999. On that date the accused pleaded guilty to forty-six counts in Bill 5A [Fraud Case]. On 9 December 1999 Mr Grant applied in person to vacate all the pleas previously entered and at the same time informed the Court that he was then withdrawing from the case. That application was adjourned to the new term and came on for hearing on Friday, 4 February. Mr Harvey QC appeared, instructed by Madden & Finucane, both appearing pro bono.

The judge then explained that Mr Harvey had spoken to witnesses to all the principal events and that included consultations with Eugene Grant and a written submission from him.

The following is a chronological record of Mr Harvey's opening of the factual background. In June 1998 following judicial review proceedings office facilities were made available to the accused at Maghaberry prison in order to permit him to cope with the volume of papers in the substantial fraud case. In July 1998 the accountants Goldblatt and McGuigan were engaged to provide their professional services. Mr Anthony Brennan of Keaney Kelly and Company was allocated to work on the case full-time.

The fraud case Bill 5A was listed for hearing on 12 April 1999, which was the first day of term following the Easter vacation. In the three week period prior to 12 April Mr Rodgers, junior counsel, attended with the accused almost daily for consultation. At no time during the course of that preparation nor earlier had the question been broached with the accused as to the appropriateness or otherwise of a plea of guilty. It had always been the accused's intention to contest these charges.

On the morning of 12 April 1999 Mr Kearney and Mr Brennan attended at Belfast Crown Court and discussed with the accused in an interview room the process of jury swearing. At approximately 11.30 the accused met Mr Grant, Mr Rodgers, Mr Kearney and Mr Brennan in a consultation room. At that consultation Mr Grant told the accused that he had been approached by the Crown prosecutor to see if he could come to an arrangement with the Crown on all his pending cases. (This was despite the fact that at this stage the accused had not yet been returned for trial on the Customs and Excise case, or the money laundering case and no judge had been allocated nor had he seen sight of the papers in those cases nor the drugs case.) Mr Grant also informed the accused that the Crown approach was to treat the fraud case as 'the number one case'. He said this was a significant shift in ground as the drug case potentially would carry a much higher or significantly higher sentence. The accused was told that an overall sentence for all the outstanding cases, including that for which it was proposed the trial would begin that day, could be achieved in single figures if the accused pleaded guilty to all outstanding charges. In addition he was told that charges against his partner Zara Lees would be taken care of. Mr Grant then went on to explain how this agreement would work. He told the accused that this arrangement would have to be ratified by a Crown Court judge but also told him that Mr Creaney would be in attendance with him and that the judge hearing the case would be a judge of Mr Grant's choice. The accused was shocked and taken aback by what he heard. Mr Grant asked the accused to consider what was on offer. He also told him that he was stupid not to accept the offer because of the risks involved in the drugs case. Mr Grant, Mr Rodgers and Mr Brennan left. The accused asked Mr Kearney to remain behind as he wished to speak to him on his own. He consulted with Mr Kearney and Mr Kearney advised him against taking the course of action set out by Mr Grant.

Later that day, Lees informed Eugene Grant in the present of other members of his legal team that he did not wish to accept the Crown's proposed arrangement and that he wished to go ahead with the selection of the jury. The judge continued:

Mr Grant's reaction to that was exceptionally hostile. He advised the accused of his experience in these matters and the need to look at all of the cases outstanding in a pragmatic way. He told the accused he ought to accept the arrangement which was on offer. In relation to the question of sentencing, the accused asked him what that would mean. Mr Grant again indicated that it would mean a single figure sentence for all the offences. The accused specifically then asked by single figures did he mean eight years and the answer was 'probably'. The accused then said could it mean 'nine'. Mr Grant answered that the chances of nine were minimal. The accused was told he would have to trust Mr Grant. The accused was distressed by the course of these developments. He then requested to speak to Mr Kearney on his own. Mr Grant responded by telling him that it would be entirely inappropriate for him to speak to Mr Kearney on his own. Mr Grant then informed the accused that he was privy to information which he could not discuss with any of those present and that he would personally guarantee the arrangement which he had set out earlier. As a result of that the accused eventually agreed to change his plea to guilty and on leaving the room stated to Mr Grant 'I am depending on you'. Mr Grant said 'Trust me'. At this meeting neither Mr Rodgers, Mr Kearney nor Mr Brennan spoke or expressed any opinion. The accused was then taken to court and pleaded guilty to Bill 5A. He was then put back for sentence. Following the appearance of the accused in court on 12 April Mr Rodgers expressed grave reservations to Mr Brendan Kearney as to what had occurred during the course of the morning and early afternoon of the 12th but on the basis that Mr Grant was privy to information that they were not, he felt he could not take those reservations further.

Following this court appearance on 12 April, there followed a number of meetings at Maghaberry Prison between Lees and Grant at which the barrister continued to reassure Lees about the commitment to an overall sentence being achieved in single figures and of eight years. But things became heated at a meeting in the prison in July. The judge's ruling continued:

Present were Mr Grant, Mr Kearney, Mr Gordon Talbot and Mr Martin Rodgers who arrived late. At this meeting Mr Grant informed the accused that he had spoken with the judge and that an arrangement had been made whereby the accused would receive a sentence of eight years for the fraud case, five years for the customs case concurrent with the eight years, and a consecutive sentence of five years for the drugs case, making a total sentence of thirteen years. The accused was devastated and told Mr Grant of the personal undertakings that he had made to him on 12 April and went over those in detail. Mr Grant suggested to him that he could fight the drugs case. The accused pointed out to Mr Grant that the only reason why he had pleaded guilty to the first case was on Mr Grant's advice as to 'a wrap up sentence in all cases'. The accused indicated at all stages his absolute reluctance to plead guilty in the drugs case. Again matters became heated, and the accused made known his feelings of betrayal. Mr Grant then left saying that if he did not agree with what was happening then he could speak to Mr Kearney. Mr Kearney was only able to stay for a matter of moments as transport had been arranged to take all the parties back. Mr Rodgers expressed his concern that the position had altered from that which he understood it to be on 12 April when Mr Grant had informed those present that he was privy to information which they were not and invited the accused to trust him. (Mr Rodgers was only involved in the one case Bill 5A and had no input in to either the drugs or the customs cases in which Mr Talbot was the junior.)

The following morning the accused contacted his instructing solicitor, Mr Kearney, by phone and an arrangement was made to meet Mr Kearney and Mr Talbot during the course of his next remand at the magistrates' court (the accused was on weekly remand at this stage in respect of the other charges for which he had yet to be returned for trial).

At this meeting both Mr Talbot and Mr Kearney were made aware by the accused of his extreme concern for the position he now found himself in and he asked for advice in relation to the pleas that he had already entered. The accused was told that Mr Grant was still hopeful of achieving the original outcome as set out on 12 April and that over the course of the summer Mr Grant would continue to negotiate on his behalf.

There was no further contact between Lees and Grant during the remainder of the summer of 1999. But in the first week of September, at Eugene Grant's request, a meeting was held outside the prison attended by Zara, Lees' solicitor Mr Kearney and the junior counsel, Mr Talbot. They discussed a note handwritten by Eugene Grant which outlined a proposed custody/probation order dealing specifically with the probation aspects of such a sentence. Arthur Harvey noted that this note appeared to indicate to the accused that he would be released within two-and-a-half years or earlier.

Lees was reassured when he met Mrs Briedge Gadd, head of the Probation Service, and Brendan Fulton, the chief prison probation officer at Maghaberry Prison, at the law courts on September 7. They spent time going through the suitability of the accused for probation and created the impression in Lees' mind that what had been outlined to him previously was correct. Mr Justice Higgins went on:

At approximately 2.30 p.m. the accused asked Mr Grant to attend. Mr Grant did so and confirmed at the meeting the matter set out in the handwritten document. The accused was still reluctant to plead guilty to these outstanding charges. When asked what he wished to do he indicated that his only option as it seemed to him at that time was to discharge those representing him and obtain new legal representation or accept what was set out in the document. Mr Grant then left the interview room and for a short time Mr Kearney and Mr Talbot went over the arrangements now proposed by Mr Grant. On the basis of those arrangements the accused was then asked to give authority to proceed to plead guilty to the Customs and Excise charges. The accused gave that authority in writing in the following terms:

'I Colin Lees have been advised by my Senior Counsel that I will serve a maximum effective prison sentence of eleven years this sentence will be in respect of all charges that I presently face outstanding money laundering charge will be tic'd. I also consent to

custody/probation order being made of two years and
understand that it is an integral part of my sentence.

Signed: Colin Lees
Witness: Signature illegible
Dated: 7/9/99.'

This authority was written by Mr Kearney. (Mr Harvey
commented that the accused was signing not in relation to
the customs charges which were before the court that day,
but a document relating to a comprehensive sentence
which was proposed in relation to all the counts which
were outstanding against him as well as those to which he
had already pleaded guilty.) The accused was then taken to
court and pleaded guilty to all the charges on Bill 336A.
[Customs case]

Eugene Grant visited Lees in prison and continued to assure
him that he would get all the benefits he had outlined. They also
discussed matters relating to the plea of mitigation. Then on 30
September, Lees was due to appear in court on the drugs charges,
as Mr Justice Higgins recounted.

On 30 September the accused met Mr Grant at the Crown
Court prior to being re-arraigned on Bill 169/1999 (the
drugs case). Mr Grant said to him 'everything is in order
now, lets just get this over with'. When the accused asked
if everything was all right he was told again 'trust me'. He
was then re-arraigned on Bill 169 and pleaded guilty.

On 20 October the accused met with his designated
probation officer, a Mr Paul Shepherd. There were three

meetings with regard to his suitability for probation. During those meetings it became apparent that Mr Shepherd had no knowledge of the 'early release scheme' referred to by Mr Grant in the handwritten document. The accused was informed that the Probation Service could not offer special case arrangements to any prisoner other than what was generally available to all. As a result of those conversations the accused contacted Madden & Finucane, solicitors, by phone and informed Kearney, Kelly and Company that he had done so.

Lees was now clearly intent on getting a new legal team for the benefit of fresh advice and a move to change his guilty pleas to not guilty. But he was on legal aid and was — for the time being at least — stuck with the legal team he had. On 11 November 1999 Lees had another meeting with a member of the Probation Service at which he had again been told there was no way the Probation Service could grant any form of early release. Mr Justice Higgins continued in his judgement to explain what happened next:

After this meeting the accused contacted Mr Kearney and indicated that he felt that he had been lied to in relation to the previous arrangements. On 17 November 1999 Mr Grant and Mr Kearney consulted with the accused at Maghaberry. At that consultation Mr Grant outlined what appeared to be the strength of the accused's pleas. The accused asked if these arrangements had been finalised with the judge and Mr Grant answered 'I won't be talking to him again, I will be doing this on my feet at the time of your sentence.' Again there was a heated exchange between Mr Grant and the accused. The accused made it clear to Mr

Grant that he believed that he had been betrayed by him over a considerable period of time and that everything that he had done over this last number of months had little to do with the presentation of his defence but was an attempt to repair the damage that had been done on 12 April. After this meeting the accused again contacted Madden & Finucane.

Lees continued meeting with Mr Kearney and on 22 November 1999 Lees was informed that his final appearance had been listed for 24 November. Lees said he was concerned he would once again be pressurised by unreliable information into following a course that he had never wished to proceed with in the first place. Mr Justice Higgins again:

On 24 November 1999 the accused was taken to Belfast Crown Court. He was put in a cell and told he was to be sentenced later that day but not before 2.00 p.m. He did not see Mr Grant during the course of the morning, but at approximately 1.50 he was taken to the consultation room. Present were Mr Grant, Mr Talbot, Mr Rodgers and Mr Kearney. Mr Grant said he had considered his position and would be asking the judge for an adjournment in order to take the matter to the Court of Appeal in the next few days. He told the accused that he would accept in his application to the Court of Appeal that he had been over-zealous in his advice and that the accused's mind had been overborne at the time of the pleas. He informed the accused that there was legal precedent for this type of case. He further told him that he would resign from the case. Mr Talbot asked the accused if this course of action was acceptable to him, to which the accused replied 'yes'. Mr Grant then left the room. The accused was then taken to court. Mr Grant asked for the adjournment, which was granted.

That afternoon the accused contacted Madden & Finucane and explained what was proposed. With a view to taking the matter to the Court of Appeal Mr Grant then prepared grounds of appeal which are set out in Form 3:

Full Name Appellant: William John Colin Lees
Grounds of application for extension of time (including reasons for delay):

'At consultation for the sentencing procedure it became increasingly clear that the appellant's mind did not go with his acts when he entered his pleas.'

Ground of application for leave to appeal against conviction:

'The appellant's mind was overborne by senior defence counsel when he entered his pleas and he lost the power to make a free, voluntary and deliberate choice of plea.'

Dated this 26th day of November 1999.

SIGNED: _____
Brendan Kearney, Kelly & Co
Clarendon House
4 Clarendon Street
LONDONDERRY BT48 7EX

As it transpired, this was not the proper procedure. The case did not go to the Court of Appeal and was referred back to the Crown Court.

On 26 November the accused appeared at Belfast Magistrates Court on remand. There he spoke to Mr Talbot. They discussed the propriety of the application to have the plea set aside and the withdrawal of Mr Grant from the case. At that stage it was felt that this was the only course of action open to the accused. At that time the accused still had confidence in his two junior counsel, Mr Rodgers and Mr Talbot.

On 8 December 1999 Mr Kearney met the accused and informed him that the attempt to refer the matter to the Court of Appeal had been found to be procedurally incorrect and that the matter would be referred back to the trial judge. On 9 December 1999 the accused appeared at the Crown Court where Mr Grant attempted to vacate the pleas. As the procedure which Mr Grant proposed to adopt on that occasion was not appropriate, the case was further adjourned. There were then a number of meetings in relation to the case and the application then came on for hearing, as I have indicated, on 4 February 2000 and was moved by Mr Harvey.

In his ruling Mr Justice Higgins said that it was Arthur Harvey's opinion that Eugene Grant's behaviour represented a significant departure from the standards expected of senior counsel. Continuing to draw on the record of Mr Harvey's representations, Mr Justice Higgins went on:

He [**Arthur Harvey**] submitted that when one looks at the facts as outlined, the Court would be driven to the conclusion that a serious error of judgment was made on 12 April 1999 and that subsequent events were 'an attempt to repair that which was irreparable and to achieve by a circuitous route that which was unobtainable'. While counsel are entitled to be robust, he submitted there is a distinction to be drawn between what is robust and what is not acceptable. In this instance he submitted that events became so bad that senior counsel, Mr Grant, entered into a series of arrangements which were beyond his professional competence and in so doing deprived the accused of the opportunity to make a decision to plead guilty with a full appreciation of what he was doing and with an adequate understanding of what his pleas involved. He submitted that in circumstances where counsel had erroneously taken it upon himself to guarantee a sentence which was solely within the province of the court, and at the same time indicated to the accused that he was able to do so because he was privy to specialised information, he deprived the accused of that complete freedom of choice to which he was entitled, whether to plead guilty or not guilty. He further submitted that for defence counsel to allege that he could select a judge or make arrangements for senior probation officers to see an accused before sentence is passed to explain a sentence which had not yet been handed down, was something which deprived the accused of a proper appreciation of how the criminal justice system operates. It had the effect of distorting the function of defence counsel, prosecuting counsel and the judge as well as the position of the accused himself. He went on to submit that this situation was not one in which the accused had received a higher sentence than what he was expecting as occurred in several of the English cases to which he referred. This was a case in which an indication was given to the accused as to the precise nature of a sentence that he would receive at a time when no judge was in possession of all of the papers and could not have made an appropriate decision. He submitted that no conscientious counsel should allow himself to fall into the position of guaranteeing such a sentence and that there was only one course open to the court and that was to vacate the pleas.

The prosecution QC, John Creaney, agreed. Indeed, the judge agreed with Arthur Harvey's submission and he ruled that Lees' application to vacate his guilty pleas in all three bills — the drugs, drink and fraud cases — must be granted. But he did so only after adding his own observations on the chain of events that had thrown the Lees trials into chaos:

It was only when the junior probation officer sowed doubts in his [Lees] mind about the early release scheme did the accused seek to unravel his pleas of guilty in all three cases. The accused is no fool. He is a mature man with many years experience in business behind him. If he was not guilty of all or any of these charges would he have pleaded guilty to all of them. If he was guilty of some but not all, he might be tempted to plead guilty to all on a 'wrap up' basis, in the knowledge that the sentence which he might have received for all Bills was modest but justified for one or perhaps two of the Bills.

On the other hand it is difficult to dismiss Mr Harvey's analysis of the conduct of senior counsel — having promised that which he could not achieve he set about trying to

do so by other means, at the same time securing the com-
pliance of the accused to enter guilty pleas on two further
occasions. At the same time the accused was complicit in
permitting Mr Grant to do what he could for him.
However, the information he was given in September was
both incorrect and incomplete.

This is a unique situation. The accused has pleaded
guilty to sixty-eight counts, entered on three separate
occasions over a period of almost five months. He has had
throughout that period available to him the assistance of
two experienced junior counsel and a number of solicitors.
No court would vacate pleas in such circumstances lightly.
Furthermore, each Bill of Indictment requires to be considered separately as they occurred on widely separated
dates and in different circumstances.

An accused is entitled to complete freedom of choice in
the plea which he makes in response to a criminal charge.
No undue pressure should be exerted on him nor should his
situation then or in the future be misrepresented to him.
How do these circumstances measure up to those princi-
ples? Regrettably they do not. The statements made by Mr
Grant on 12 April 1999 were in effect inducements. Such
inducements (or even one of them) are sufficient to deprive
the accused of that freedom of choice as to his plea to
which he is entitled. Can a distinction be drawn between
the events of 12 April and the pleas entered in September?
Six matters appear to be relevant. First, the statements
made on 12 April referred to all the charges which the
accused faced. Second, the interlinkage of the second and
third pleas with each other and the first. Third, the hostile
nature of some of the exchanges. Fourth, the gross nature of

several of the misrepresentations. Five, the terms of the authority signed by the accused. Six, the statement by senior counsel that he was privy to information which he could not disclose and which was not known to the other lawyers. For counsel to proffer or promise inducements of this type or make statements of this nature to an accused person, is a grave departure from the duty of counsel in a criminal case and from the code of conduct of the Bar of Northern Ireland, as well as a desertion of the professional standards and ethics of the Bar which the judiciary and the public are entitled to expect from all members of that profession.

Having reviewed the facts as presented I find impossible to differ from Mr Harvey's submission that a serious error of judgment was made on 12 April 1999 which was irreparable and that subsequent events were an attempt by senior counsel to achieve by a circuitous route that which he had promised to the accused. The only conclusion I can come to therefore is that the accused was placed in a situation in which he no longer had that freedom of choice to which he was entitled and that his position in the event of the pleas of guilty was misrepresented to him. Therefore the application to vacate the pleas in all three Bills must be granted.

Eugene Grant was investigated. He was disciplined and he repaid the fees he had earned from the Lees case. A plea of mitigation was entered on his behalf in which it was made clear that he unreservedly accepted and apologised for the *grave departure from the duty of Counsel in a criminal case from the Code of Conduct of the Bar of Northern Ireland as well as the desertion of the Professional Standards and Ethics of the Bar which the judiciary and the public are entitled to expect from all members of his profession. Such conduct is unacceptable in any circumstances but it is of particular regret to him that his conduct has affected such an important case.'*

In mitigation, it was claimed that Eugene Grant was at all times attempting to *'act in the best interests of Colin Lees who faced what Mr Justice Gillen has described as overwhelming evidence and the risk of consecutive sentences in view of the seriousness of the offences and the fact that the drugs and Customs and Excise offences had been committed whilst on bail. Mr Grant did not knowingly attempt to mislead. He was at all times seeking to act in the best interests of Mr Lees. He did not set about to mislead nor did he stay in the case to or subsequently attempt to repair that which was in fact irreparable and achieve that which was unattainable by a circuitous route.'*

Further, in mitigation, it was stated on Eugene Grant's behalf: *'Mr Grant appreciates and accepts that by overbearing the will of an accused person he transgressed the role of Counsel in the administration of criminal justice. In the event, any risk of an innocent person being convicted has not materialised. Mr Lees has been convicted of the drugs charges (there was a conclusive document referred to as 'the game plan' in his handwriting, to which there was no explanation and no answer) and has now pleaded guilty to all the other charges including the fraud charges (in relation to which Mr Justice Gillen has said that 'the evidence was so overwhelming the result would have been virtually inevitable . . . .')*

It now appears that Colin Lees' solicitor has written on his instructions by letter dated 1 November 2000 that he appreciates the professional work carried out by Mr Grant and wishes him success in his professional career. This was not solicited by Mr Grant and is indicative of either a lack of sincerity in Mr Lees' original allegation that his mind did not go with his pleas or of his manipulative approach. The following factors are relevant to both such views, namely:

(a) At no stage did Mr Lees appear to Mr Grant to be shocked, distressed or under pressure or taken aback by Mr Grant's remarks to him.

(b) Mr Kearney is of the view that Mr Lees knew that he was taking a gamble and that he was prepared to take a risk.

(c) Mr Lees was a mature man with many years experience in business behind him and in the words of Mr Justice Higgins was 'no fool'.

(d) Mr Lees has now pleaded guilty to the fraud charges, the Customs and Excise charges and the money laundering charges.

(e) The assessment of Mr Justice Gillen was that Mr Lees was 'a man of some intelligence' with 'undoubted ability' but that 'once apprehended [he] skilfully, albeit unsuccessfully, attempted to outwit those who were questioning [him] and showed absolutely no remorse for what [he] had done, exhibiting only a criminal defiance in the face of overwhelming evidence'. Also that the fraud that he committed 'was a crime motivated by sheer greed and actuated by clever manipulation and planning'.

Lees had indeed been found guilty of the drugs charges . . . but not before another hitch in the proceedings. His drugs trial began in September 2000 but was soon aborted for legal reasons. It appears that during an officer's testimony in which he was reading aloud from transcripts of the tape-recorded interviews with Lees, the jury got sight of material they should not have seen on special screens provided to help them understand what was going on. It was material that had been edited out of all copies, except those given to the jurors.

The re-trial began a few weeks later. By 19 October 2000 Lees was found guilty of drug smuggling. Prosecuting, John Creaney QC had opened the trial by describing the events at Malin Head, describing the people involved there with particular interest in Noel Morrison as the individual responsible for the purchase of the *Plongeur Wisky*, along with his friend and co-conspirator Colin Lees. He carefully explained to the jury the significance of the communications from Dame Hill Ltd in Dublin to the boat owners in Gibraltar — Morrison using the name David Reid but letters on 'Reid's' behalf being in Lees' handwriting. He highlighted the details of the telephones used by those on the boat and those waiting at Malin Head.

But the clinching documents were those referred to by the prosecutor as 'the Game Plan.' He addressed the jurors: 'I use the term Game Plan here and really [it is] of considerable significance because this is on the back of a sheet [on which] the names Kevin Lafferty and McElroy are written. If you recollect, the people who arrive in Kilrush or are found in Kilrush on the boat are Kevin Lafferty from Donegal and Dessie McElroy from Ballymena. So, members of the jury, these documents which were found were the key to, very largely, the key to Mr Lees' involvement. They speak for themselves; they speak out; they are a thread. What we say basically — starting with that letter and this document, that puts this man [Lees] in the heart of the plan.'

John Creaney referred briefly to some of the contradictions in Lees' answers to the police in relation to, for example, the boat about which he first claimed to know nothing . . . but then admitted to having written faxes about its purchase — at someone's dictation, of course. The same handwriting used to arrange the boat purchase then featured on 'the Game Plan.'

He pressed home the point for the jurors: 'So again what was set out in his handwriting, I use the term 'Game Plan', is the expenses associated with this enterprise and what outgoings, as it were, were required for getting this boat purchased in Gibraltar and getting it out of Gibraltar and also getting a boat to Malin and some of the expenses for Malin. So, both of those first two legs of the case, the two areas which I opened earlier this morning, are seen to be brought together in documents in the handwriting of Mr Lees.' He told the jury that he was asserting this, and that it was a matter ultimately for the jury to decide. And they decided that they could see through Lees' arrogant belief that he could hoodwink them as well as everyone else . . . they found him guilty.

But Mr Justice Gillen did not sentence Lees immediately. There were other trials to consider and so he adjourned the case, with the defence intimating that it would appeal the conviction. On 23 November 2000, Lees decided to plead guilty after all to nineteen charges in relation to the drinks scam; forty-seven of theft and fraud with a further two of money laundering. A week later, on 30 November, he was brought into court to receive his sentences on all charges . . . they ranged from five years for evading £2m customs duty on the drinks scam; nine years for the £23m fraud; three years for laundering £125,000 and twelve years for masterminding the £17m drugs shipment.

The media remained muzzled because of other cases pending in relation to Lees and because in the eyes of the judge, publication might damage the chances of a fair trial for Lees if his appeal was successful. Normally when someone is convicted of serious crimes, the media is free not only to report the outcome of the case but also to include any other material gathered in relation to the crime and the criminal. It's widely accepted that the three judges in an Appeal Court cannot be influenced by events in the media. But here the consideration was not for the Appeal Court but for the prospect of a successful appeal and a re-trial before a jury. To many observers it seemed as though Lees was being protected from adverse publicity. Many people in his hometown were still in denial about Lees. They just simply did not believe that he was guilty of serious crimes like drug running.

The judge eventually agreed to allow Lees' conviction for drug smuggling to be reported — but that was all. There could be no background report giving the life and times of the bankrupt businessman. This had become an issue of press freedom. Two judges involved in Lees' cases had imposed reporting bans — Mr Justice Higgins and Mr Justice Gillen. But only the BBC was prepared to challenge it in court on the grounds of public interest. But to no avail as Mr Justice Gillen stood by his order banning publication. As he put it: 'This order simply postpones the right to publish the details of these offences, the details of which have already lain dormant for many months. The restriction on the press by a postponement, for what is unlikely to amount to more than some weeks, is insufficient to dissuade me from discontinuing the order which I have already made. Accordingly the order which I have already committed to writing shall remain in force as therein set out.'

It wasn't until October 2002 — more than a few weeks — that Lees decided to withdraw his appeal and then, and only then, was the ban on publication lifted. Finally the world could learn the truth about one of Ireland's most dedicated and determined criminals . . . the man who fell from grace.

But Lees had one more scheme up his sleeve. I had been waiting for the day I could tell the story of Colin Lees on UTV's *Insight* programme. While we were busy editing, we transmitted short 20-second trailers advertising the programme and on the day the reporting restriction was lifted I prepared a short report on the UTV *Live at Six* programme and then was interviewed in the studio by Mike Nesbitt.

Later that evening I received a telephone call from Lees' solicitors, Madden & Finucane. At the other end of the phone was Patricia Coyle. She said her client had been in touch, having seen the news item earlier, and he had expressed concern about a couple of things. He was considering offering himself for interview. She wanted to know if I intended to tell the story about him in the United States — even though he had not been charged with anything there. I said we were planning to include the details of how he had defrauded Richard Worthy of almost $1m. She wanted to know if we were going to broadcast details of Lees' activities in Scotland — even though he was not before the court there. I said we were.

She then said her client was upset by these revelations and she added that they were thinking of seeking an injunction to prevent us from transmitting these aspects of the Lees story. I told her she should have mentioned that from the start of the conversation. I told her she had misled me. She remarked that there was unlikely to be a successful application. A barrister had already given opinion. She asked me to provide questions for him to consider. I pointed out that he was in jail. She said he got out on home leave. I reminded her the programme was being transmitted in about forty-eight hours. I sent a fax with the questions the following morning and later that day got a call from Patricia Coyle to say that there would be no interview because it was against prison rules. So even from his prison cell, Lees tried to have the truth buried. It did not work . . . just as it did not work in the courts.

But Lees' solicitor was not the only unusual call that week. On the same day I received a call from Billy Cousins, a convicted loyalist with links to the Ulster Volunteer Force (UVF). I knew he had attended many of Lees' courtroom appearances — most often sitting in the public gallery alongside Lees' common-law wife Zara. Perhaps my curiosity was about to be sated. Billy Cousins first explained that, like Colin Lees and his solicitor, he had seen our news report and he just wanted to try to present another side to Lees that few people knew. He stressed that he had made the call of his own volition and not at the behest of Lees. Lees and Cousins had met in jail and had become friendly. Billy Cousins said Lees' convictions meant he had done the crime and now had to do the time and he had no problem with that. What he wanted to tell me was not relevant to our proposed UTV *Insight* programme, which was due for transmission in about forty-eight hours time. He said he would meet me after our show was transmitted. We arranged to meet at his house in North Belfast the day after our film about Lees, called 'Racing to Destruction', was shown on 17 October 2002. But on the afternoon of the 17th, Billy Cousins called me to say he would not be able to go ahead. It was clear from his comments that he had been in touch with Lees. We agreed to talk again later. There were several conversations with Billy Cousins in the days and weeks after our film was shown. But no meetings took place. In December 2002 I asked Billy Cousins to find out from Lees if he would be prepared to meet me for an interview for this book. I have not heard from him since. I take it from the long delay that Lees' answer was no. He was not going to risk anything which had the potential to show him up in a bad light. He still wanted to maintain an aura of secrecy around his

269

nviction as a drug runner and fraudster. When it came to protecting Colin Lees, Colin Lees excelled himself. He was selfish when it came to looking after his own interests. No one else mattered. And it was something the trial judge picked up on.

Mr Justice Gillen said Lees would not allow the fear of consequences for himself, for his family or the knowledge of the financial havoc he could wreak on others, or even arrest to deter him. He summed Lees up as someone who 'unsuccessfully attempted to outwit those who were questioning you and showed absolutely no remorse for what you had done, exhibiting only a criminal defiance in the face of overwhelming evidence'.

The judge went on to describe Lees as 'a man of some intelligence who — unfortunately — choose to redirect that ability into crime on a massive scale'.

Of course, others also paid the price of their association with Lees. They included his 41-year-old former company associate Michael Wightman, who in June 1999 was given an eighteen-month suspended jail term for involvement in the fraud on the Lees Group of Companies.

Jonathan Murphy from Dublin escaped jail but was fined £6,000 after he admitted helping Lees as an undischarged bankrupt.

James O'Kane (53) from Clifton Drive, in Lytham St Anne's in England, was not so fortunate. He was not only jailed for three years for his involvement in the drinks scam, but also lost £4,500 by way of a confiscation order.

One of those involved in the drug smuggling operation, Samuel Philip Adams (49) from Abbeydale Park in Belfast, received four years. Two others — Ian Symington (36) of Sendmarsh Road, Surrey, in England, and 41-year-old James Millar from Toome Road, Ballymena, were freed when their jail terms (two years in Symington's case and three years in Millar's case) were suspended.

Noel Johnston from Meadow Street in Ballymena was not brought before the court because he was already serving a sentence from drug offences committed after Malin Head. He had been caught with £250,000 worth of cannabis after a car chase in Cullybackey outside Ballymena and was jailed for three years. Noel Morrison is still on the run — and is still wanted by police in Northern Ireland.

Lees languishes in prison most nights. But in preparation for his eventual release in October 2003 he has been getting weekends at home for some considerable time. The police did not recover all his ill-gotten gains and suffered a setback when they applied to court for an order giving them the right to confiscate all Lees' property as the proceeds of crime. They lost the case on a technicality, but are hoping new legislation will give them another opportunity to pursue him.

Det. Const. John Horan believes there is a lot to pursue; that Lees has cash secreted in various corners of the globe which he hopes to retrieve when he is released from prison: 'It's very hard to quantify but exactly what you said — you're talking about £23m fraud. Now of course there's an argument that a certain amount of that gets used up in buying the drugs, there's a certain amount of that gets used up in buying a pub. There's a certain amount of that gets used up in buying the haulage companies, but I still think you're talking conservatively £10 to £15 million. I think Mr Lees feels that when he gets out of jail he will go back to his millionaire lifestyle because we haven't taken his assets from him, yes.'

The experience of investigating Colin Lees has had a far-reaching impact on the police service in Northern Ireland, as Det. Ch. Supt. Jimmy Molloy and Det. Const. Horan explained. First, Jimmy Molloy: 'We were staggered at the complexity of this investigation and the link between the criminal fraternity in

271

Northern Ireland and America — and in this particular case, the Mafia. It made us aware of the need to carry out a fundamental review as to how we carry out investigations into financial crime.'

Det. Const. Horan put it this way: 'What the Lees case taught us was that while Northern Ireland isn't exactly the biggest place in the world, crime of this volume and of this sophistication was going on here. I mean for us it was very much a learning curve, the amount of international enquiries that we had to conduct and the amount of resources that had to be devoted to this one investigation, it was very much a learning curve, and I think that surprised me the most. You're taking telephone numbers, which is not what I expected.'

Northern Ireland has now followed the example of the Republic's Criminal Assets Bureau by establishing the Assets Recovery Agency which aims to take on organised crime by attacking the assets of the criminals who run it.

But for some individuals like the late Malcolm Baillie, there's no action the police could take to remove the deep sense of betrayal left in the criminal wake of people like Colin Lees. Like the unfortunate bar staff at the Loughside Inn who discovered that the National Insurance and tax contributions removed from their wages by Lees had not been paid to the authorities. Like Malcolm Baillie, who was left a broken man. What they have in common is the painful breach in trust . . . the realisation that Lees cared for no one but himself. And yet the very trait in Lees that led them into the despair of distrust is the one endearing characteristic they most fondly remember about the man who destroyed their lives.

While Lees displayed his arrogance and lack of remorse to the bitter end of his trials, from his deathbed Malcolm Baillie displayed great dignity when asked if, given the opportunity to speak to Lees face-to-face at that moment, what would he say: 'I don't know. I don't know. I don't hate the man in the sense of . . . you know . . . there's two things that strike me. You can hate a man because he's bad and you can dislike a man because of some things he does. Aw, I hate him for what he did. But as a person — as a person to person socially he was like most of us . . . quite sociable. What he did was dangerous. I think he had the ability to do what he was doing because he had power and when a man has power and he uses it to defraud, that's dangerous. When the Northern Ireland police came to see me, I said to a female officer, 'You know, Lees is not all that bad a man.' Well, she just glared at me.

'Then I thought about it. I had spent twenty-five years paying a mortgage and you end up with a decent house and no mortgage. And you suddenly get Lees doing a thing like that and it costs you £60,000 and it puts you back in debt. And then the cost of the court and getting a flat in Edinburgh . . . and my daughter who's a lawyer helping out with her finances to help us. Maybe if I was thirty-five years younger or forty years younger, Mr Lees would better get out of the way because as a footballer I never looked for any mercy or gave any and I wouldn't have given him any, I'm sorry to say. I hate to think what he's done to a lot of other people. But if it's anything like what he's done to us, then he couldn't care less . . . couldn't care less.'

Malcolm Baillie died a broken man . . . Colin Lees lives to enjoy the fruits of his dastardly labours.

Index

Loughside Inn, 186–7, 190, 194, 201, 227–30, 272
Lyle, Stewart, 47
Lynch, Thomas, 165
Lynn, Stafford, 193
Lyons, Ellen, 176, 177
Lyons, Jonathan
  career and lifestyle, 164, 165–6
  fraud, 164–5
  investigated, 160–64, 170–73, 176–80
  Jones and, 155, 160, 161–3, 171–3, 176–80
  Lees and, 178–80
  Mafia and, 123–4, 126, 155, 166, 168–70, 171–2, 176

McCartan, Fergus, 118
McCorkindale, Alastair, 72
McCorkindale, Archie, 37–8
McCoy, Ed, 225
McCrea, Rev. William, x, 93
McCurran, B., 107
McElroy, Dessie, 183, 189, 219, 235, 239, 265
McEwan, Judge Robin, 241, 244
MacIsaac, Donald, 32–3, 34–5, 37, 47
McKenzie, Alan, 77
McLaughlin, Derek, 99
Madden & Finucane, 247, 255, 256, 257, 268
Mafia, 126–7, 152–3, 159, 162
  Lyons and, 123–4, 126, 155, 171–2, 176

methods, 166–9
Operation Thorcon, 169–70
Magherafelt, ix
  civic reception for Lees, x
  job losses at Lees Group, 98
  shopping centre, 19–20, 53–5, 59, 68, 74
Magowan, Professor Jim, 25, 27, 30–31
Malin Head, boat wrecked, 128–30
Mallock, Ray, 7, 8
Manley and O'Reilly, 11, 40, 41
Marine Structures Ltd, 26, 32–3, 37, 45–7, 63–4, 67, 69–74, 81, 242
Market One International Ltd, 228, 230, 231–2
Martino, Carol, 115, 159, 171
MASA, 48
Maurer, David W., 112–13
Meaghan, Anthony, xix, 134, 146, 225–6
Metro Factors Inc., 102, 109, 110, 114 see also Worthy, Richard
Meyers Pollock, 152, 168–9
Midland Walwyn, 172, 174–5
Mid-Ulster Mail, 36–7, 98
Millar, James, 130, 132, 133, 135, 136, 138–9, 148–9, 212, 270
MI6, 22, 25, 27, 80, 241
Misuse of Drugs Act (1971), 237–8
Moira Direct Furnishings, 228, 230
Molloy, Det. Chief Supt Jimmy

It's
Who
we
Are

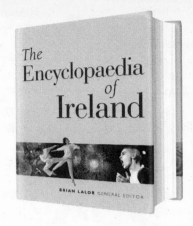

The Encyclopaedia of Ireland

BRIAN LALOR GENERAL EDITOR

The first modern, single-volume, Irish encyclopaedia

Over 1,256 pages

More than 900 contributors

An incredible 5,000 articles

1,000,000 words

In excess of 700 illustrations

'A marvellous, multitudinous and instructive compendium, up-to-date and up to speed.'
Seamus Heaney